Locating the Destitute

I0891884

New World Studies

J. Michael Dash, *Editor*

Frank Moya Pons and
Sandra Pouchet Paquet,
Associate Editors

Locating the Destitute

Space and Identity in Caribbean Fiction

Stanka Radović

University of Virginia Press
Charlottesville and London

University of Virginia Press
© 2014 by the Rector and Visitors of the University of Virginia
All rights reserved
Printed in the United States of America on acid-free paper
First published 2014

9 8 7 6 5 4 3 2 1

Library of Congress Cataloging-in-Publication Data

Radović, Stanka, 1974–
Locating the Destitute : Space and Identity in Caribbean Fiction / Stanka Radović.
pages cm. — (New World Studies)
Includes bibliographical references and index.
ISBN 978-0-8139-3628-4 (cloth : acid-free paper)
ISBN 978-0-8139-3629-1 (pbk. : acid-free paper)
ISBN 978-0-8139-3630-7 (e-book)
1. Caribbean fiction (English)—History and criticism. 2. Caribbean fiction (French)—History and criticism. 3. Space and time in literature. 4. Personal space in literature. I. Title.
PR9205.05.R33 2014
810.9'9729—dc23

2013046705

THE AMERICAN LITERATURES INITIATIVE

A book in the American Literatures Initiative (ALI), a collaborative publishing project of NYU Press, Fordham University Press, Rutgers University Press, Temple University Press, and the University of Virginia Press. The Initiative is supported by The Andrew W. Mellon Foundation. For more information, please visit www.americanliteratures.org.

This book is dedicated—with love—to Joshua and Daniel Dittrich,
who helped me write it, and to the memory of my father,
Ranko Radović, architect, who made everything possible.

Contents

Acknowledgments

I WISH TO THANK my Cornell graduate advisors—Natalie Melas, Satya Mohanty, Biodun Jeyifo, and Timothy Murray—for their continuous support and invaluable guidance in shaping my work.

During my year as Mellon Fellow at Cornell's Society for the Humanities in 2006–7, I developed the central ideas of this book. I wish to thank all my coparticipants in the seminar Historicizing the Global Postmodern for their constructive and generous feedback.

I am also grateful to the English Department at the University of Toronto for collegial and financial support, particularly for granting me the semester of leave that allowed me to write and for funding my trip to the V. S. Naipaul archive. I thank my colleagues Ato Quayson, Neil ten Kortenaar, and Dan White for their helpful comments on an early draft of the manuscript.

I also wish to acknowledge the expert help I received at the V. S. Naipaul archive at the University of Tulsa's McFarlin Library from Marc Carlson, librarian of Special Collections and University Archives, and Jenny Eagleton, who helped me navigate the collection.

I am grateful to the University of Virginia Press, particularly its humanities editor, Cathie Brettschneider, as well as the two anonymous reviewers who found merit in this project, offered many insightful suggestions, and supported its publication. Many thanks to Tim Roberts for managing the editorial process, to Judith Hoover for her expert copyediting, and to Martin L. White for the index.

For their intellectual rigor and the inspiring generosity of their research and teaching, I remain indebted to professors Wlad Godzich, Neil Hertz, and Richard Waswo, who taught me during my BA years at the University of Geneva and helped me make it to graduate school.

Finally, special thanks to my brother, Rajko, and mother, Mirjana, whose inquisitiveness, generosity, and genuine talent for dialogue helped me shape many ideas in this book.

Abbreviations

As a convenience to the reader, some of my most often used sources are referenced in the text using parenthetical abbreviations. The list of these abbreviations is given below. When the source of the reference cannot be deduced from the text itself, it is clearly indicated in the endnotes. All sources used in this book are also listed in the bibliography.

"DS"	"Different Spaces," Michel Foucault
FH	*Frangipani House*, Beryl Gilroy
HBP	*L'Hôtel du Bon Plaisir*, Raphaël Confiant
HMB	*A House for Mr. Biswas*, V. S. Naipaul
"IPC"	"In Praise of Creoleness," Jean Bernabé, Patrick Chamoiseau, and Raphaël Confiant
PS	*The Production of Space*, Henri Lefebvre
RI	*The Repeating Island*, Antonio Benítez-Rojo
T	*Texaco*, Patrick Chamoiseau

Locating the Destitute

Introduction

But thought in reality spaces itself out into the world.

—Edouard Glissant, *Poetics of Relation*

THIS BOOK ENGAGES QUESTIONS of space and spatial imagination in Caribbean fiction. Through the lens of contemporary spatial theory, I offer a comparative and interdisciplinary view of Caribbean postcolonial discourse. This discourse, in its inherently spatial orientation, contributes to and even anticipates the growing interest in space and place as critical categories fundamental for our understanding of social and political identity. Many Caribbean writers emphasize not only the cultural and linguistic legacy of colonialism but also its impact on space and spatial hierarchy. This question of spatial hierarchy has an even broader relevance: How are ordinary people, whom the Marxist sociologist Henri Lefebvre designates as "users" of space, excluded from active and autonomous participation in shaping their daily spatial reality, and, more important, how do they challenge this exclusion through practices of spatial imagination? My aim is to examine space as a political fact and as a metaphor whose imaginary potential continually challenges its material limitations. Literary responses to colonial hierarchy in the Caribbean conceptualize the spatial identity of the region as a necessary battleground for individual and collective autonomy in the face of external domination. Space and housing, in particular, become the most salient means to enact various strategies of resistance to colonial and neocolonial spatial discrimination based on wealth and private property. My readings of Caribbean literary texts foreground the impact of socioeconomic deprivation on (post)colonial self-understanding. This socioeconomic deprivation is not only socially produced but derives its structure and modes of operation from an established practice of capitalist exploitation so cogently exposed by Lefebvre, whose theories of space guide my intervention.

In *The Production of Space* (1974), Lefebvre warned that obsessive references to "space" might degrade this valuable concept into a figure of speech: "We are forever hearing about the space of this and/or the space of that: about literary space, ideological space, the space of the dream, psychoanalytic topologies, and so on and so forth" (3). This indiscriminate invocation of space is, in Lefebvre's view, a sure sign that space is paradoxically absent from most epistemological studies. The growing interest in spatial analysis, not only in geography, urban studies, and architecture, which traditionally deal with space, but also in philosophy, sociology, globalization studies, environmental criticism, and literary studies, signals a profound concern with space and place as such and also, often indirectly, with the role of spatiality within broader questions of culture, identity, and distribution of wealth. Beyond serving merely to invigorate tired discourses in search of new directions, spatial analysis reveals us clinging to the notions of space and place in fear of losing them. Already in his 1967 lecture "Different Spaces" ("Des espaces autres"), Foucault suggested that "today's anxiety concerns space in a fundamental way" (177). Deprived, through the complex processes of globalization, of the imagined simplicity of physical location, we seem to discover ways of reinserting space into discourses that are not explicitly concerned with spatiality. Consequently, "the language of social and cultural investigation is increasingly suffused with spatial concepts" (Smith and Katz, 66). Space thus becomes a metaphor, offering an inner geography of discovery and appropriation. The fact that we are increasingly "mapping" everything may well signal the disorientation of our age, but it is also the sign of a craving for the sensuous world, which we seek to reclaim.[1] At the same time, the proliferation of spatial metaphors suggests an act of substitution: if space is indeed absent from most epistemological studies and is always somehow beyond our reach (we are most often its compliant users but rarely or never its active planners), the abundance of spatial metaphors substitutes for active engagement with the social production of space. Increasingly out of place (or "destitute," as I aim to argue in this book) in an overadministered and closely surveilled global world, we substitute for real space by finding and shaping it imaginatively.

Adopting Lefebvre's perspective on space, I argue that beyond the moment of our inherent place-bound existence, we also occupy space in excess of our ontology, producing a kind of spatiality that shapes our understanding of the world. Our spatial existence is thus given and passively experienced and also continually produced and reproduced, allowing space to be actively transformed through our everyday engagement with it. This vital spatial dynamic, which emerges in and from a particular social practice and in turn shapes it, leads me to consider the complex correlation in Caribbean literature between dominated space inherited from the colonial world order and the imaginative contestations of that inheritance. Keeping in mind the dual problematic of space—its material relevance and its metaphorical resonances—my readings of selected novels of the Anglophone and Francophone Caribbean focus on the house as a literary site of convergence of material facts and metaphorical revisions of spatial practice. Marginalized people's imagination of alternative spaces thus becomes intrinsic to the structures of spatial exclusion, which motivates the production of imaginary alternatives in the first place. In the case of my analysis, Caribbean literary engagements with space often break the binary logic of space-as-real and space-as-metaphor by carving out, through narrative, a "third space," where the imaginary and material aspects of spatiality are treated as inextricable and complementary facets of our daily spatial practice.

Although my treatment of the imbrication of space and identity centers primarily on the built environment and the Lefebvrian notion of "produced" space, it is important to mention here that my work has profited from the increasing interest in the environmental approaches to Caribbean and postcolonial literatures. My emphasis on the correlation between spatial practice and spatial imagination is in dialogue with recent studies in postcolonial environmental criticism, namely DeLoughrey and Handley's edited collection *Postcolonial Ecologies* (2011), whose explicit aim is "to foreground spatial imagination made possible by the experience of place" (4). I address some aspects of the emerging ecocritical interest in Caribbean literary spatiality in chapter 1. My central focus, however, remains on the identity of space and self rather than space as alterity, and so my treatment of spatiality favors built environments in which the social can be read and transformed, leaving aside questions of landscape and natural environment.

The interplay between imaginary and material concerns in Caribbean postcolonial fiction is echoed in various contemporary theories of space. Space itself is often discussed as an inherently dual category understood both as a concrete physical phenomenon we experience daily and as a potent metaphor for various reflections on our material, social, and imaginative existence. Contemporary spatial analysis seeks to undo this tendency toward binary readings of space by emphasizing its complexity. Yet, as Neil Smith and Cindi Katz point out, "there has been little, if any, attempt to examine different implications of material and metaphorical space" (67). In an effort to fill this gap, they argue for the inherent interconnectedness of material and metaphorical space. Ever since Lefebvre's critique of social space, spatial discourses have registered an increasing effort to disrupt the binary readings of space (space vs. history, space vs. place, social space vs. natural space, private space vs. public space, etc.) with a move toward triple structures in which a third term is introduced to add dimension to the potentially reductive facets of binarism. Foucault's often-cited observation that we might now be living in "an era of the simultaneous, of juxtaposition, of the near and the far, of the side-by-side, of the scattered" ("DS," 175) rather than an era of gradual temporal development emphasizes the common dissociation of time from space, history from geography, as if they existed separately and were unrelated. This artificial binary, which, in Foucault's ironic formulation, divides "the devoted descendants of time and the fierce inhabitants of space" (175), contributes to the sometimes clandestine, sometimes manifest ubiquity of "space" in various discourses and puts this concept, time and again, in the position of either subsuming all other considerations because it always already contains them, or of being subsumed by them as a static and fixed category. Instead, as Doreen Massey argues, what is needed is "to uproot 'space' from that constellation of concepts in which it has so unquestioningly so often been embedded (stasis; closure; representation) and to settle it among another set of ideas (heterogeneity; relationality; coevalness . . . liveliness indeed) where it releases a more challenging political landscape" (*For Space*, 13). Massey proposes to challenge the fixity of interpretations that deprive space of its inherent dynamism, which she locates in the fact that space is always relational, heterogeneous, and under construction. As such it should be capable of shaping a different political landscape and opening more challenging political questions.

From the perspective of postcolonial studies, this view of space and place is not new. I argue that notions of relationality, heterogeneity, and openness characterize the entire Caribbean discourse, both in its profound spatial focus and in its attendant reimagining of individual, communal, regional, and global identity of the Caribbean. While I investigate the mutual interdependence of space and identity in select examples of Caribbean literature by means of Lefebvre's triple model of space, I also show the extent to which the conclusions and concerns of contemporary spatial theorists find resonance and further development in the postcolonial Caribbean discourse.

My inquiry into the geography of identity, which emerges from the various configurations of Caribbean literary spaces, does not imply a denial of time or history but aims to emphasize instead the manner in which colonial history makes its spatialized appearance in a literary text and is made tangible as a situated protagonist of fiction.[2] If postcolonialism is, above all, a study of "the various cultural effects of colonization" and colonialism itself the settlement and exploitation of distant territories (Ashcroft et al., *Post-colonial Studies*, 186), the problem of spatial—and not only historical or cultural—dispossession of the occupied or resettled places must be taken very seriously. The historical and linguistic emphasis characteristic of postcolonial theory cannot overlook the intrinsically spatial nature of colonization and its effects. As Wlad Godzich reminds us, "Decolonization was followed by a reterritorialization that became rapidly conceptualized through notions of core and periphery, in which the former colonial powers together with other economically dominant nations constitute the core whereas the former colonies form the periphery" (xi). For Edouard Glissant, the historical relations of dominance, exploitation, and displacement, which define colonialism, have been understood precisely in terms of their spatial structures: a "vertical" cultural hierarchy between the colonizer and the colonized is systematically mapped onto the horizontal plane of geography and results in multiple cross-cultural relations whose promise of encounter is always undermined by the hierarchical origins and exploitative aims of colonial trajectories. Similarly, Homi Bhabha's definition of the postcolonial project focuses on the unequal geopolitical ordering of the world, whose enduring hierarchy motivates various forms of cultural representation and contestation: "Postcolonial criticism bears witness to the unequal and uneven forces of cultural representation involved in the contest for political and social authority within the modern world order. Postcolonial perspectives emerge from the colonial and anticolonialist testimonies of Third World countries and from the testimony of minorities within the geopolitical division of East/West, North/South" ("Freedom's Basis," 46). According to Bhabha, the postcolonial critic takes up the task of questioning the inequality of geopolitical power distribution; he also sees himself as "bearing witness" and offering "testimony" about the very experience of such inequality. Emphasizing the implicit spatiality of colonial contact, Bhabha suggests that culturally and economically oppressed peoples create "cultures of survival," whose meaning and status have to be understood outside of the usual grid of national preservation because "various contemporary critical theories suggest that we learn our most enduring lessons for living and thinking from those who have suffered the sentence of history—subjugation, domination, diaspora, displacement" (47). Taking this geopolitical distribution of power as its central concern, postcolonial discourse furthers the scope of the materially grounded spatial theory while providing, at the same time, a valuable opportunity for examining the metaphorical aspects of colonization and decolonization deployed, as Smith and Katz argue, "to convey the dynamics of social domination in the everyday lives, thoughts and practices of social groups and historical subjects" (69). Since colonization is not just physical and cultural but also symbolic appropriation of space, decolonization becomes, in turn, a struggle for physical liberation and also "a metaphor for the process of recognizing and dislodging dominant ideas, assumptions and ideologies as externally imposed—literally of making a cultural and psychic place of one's own" (69). Narrative configurations of Caribbean postcolonial location thus force us to read, through the metaphors of space, the endurance of colonial hierarchy through various institutions and ideologies as well as the struggle for autonomy and independence of postcolonial societies against this oppressive historical legacy. Most important, these narrative representations of Caribbean spatiality offer a view of quotidian, "miniature" embodiments of resistance where the material and symbolic maintain their dynamic relationship.[3] In reading spatially oriented Caribbean fiction, I focus on the quotidian manifestations of colonial hierarchy as well as the small but persistent gestures of resistance to that oppression. I work with the underlying assumption that the exercise of power as well as its contestation emerge from a struggle to dominate or liberate, as the case may be, the daily individual imaginary before any such power can achieve the status of a sociocultural rule. This aspect of my discussion relies primarily on Lefebvre's notion of everyday life and its value for interpreting the intimate relationship between human sociality and spatial production.

In the Caribbean context, the house, more than any other type of space, allows me to address the following set of central issues: (1) colonial dispossession and the need for solid ownership; (2) the porous sense of private space and its relation to communal spaces; (3) the utopian dream of autonomous postcolonial space in response to the lack of independent and secure social grounding; and (4) individual and communal destitution, for which the house serves as an imagined or real substitute. In order to address these questions in their continuous interplay, I introduce the concept of *destitution* as the organizing principle for my reading of postcolonial spatial exclusion and the imaginative efforts to contest it in V. S. Naipaul's *A House for Mr. Biswas* (1961), Patrick

Chamoiseau's *Texaco* (1992), Beryl Gilroy's *Frangipani House* (1986), and Raphaël Confiant's *L'Hôtel du Bon Plaisir* (2009). I focus primarily on the etymological sense of the word *destitution*—to be put away or placed outside—in order to raise the question of what it means to be made, paradoxically, *exterior within* a dominant power structure and consequently alien to oneself. This etymological interpretation, which emphasizes the word's combined relevance as a spatial category and as a methodological device for reading postcoloniality, does not exclude its common designation of poverty and material deprivation. Instead the notion of spatial marginality goes hand in hand with the representation of inadequate material means that limit the social and human possibilities of the protagonists. In response, the efforts at constructing imaginary spaces attest to the need of the destitute to create a utopian substitute for their deprivation. The dialectical pair of *destitution* and *substitution* thus allows me to interrogate the continuous interplay between the reality of material lack and its narrative substitutions without losing sight of the ultimate inadequacy of this contest. The utopian and metaphorical responses to spatial exclusion and poverty only underscore the absence of basic opportunity for the marginal and poor. At the same time, these imaginative contestations of adverse material conditions reveal the creative resourcefulness of the "cultures of survival" without indulging in facile survivalist rhetoric (Bhabha, "Freedom's Basis," 46). My select authors construct narrative "houses," which reflect their need to reclaim actual or imaginary places and also the very conditions of self-representation. The "destitute" in these novels attempt to repossess their denied location (a house, a self) both materially and narratively. Since the spatial identities thus created weld together the *where* and the *who*, I proceed to question the implications of narrative representation itself: What does it mean to resolve the material through the imaginary or, conversely, to treat fiction as material?

Throughout this project I define identity itself as location: a place one chooses or is assigned, the site where one is, stands, exists, is situated. As a matter of fact, these words share the same root: the Indo-European *sta*,[4] which designates standing. The particular physical location, a site, thus is closely related to the notion of identity and also to a whole set of concepts important for my discussion: words like *state, status, establish, exist, destitute,* and *resist*, among many others, all derive from this same root, serving in this project simultaneously to emphasize the colonial imposition of a social location and its diverse anti- and postcolonial revisions. The imaginative and imaginary contestations of dominated space are, in this project, understood as profoundly necessary to the production of alternative social space and political practice. In Caribbean fiction the linguistic image of a standing person encapsulates communal autonomy and the right to self-determination, personal dignity, cultural specificity, and revived memory that all depend on being housed in the place of one's own choosing. Consequently, standing upright in order to resist socioeconomic and cultural destitution becomes a fundamental concern for the novels I address: the outcome determines the scope of individual and communal freedom. The physical places described in *A House for Mr. Biswas*, *Frangipani House*, *Texaco*, and *L'Hôtel du Bon Plaisir* crystallize the protagonists' ambiguous and complex relationship to the New World, where, through the Atlantic slave trade and the subsequent practice of indentured servitude, their ancestors faced the loss of their geographic, cultural, and linguistic grounding. In the novels I analyze they now struggle to redefine their understanding of this diasporic location and of their identity in it. Incomplete memories, inadequate homes, and partial self-understanding threaten to turn these protagonists' identity into either a pure fiction or an ossified token of some historically frustrated "original" existence. Like Salman Rushdie's Saleem Sinai, they are "handcuffed to history"—a history of colonialism through which they became destitute in the first place.

What transpires here is a complex coupling of two related yet quite dissimilar uses of the verb *to own*, meaning, on the one hand, "to possess" in terms of material ownership while suggesting, on the other hand, a figurative act of being able to "lay claim to" or simply "call" something one's own. In this distancing of material possession from the idea of being, or what Lovelace calls "the right to a humanness unlinked to the possession of any goods or property" (151), we rediscover the kind of intervention that characterizes spatially oriented Caribbean novels. They are concerned with substituting the notion of material possession, which is either unavailable or severely limited for most people in the islands, for cultural and self-ownership, which involve control over the way people live and express their specificity. This kind of ownership, a more figurative one, of calling something one's own, of naming and authoring one's way of living, is precisely what concerns most Caribbean writers and is explicitly addressed in the novels under discussion. Apparent destitution is therefore recast as potential, stripping the idea of material possession of its artificial, although historically engrained, relation to identity.[5] Instead, people affirm their identity through daily social practice, claiming authorship of their lives through the way they inhabit space, relate to one another, and shape their experiences in language. Most "yard novels," which I discuss in chapter 2, are characterized by extensive and sometimes almost exclusive use of dialogue as a narrative device. This dialogical dimension of the novel emphasizes oral, public, and communal forms of belonging over written, private, and individual forms. And although the practice of writing and its relation to individual autonomy are both quite central to many of these reflections on what is Caribbean culture and, above all, where it is located, most spatially inflected Caribbean narratives maintain their preference for stepping outside the enclosed walls of individual houses into spaces, such as yards, streets, and squares, that involve the presence of a larger community even as they emphasize the need for a house as a sign of accommodation for a culture. This physical stepping out of the enclosed into open spaces is paralleled by the disruptions of the written form through orality, which I discuss in chapters 4 and 6.

The struggle to reinvent and, in the process of storytelling, bring into being another form of spatial and historical identity thus constitutes the central and most original contribution of these novels. Caribbean postcolonial authors recognize both the historical horrors of slavery endured by their ancestors and their own contemporary dispossession and minor status in the global capitalist distribution of wealth among nations. In response, they offer a view of destitution as productive of narrative resistance. Although this imaginative contestation of coercive history may fail to transform the reality of postcolonial destitution, the construction of alternative spaces and identities in these texts offers the literary itself as an area of autonomous living. In keeping with Lefebvre's notion of produced space, I argue for postcolonial literature's transformative potential in producing alternative images of space and identity. The utopian potential of such literature underscores the necessity to resist and transform the reality of political and economic limitations; the absence of place is productive of imaginary spaces, whose existence is often shown as more powerful than the reality of material deprivation. At the same time, we are made aware that the utopian dimension of the narrative, which contests destitution by formulating it, cannot and should not substitute for the fundamental question of what it really means to marginalize people and deprive them of their ability to stand on their own.

As we well know, transatlantic colonialism was driven by economic profit based on the exploitation of distant territories and trade in human beings. This problem is, obviously, not only ethical or historical but also profoundly geographical: it characterizes the relationship of the colonizer to the colony, of the colony to the metropole, and of all the people involved in this transaction both to their place of origin and to the destination of their displacement. The focus on New World postcolonial literature thus implies an examination of not only historical but also spatial consequences of slavery and the continuous struggle for a place of one's own, necessarily denied by the slave trade and the institution of slavery. In Maeve McCusker's view, "It is a familiar observation that colonialism was, first and foremost, a spatial enterprise, concerned with appropriation and expropriation of territory, and that notions of space, displacement and location are central metaphors in postcolonial writing" (41). The postcolonial criticism that I am interested in focuses, of necessity, on the placement of subjects and subjugation of places, negated by the racially structured exploitation that found one of its systematic applications in the practice of slavery. As a discourse of socioeconomic and conceptual change, such criticism insists, among other things, that the colonized territory and the enslaved person *are* and *require* autonomous space, which the violence of conquest has exploited and denied.

This inherent spatiality of postcolonial theory reveals its deep affinity with and a dialogical relation to critical spatial discourse. For example, parallel to postmodern spatial theory's impatience with binary oppositions, postcolonial critique expresses its own wariness of these same structures predicated upon hierarchical and exclusionary relations. In Bhabha's reading of colonial discursive legacies, there is, for example, a concerted effort to disrupt simple binaries by introducing a third term into the traditional opposition of colonial and postcolonial history. This third space is a space of interstitiality, or the space "in between," by which rigidly established analytical and social categories need to be reassessed for their own exclusionary impulses and account for "the hybrid moment of political change," which allows us to recognize and articulate a position that is "*neither the One, nor the Other, but something else besides*" (*The Location of Culture*, 28). Bhabha's hybrid or third term thus shares the political goal of Massey's rereading of space: a different and radically more open political landscape. But it is the postmodern spatial turn in particular (best exemplified in Edward Soja's *Thirdspace*, 1996) that finds its conceptual twin in postcolonial theory inasmuch as they are both invested in rejecting the prescriptive limits of dual structures in favor of a third option, which values the inherent ambiguity of any conceptual category and of any direct engagement in the political world. Although Soja hesitates to embrace Bhabha's "third space" whenever it teeters on the edge of being "a spatially ungrounded literary trope, a floating metaphor" (141), revealing Marxist spatial theory's justified impatience with the potentially conciliatory uses of imaginary space, he admits Bhabha's theorization of cultural location by broadly relating it to his own theoretical coinage, "thirdspace," a term he uses to designate an interconnected and transdisciplinary understanding of the complex relationship between space, history, and society (143). From these cursory connections between spatially inflected postmodern and postcolonial theories, we discover that many central postcolonial "master tropes," such as hybridity, interstitiality, diaspora, and exile, lend themselves, as Clive Barnett reminds us, to being read as geographical metaphors. At the same time, they are also metaphors of impurity and mixing and as such "retain a strong sense of the importance of thinking about the geography of identity, but do so without modelling this geography of identity on an image of clear-cut and indivisible demarcations of belonging" (157).

My own interdisciplinary reading of spatial theory alongside postcolonial and Caribbean discourses seeks to address the necessity, potential, and limitations of this "thirding," by which all three critical discourses, each in its own way, aim to account for the irreducible complexity of the global world while recognizing the danger of its enduring binary structures and the fundamental need for conceptualizing an alternative political practice through alternative spatial imagination. My approach to these questions relies on Lefebvre's three-dimensional analysis of space based on the continuous interplay between material production, the production of knowledge, and the production of meaning, insofar as I seek to maintain the simultaneous interdependence and contradictions between material spatial practice and its imaginative appropriations. I focus on the intricate literary representations of Caribbean postcolonial space by suggesting that Lefebvre's *lived space* of daily human experience is reconceived through fiction into new forms of knowledge (*conceived space*), which in turn seek to critique and transform the material social practice (*perceived space*). As Christian Schmid emphasizes, for Lefebvre, "the materiality in itself or the material practice per se has no existence when viewed from a social perspective without the thought that directs and represents them, and without the lived-experienced element, the feelings that are invested in this materiality" (41). Space thus emerges only from the interplay of all three dimensions. In my analysis of Caribbean literary space, it may sometimes seem that I isolate and deal with only two poles of this triple structure: the material and the imaginary. I would like to emphasize, however, that in my treatment of literary texts, the imaginary dimension of quotidian space always contains all three aspects of Lefebvre's triple structure and provides us with a powerful critique of the material reality through the spatial image, which itself persistently merges the symbolic and the conceptual. In other words, the literary spatial image gestures toward a metaphorical reappropriation of space and, at the same time, offers its metaphoricity as a means of reconceptualizing space. The obvious limitation of mapping Lefebvre onto a literary analysis lies in the fact that his Marxist critique of the social production of space focuses on material spatial practice. As an art of representation, literature is already at a remove from this concrete spatial practice. Yet literature's imaginative engagement with daily reality has a transformative potential, and, instead of understanding it as a passive formulation of utopian fantasy or ideological acquiescence, we may also think of its undeniable capacity to reshape the very terms of our engagement with the real. My use of Lefebvre's theory should therefore be understood as a frame of reference for a particular kind of literary reading, which seeks to preserve the continuous dialectical correlation between materiality, its conceptualization, and its symbolic meanings. Lefebvre's work addresses precisely this correlation and allows me to explore its critical potential in shaping our understanding of socially produced space in Caribbean postcolonial discourse. With Lefebvre's help, my work seeks to resist the postmodern tendency to resolve contradictions within the realm of the linguistic sign (no matter how flexible it might be), while avoiding the reductive notions of economic materialism through which human subjectivity and modes of resistance risk being reduced to a determined set of "objective" historical conditions. I argue instead that the Caribbean context represents a compelling instantiation of the problem of space understood as both concrete and metaphorical, squarely material and persistently imaginative.

Lefebvre's three-dimensional dialectics of spatial practice constitutes one of the most progressive and inclusive critiques of spatial binaries and their ability to render social experience of space increasingly abstract and regulatory. I turn to this particular interpretation of social space not only because "Lefebvre's urban and spatial writings are of more general interest for radical social and political theory" (Goonewardena et al., 4), beyond the strict confines of the specialists' research on space, but also because Lefebvre's inclusion of the imaginative symbolic dimension of the users' spatial practice into the broader structure of social production of space marks a significant opening of spatial theory to the insights and considerations acquired through literary and artistic practice. The interplay between the everyday experience of space and the diverse conceptual and imaginative attempts to reclaim it is a significant contribution of Lefebvre's theory, which is of particular resonance for literary engagements with space in general and for postcolonial literary spatiality in particular. Lefebvre's recognition that material spatial practice depends upon and in turn mobilizes various conceptual and imaginative interventions points to his innovative and idiosyncratic revisions of Marxist theory to include the daily and symbolic relations of actual users to their space and not only the systemic, structural, and institutional versions of spatial practice. This attention to the impact of imagination on actual space through the almost imperceptible daily interventions of its users suggests Lefebvre's interest in linking the cultural and economic readings of space. The importance of art as a form of everyday poetic practice in Lefebvre's analysis of social space allows me not only to extend his insights to the literary considerations of Caribbean spatiality but also to examine the specific contribution that the postcolonial Caribbean narratives may offer to those contemporary spatial theories that seek to bridge the gap between material and imaginative engagements with space.[6]

In *The Production of Space* (*La production de l'espace*, 1974), Lefebvre introduces space as a concept that has had thus far a strictly geometrical or classificatory meaning, evoking no more than an empty area ("un milieu vide"), traditionally treated as separate from politics and ideology. His central contribution is, on the contrary, to theorize space as *produced*. It is therefore not only inherently political but also comparable, according to Rémi Hess, to any merchandise (foreword to *La Production de l'espace*, xi). Aiming to overcome a contradiction between theories of space and spatial practice, Lefebvre describes his work as "an effort to overcome confusion by considering (social) space as well as (social) time no longer as facts of a more or less modified 'nature' nor as simple facts of 'culture,' but as *products*" (*La production de l'espace*, xix, my translation). This notion of space-as-product requires a broader sense of production, as the systematic generation of "things" having a global impact of the second upon the first nature. Moreover space as product retroactively intervenes in the production itself and becomes, in Lefebvre's system, a rather complex "produit-producteur" (product-producer or productive product [xx]).

Lefebvre's intervention is then announced as a turn toward something crucial but overlooked—a forgotten concept of social space, which must now be remembered. Lefebvre's opus thus offers, as Gabriele

Weigand suggests, a productive confrontation between sociology and history from the point of view of a philosophical anthropology. Perhaps unintentionally, Lefebvre's project evokes something of the Freudian "uncanny" by bringing space back to life as an idea that was either repressed or taken for granted. The monumental scope of the book suggests a major intervention and a need to fill the gap of perceived theoretical oblivion. Although Lefebvre's text was first published in 1974, the same kind of urgency permeates many subsequent theorizations of space by other proponents of the centrality of space in social life. But why is space perceived as forgotten and haunting, and how do spatial theories of social life propose to remedy the erasure? Or, more practically, what is gained by looking at space?

Lefebvre notes, on the one hand, an a priori and therefore mostly unquestioned existence of space in philosophy and, on the other hand, its constant generalization. He laments, as I have already mentioned, the ubiquitous and indiscriminate use of the concept: "Conspicuous by its absence from supposedly fundamental epistemological studies is not only the idea of 'man' but also that of space—the fact that space is mentioned on every page notwithstanding" (*PS*, 3).

Lefebvre is particularly critical of the linguistically oriented structuralist school (in which he places Kristeva, Barthes, and Derrida) for its tendency to posit the existence of "mental space," thus forgetting the urgent questions posed by the spatial reality of everyday life. This school of thought, whose "growing renown may have something to do with its growing dogmatism, is forever promoting the basic sophistry whereby the philosophico-epistemological notion of space is fetishized and the mental realm comes to envelop the social and physical ones" (*PS*, 5). Here Lefebvre critiques the circular movement that establishes a particular "theoretical practice," which then produces a "mental space," which in turn becomes the locus of a "theoretical practice."[7] In this circularity he sees, and seeks to contest, the unconscious ideological tendency of the dominant class to presuppose a separation of mental space from social practice and to set itself up as a reference point of "knowledge" (*PS*, 6). His ultimate quarrel is aimed at the reductionist division between mental space on one side and social spheres on the other and the preeminence of an absolute knowledge of history, philosophy, and science over ideology and nonknowledge (seen mainly as lived experience). It is ultimately in this critique that Lefebvre's "triplicity" defines itself as a connection and constant motion between the actual, theorized, and lived dimensions of human existence. Space connects the mental and the cultural, the social and the historical. As a product, space can be decoded from the relations of the subjects who inhabit it, while their subjective relations are in turn shaped by the kind of space-product in question.

Yet two mutually constitutive illusions, argues Lefebvre, shield space from our knowledge: it is perceived as either transparent or obscure. The illusion of transparence belongs to philosophy, which posits "innocent" space illuminated by piercing thought. Another illusion—that of impenetrable opacity—suggests that there is really no link between the concept and the thing it designates. From this perspective, it is a mistake to consider language as substantial, as designating anything real. While the illusion of transparency belongs to the world of philosophers, the second illusion, that of opacity, suggests a form of dogmatic materialism. These two in effect contain and generate one another: the dark symbolism of nature obscures its alleged philosophical transparency, while a transparent history finds itself entangled in the nostalgia for mute physical nature.

Lefebvre's analysis aims at undoing this binary relation between the material-real and the conceptual-imaginary. He thus provides some important conceptual tools for my own reading of the common postcolonial binarism between the actual and the literary, between historical materialism and its literary utopias. Instead of an either/or paradigm, he argues for the triplicity of space and sees space, more than any other concept, as emphasizing the mutual dependence of the different aspects of human existence. To put it simply, everything human intersects in space and is made perceptible by a set of specific coordinates.

Lefebvre's spatial triplicity then takes the following shape:[8] (1) spatial practice ("la pratique spatiale") or space as it is *perceived*: this is the social space of production and reproduction, of everyday networks of interaction and communication; (2) representations of space ("les représentations de l'espace") or space as it is conceptualized and *conceived*: this dimension of space expresses the way space is socially represented and designates various relations of power, which shape that representation; and (3) representational spaces ("les espaces de représentation"), which refer to the *lived space*, with its symbols and images: this is the space of inhabitants, artists, and some writers/philosophers "who describe and aspire to do no more than describe. This is the dominated—and hence passively experienced—space, which the imagination seeks to change and appropriate. It overlays physical space, making symbolic use of its objects" (*PS*, 39). This triple configuration of space is essential for Lefebvre and will remain so for his postmodern followers because it constitutes a passionate critique of dual structures and their misleading clarity:

> A triad: that is, three elements and not two. Relations with two elements boil down to oppositions, contrasts or antagonisms. They are defined by significant effects: echoes, repercussions, mirror effects. . . . Such a system can have neither materiality nor loose ends: it is a "perfect" system whose rationality is supposed, when subjected to mental scrutiny, to be self-evident. This paradigm apparently has the magic power to turn obscurity into transparency and to move the "object" out of the shadows into the light merely by articulating it. In short, it is the power to *decrypt*. Thus knowledge (*savoir*), with a remarkable absence of consciousness, put itself in thrall to power, suppressing all resistance, all obscurity, in its very being. (*PS*, 39–40)

Although his point suffers in the English translation, Lefebvre insists here on the semblance of meaning or the signifying effect ("un effet signifiant") of a dual structure in which one element immediately derives its value from its relational opposition to another element. By focusing on the mirror effect within a binary system, Lefebvre is evoking not only Western philosophical traditions, such as the Hegelian dialectic, but also de Saussure's linguistic premise that the meaning of one term and its value depend entirely on another, differential term within the same system.[9] The ensuing systematic duality, which lies at the core of structuralist thought, has the appeal of clarity and promises transparence. By relying on dual relations, the process of reflection appears capable of deciphering the world without residual opacity or contradiction. But in such a system, Lefebvre insists, the body itself has been left out or neutralized and can be recovered only in a triangular relation: "In seeking to understand the three moments of social space, it may help to consider the body. All the more so inasmuch as the relationship to space of a 'subject' who is a member of a group or society implies his relationship to his own body and vice versa. Considered overall, social practice presupposes the use of the body: the use of the hands, members and sensory organs, and the gestures of work as of activity unrelated to work" (*PS*, 40). The body erased by the seemingly transparent processes of production and specialization leads us to the residual nature of everyday life, which is itself, according to Lefebvre, a kind of leftover of our alienating specialized occupations: "Everyday life, in a sense residual, defined by 'what is left over' after all distinct, superior, specialized, structured activities have been singled out for analysis, must be defined as a totality" (*Critique of Everyday Life*, 97). Yet it is precisely this flotsam of daily life and the forgotten body that inhabits it that in Lefebvre's view constitute the human and the human relationship to the real, no matter how partial or incomplete. Those parts of human life and activity that appear secondary to the principles of incessant productivity (i.e., relations and needs such as friendship, comradeship, love, play, conversation, etc.) become, according to Schmid, essential to Lefebvre's idea of social practice and its urban manifestations: "Central to Lefebvre's materialist theory are human beings in their corporeality and sensuousness, with their sensitivity and imagination, their thinking and their ideologies; human beings who enter into relationships with each other through their activity and practice" (29).

As Andy Merrifield points out, Lefebvre's long-standing interest is in the life "outside the factory gate and the office cubicle, beyond the school staffroom or store checkout" (9). Yet even this residual everyday, where people, in their opaque physical existence, always remain beyond knowledge and theorization, is slowly "colonized" through commodity and consumerism. By means of media and advertisement, and today we could add social media and an increasing dependence on technological aids for all forms of social relations, the quotidian totality slowly becomes another field of fragmentation. Despite this degradation of the everyday and its potential, Lefebvre remains faithful, Merrifield argues, to the notion of *Homo ludens* and the possibility of freedom and fulfillment beyond labor and consumption contained in the hierarchized, specialized, and abstracted world of capitalist production. Devoted to the disorderly spontaneity of the festival and its Rabelaisian laughter, Lefebvre envisages it as "a special, potentially modern form of Marxist praxis that could erupt on an urban street or in an alienated factory. The festival was a pure spontaneous moment, a popular 'safety [valve],' a catharsis for everyday passions and dreams, something both liberating and antithetical" (Merrifield, 17). Moreover, the festival is an intensified version of the everyday, where the *un*productive, playful, and excessive dimensions of performance and laughter serve as a liberating political force and challenge the dictates of bureaucratic dogma. This view finds resonance in many theorizations of the Caribbean, where the carnivalesque, comedic, and excessive approaches to quotidian limitations serve to counter the alienating circumstances of the postcolony. Benítez-Rojo's Caribbean performativity, Glissant's errantry, Brathwaite's "tidalectics," Wilson Harris's "living landscapes," and the carnival, along with many other representations of the Caribbean in both theory and literature, seek to capture and celebrate the geocultural specificity of the location while imaginatively exceeding the limits of its inherited colonial order. This contestation through excess is, according to Lefebvre, already contained and firmly rooted in the bodily dimensions of human life.

Lefebvre's theorization of bodily opacity and its enduring relevance for the untamed aspects of *lived space*, which engages our creative responses to domination and external order, encourages my own reading of transatlantic postcoloniality: it is the level of actual daily experience, which, out of necessity and despair, finds its rearticulation in the imaginary. In this relation of the lived to the imaginary, there is no room for the binary: one element cannot survive without the other, but neither can one resolve the other. By positing the triplicity of space and spatial sociality, Lefebvre argues for the value of living contradictions but denies the impulse to synthesize them. As Soja argues in *Thirdspace*, the open logic of "both/and also" instead of "either/or" motivates the entire spatial critique. This "additive" impulse makes postmodern geographers' critique useful to the postcolonial problematic insofar as it recognizes the embattled relation between the actual and imagined as they unfold, inseparably, in a concrete spatial context. It would be easy and obvious to divide the world into legible binary chunks. It is less obvious and more slippery to look at the world as an ever-growing set of entangled threads and planes of coexistence, without nonetheless abdicating responsibility for the *kinds* of entanglements and coexistences that we witness or participate in. As Peter Hallward rightly insists, "That we *are* relational in no way determines the kinds of (political or ethical) relations we should pursue" (xv). The real and imaginary or, to borrow Lefebvre's language, practice and representation, cannot be isolated one from the other but require some third articulation.

Of course, Lefebvre's argument makes the notion of the "real" very difficult to pin down because nothing can be "unreal" when it comes to human spatiality. What in his triple structure of space can be said to be real, and what is imaginary? Lefebvre's *lived space*, more than any other, carries the burden of reality since it reflects and encompasses the actual relationship between the user and his or her environment. Yet it is precisely in the lived experience of space that Lefebvre also locates the impulse toward imaginative reappropriations of space. This recapturing of spatial experience seeks to challenge the fact that most forms of spatial practice are otherwise designed for and imposed on their users. To conquer space, one must first imagine the conquest and then accomplish it.

For Lefebvre, there is ultimately no significant distinction between the lived and the imaginary. Rather, what is lived is always lived through the symbolic and imaginary relations between the inhabitants and their space. Moreover, it is in the imaginary that we find the opposition to space dominated by the institutions of power. By its very nature, the imaginary refuses the logic of normative coherence in favor of the intimate affective life: "Representational spaces need obey no rules of consistency or cohesiveness. Redolent with imaginary and symbolic elements, they have their source in history—in the history of a people as well as in the history of each individual belonging to that people. . . . Representational space is alive: it speaks. It has an affective kernel or centre: Ego, bed, bedroom, dwelling, house; or: square, church, graveyard. It embraces the loci of passion, of action and of lived situations, and thus immediately implies time. Consequently, it may be qualified in various ways: it may be directional, situational or relational, because it is essentially qualitative, fluid and dynamic" (*PS*, 41–42). In his explanation of *lived space*, Lefebvre makes clear the connection between the details of experiential bodily life (bed, house, square, graveyard) and their historical memory: as soon as we address the affective core of the human imaginary, we must also see it as simultaneously individual, relational, historical, and geographical. Led to the historical dimension of human life through its spatial manifestations, Lefebvre explains his understanding of the relation between location and its history: "If space is produced, if there is a productive process, then we are dealing with history" (*PS*, 46).

I adopt one version of Lefebvre and his postmodern followers for my own discussion of postcolonial spatial (im)possibilities: historical exploitation of the colonies can be read retroactively from the contemporary realities of the spatial distribution of privilege. From this perspective, the inequality of global relations of power among the so-called nation-states can be reinterpreted through the history of colonial exploitation. In other words, space may hide consequences from us, as Soja has it, but it can also reveal them. Yet this reading of history *from* space is not all. It would be more important, I argue, to return not to historical or geographical abstractions but to the notion of the quotidian bodily experience of both, especially as they are understood and reconstructed in literature. The quotidian human may, in the end, be the only question that preserves an almost atemporal urgency. That political history and political geography shape and often destroy this banal human seems to me beyond discussion. Yet if a literary text can bring these quotidian human concerns back into focus, this is its best and most revolutionary contribution. My reason for looking at the spatial configurations of the Caribbean postcolonial novels ultimately has to do with the potential of the narrative space to zero in on the physical, bodily, and seemingly trivial way people live and die, exploited and unaccommodated within the systems of thought and action they still need to change.

The spatial dimension of my argument triggers the following question: In the context of postcolonial displacement, is it possible to build a house within a novel, or to treat the novel as a substitute house? In order to answer this question, I explore the fictional and material dimensions of spaces represented in Caribbean literature, which, at its historical core, grapples with colonial displacement and the (re)claiming of place. Starting with the fact that colonialism, a profit-driven territorial conquest, produces a hierarchy of cultures and languages and also a deeply felt and lasting geographic discrimination, the etymologically understood concept of destitution allows me to examine the problematic of spatial exclusion of the individuals and communities represented in Naipaul's *A House for Mr. Biswas*, Gilroy's *The Frangipani House*, Chamoiseau's *Texaco*, and Confiant's *L'Hôtel du Bon Plaisir.* With the etymological sense of the word *destitution* (to be put away or placed outside) in mind, I question the insider's exteriority in the postcolonial social practice, the centrality of its spatial manifestations, and its impact on the individual and communal ability to challenge and reinvent the existing social order.

The symbolic meaning of real spaces, which I address in this introduction, will continue to permeate the rest of my inquiry. Lefebvre considers space to be legible because it results from and in turn creates a signifying process. This claim allows me to argue that the use of spatial metaphors in Caribbean postcolonial fiction necessitates a critical rereading of the imaginary solutions to the real problematic of spatial existence. By examining Lefebvre's triplicity of space and particularly his third term, *lived space*, I suggest that the material reality of space is inextricably bound to and dependent upon the symbolic meaning of its inscription. Lefebvre's third space allows me to link, inextricably, imagination to lived experience. In so doing I offer a critique of the underlying binarism of postcolonial theory as well as its often inadequate escape into the terminologies of *in-betweenness* and *interstitiality.* Instead I focus on the way the symbolic space serves radically to question and reconfigure the material structures of hierarchy and discrimination in the postcolonial context. Although the narrative rendition of space cannot resolve the problems of real spatial destitution, it is of crucial importance to examine the recurring spatial metaphors in the Caribbean literary context and their lasting impact on our understanding of location—ideological and material. The narrative reflection on the material inequalities and racialized hierarchies, which characterize the postcolonial world, ultimately speaks to the literary text's power to take issue with the material conditions it invokes and thus redefine them.

In chapter 1, "Caribbean Spatial Metaphors," my aim is to put Caribbean postcolonial discourse in dialogue with contemporary spatial theory in order to elucidate how they can enrich one another. The recent popularity of spatial theory signals an increasing interest in the phenomenon of space and its sociopolitical significance in the global world. Yet the proliferation of spatial metaphors within this discourse causes some concern among theorists who favor a materialist approach to spatial problems. They warn that the excessive use of spatial categories runs the risk of diluting the political urgency of spatial analysis and diverting attention from space as reality to space as image or narrative device. In response to this genuine concern, I argue that Caribbean postcolonial discourse evinces a strong engagement with spatial questions without, however, losing sight of their material roots and relevance. Since colonialism and its postcolonial contestations are not only historical or cultural but also inherently spatial phenomena, I show that the reliance of Caribbean discourse on spatial metaphors, far from weakening the problems of spatial reality, draws attention to the complex interplay between the concrete fact of spatial destitution and its metaphorical substitutes created by narrative images of space. These images offer spatial metaphoricity as an inadequate yet necessary gesture of substitution in response to the realities of colonial and postcolonial destitution. Using Lefebvre's triplicity of space as my theoretical basis, I argue that every engagement with the reality of space also requires us to recognize the imaginative uses that we make of space and the manner in which this symbolic practice reflects and transforms spatial reality. In the case of Caribbean fiction, the narrative substitutions for spatial destitution signal the authors' keen awareness of the reality of inadequate living conditions while offering a powerful narrative contestation of that reality. In my survey of spatial metaphors in both spatial theory and Caribbean discourse, I show the limitations of the binary division between material reality and its imaginative revisions and argue instead for a third option: the properly Lefebvrian recognition of their dialectical interplay in which new solutions and approaches to space are produced.

In chapter 2, "A House of One's Own: Individual and Communal Spaces in the Caribbean 'Yard Novel,'" I focus on the figure of the house as a space whose ambiguous nature, reflected in its being both a material structure and a metaphorical construct, allows me to explore the overlap between space and identity in Caribbean fiction. My focus on the spatial and architectural significance of the house and housing conditions draws attention to marginalized people's struggle for a place of their own, that is, their meaningful and clearly demarcated place. For the formerly colonized and their descendents, houses crystallize the need for independence and autonomy through a place of one's own while at the same time emphasizing the enduring impact of inherited colonial hierarchies played out in spatial terms. The insistence on the acquisition and possession of a house, even if this is often a purely utopian quest, is a form of resistance to the imposed structures of administered and dominated spatial practice. In order to show the complexity and specificity of this spatial problematic in the Caribbean novel, I discuss a unique genre of Caribbean fiction, namely the "yard novel," which chronicles the shortage of adequate living conditions and the impoverished communities' struggle to substitute for this lack by forging communal bonds within their destitute dwelling spaces. By surveying a number of representative yard novels and their major themes and narrative methods, from C. L. R. James's *Minty Alley* (1936) to Earl Lovelace's *The Dragon Can't Dance* (1979), I emphasize the centrality of spatial considerations in Caribbean fiction and their role in destitute people's imaginative challenges to their daily experience of dispossession. The narrative triumph of the destitute only emphasizes the real conditions of deprivation that the literary texts obviously cannot resolve. This complex slippage and overlap between the imaginary and the real is reflected in the ambiguous spatiality of the house and thematized by all the novels I address in this book.

In chapter 3, "'No Admittance': V. S. Naipaul's *A House for Mr. Biswas*," I pursue the symbolic and material dimensions of spatial identity by focusing on Naipaul's celebrated novel, in which spatial ambiguity between ownership and dispossession emerges from the protagonist's desperate quest to acquire a house of his own. The ever-elusive image of one's own space, constructed in opposition to unaccommodated existence, crystallizes the problem of postcolonial space as a contested territory of self-invention. Although Mr. Biswas remains stranded between autonomy and dependence, I focus on his attempts at creative writing and journalism to show how this historically destitute protagonist attempts to resolve the need for physical shelter through the allegedly stabilizing dimensions of writing. Since Mr. Biswas's sense of self coincides with his utopian house, and the house ultimately exists only in writing, Naipaul's novel interrogates what it means to be an outsider within the established system of material and symbolic hierarchies, which determine and threaten the scope of one's identity. The lingering questions that Naipaul leaves us with are why the ownership of a house in our possession-oriented world should represent such a bold act and why a man like Mr. Biswas should dream of a house as if it were an act of defiance. What kind of historical and spatial experience jeopardizes this simple need for housing and property, which is, in another context (that of Europe and North America, for example), defined as the most basic human right and a sign of the social relevance of the owner? Naipaul shows us in *A House for Mr. Biswas* not only the way a house crystallizes the link between possession and autonomy but also the cross-cultural hierarchy that applies to those who own and those who do not.

From Naipaul's isolated individual displacement, I turn in chapter 4, "Squatters in the Cathedral of the Written Word: Patrick Chamoiseau's *Texaco*," to the Martinican writer Chamoiseau's collective place in order to examine the communal dimension of spatial belonging. Drawing on the urban theory of *terrain vague*, a concept that translates into English as "wasteland," "derelict area," or "vacant land," I examine Chamoiseau's Texaco as an abandoned portion of urban land, which remains available for spontaneous use by its destitute community. In his famous essay "Terrain Vague," the architect and urban theorist Ignasi de Solà-Morales describes *terrains vagues* as those spaces that are internal to the city yet external to its everyday use, echoing in spatial terms exactly the role that destitute populations, such as the community of Texaco, play with respect to the hierarchical social structure of the city. The derelict location and its squatters represent the internal outsider to the (post) colonial city. When the "insalubrious" slum of Texaco is scheduled to be demolished and its squatters displaced, the slum leader Marie-Sophie offers to recount to the urban planner the genesis of Texaco in order to save it. Chamoiseau's act of storytelling counters the official history of colonial dislocation with the celebratory representations of squatting and rhizomatic growth through which the space of unauthorized communities, languages, and histories is asserted. The tension between the official and the illegitimate allows me to trace the problem of contested urban spaces and argue that the act of storytelling brings place into being. I conclude that, for Chamoiseau, the notion of place owes its existence to the narrative inscription of communal experience. The apparent poverty of the living conditions is here countered by the wealth of communal relations and oral narrative connections across space and time. For Chamoiseau, in contrast to Naipaul, the very real economic limitations of the slum community do not amount to a flawed or incomplete sense of identity but instead trigger a collective struggle for group identity and collective ownership of space and self.

In chapter 5, "Heterotopia of Old Age in Beryl Gilroy's *Frangipani House*," I reconsider the representation of spatial exclusion of the elderly in the postcolonial context. Mama King, the protagonist of this novel set in Guyana, finds herself imprisoned in an "ideal" location for the old. Everyone keeps telling her how lucky she is to be placed in the retirement home called Frangipani House, yet she experiences the place as a prison. For Mama King, as for Mr. Biswas, what differentiates freedom from imprisonment lies above all in her ability to choose or change her place of "residence"—metaphorically and literally. In order to emphasize the inherent ambiguity of the house as a literary figure—offered here as an ideal shelter and a prison—I rely in this chapter on Foucault's discussion of heterotopias, those extraordinary spaces that serve to "suspend, neutralize or reverse the set of relations that are designated, reflected or represented by them" ("DS," 178). They are, in essence, actualized utopias, linked to all other spaces yet at variance with them, serving to represent, contest, and reverse the real space to which they are both inextricably linked and external. The concept of heterotopia thus allows me to examine Gilroy's use of spatial metaphors as a way of contesting the institutional exclusion of the poor and weak who are paradoxically placed, with much benevolence, where they do not wish to be: sheltered inside the institutions that keep them safely outside any daily social practice. In response to her growing isolation and incipient dementia in this infantilizing space, Mama King narrates her memories of youth out loud to no one, in the void of her retirement home. These overflowing memories are her desperate effort to challenge the reality of confinement and dependence. Through her futile storytelling, however, she succeeds in recollecting and envisioning her freedom and autonomy with respect to the administered heterotopia of old age. Gilroy's novel thus allows us to interrogate the inherent duality of the house, represented in my other literary examples as a dream of independence, and here as a nightmare of seclusion. In contrast to Naipaul's Mr. Biswas and his utopian house, for example, Gilroy's Mama King confronts the house as a space of dispossession, and her gestures at narrative autonomy only affirm the gradual loss of identity within heterotopian space, emphasizing once again the imbrication of identity and place.

Finally, in chapter 6, "Upper and Lower Stories: Raphaël Confiant's *L'Hôtel du Bon Plaisir*," the house emerges as a setting of communal struggle for socially recognized identity and a site from which collective history and shared communal experience can be read. Taking, like Chamoiseau's *Texaco*, an architectural view of Martinican history, this novel explores communal spatial relations through the vertical structuring of stories and storeys in contrast to Texaco's horizontal, rhizomatic movement. *L'Hôtel du Bon Plaisir* is characterized by a humorous and light-hearted treatment of material destitution that nevertheless emphasizes all the more effectively the lack for which the carnivalesque and comedic dimensions of the narrative must substitute. Drawing on Bakhtin's theories of the carnival and the grotesque and on Lefebvre's admiration for this Rabelaisian principle with respect to *lived space*, I discuss how Confiant's protagonists' stories resist the order and grammar of imposed hierarchies and in so doing strive to maintain the hotel as a space of creoleness. Confiant organizes the novel as a "creole comedy" in six acts but opens with an evocation of Kojève's aphorism, "La vie humaine est une comédie. Il faut la jouer sérieusement." (Human life is a comedy. One must act it seriously.) The unsettling contrast between surface humor and profound human suffering, which the humor both hides and elevates, leads me to examine Confiant's chosen building, the repurposed titular Hôtel du Bon Plaisir, as a site of perpetual struggle between inadequate living and human dignity. The undecided nature of this struggle can be reflected only in an inherently ambiguous spatial figure, the house, which simultaneously conceals and exposes the material misery of its occupants as well as the richness of their stories and relations. Moreover, as Confiant insists in the epilogue, in the course of its existence the building takes on the qualities of a living being (it is literally Lefebvre's *lived space*) that reflects the characters of its inhabitants. The hotel is therefore more than just a building; it is a tangible trace of the life of its tenants, their dwelling place and the monument to that dwelling. When it finally burns down, the hotel takes with it the history it embodies. The makeshift parking lot that replaces it suddenly appears as a faceless site with no memory and no character. The clash is again between the utopian desire for a space of one's own and the bold attempts to repossess such a space through storytelling, communal loyalty, and a sense of shared experience where the "poetics of relation" (Glissant) challenge the limitations of the material living conditions and their colonial roots.

1 Caribbean Spatial Metaphors

I myself consider literary documents as *realities of the imagination*, pure products of the imagination. And why should the actions of the imagination not be as real as those of perception?

—Gaston Bachelard, *The Poetics of Space*

CARIBBEAN DISCOURSE AND LITERATURE open a unique possibility for an innovative rereading of spatial and postcolonial theories in conjunction. The Caribbean has always been contested space, historically fought over and swapped among various colonial powers while conceptually cast as either the abyss of the slave plantation or the garden of worldly paradise. Engaging with various discursive representations of this ambiguity of Caribbean space, I address in this chapter the polarized visions of Caribbean postcoloniality between brutal colonial facts and powerful images of their contestation. These gestures of creative resistance, often formulated through spatial metaphors, offer deliberately provisional "third" solutions against perceived historical binaries. In the novels I analyze, space in general and Caribbean space in particular are always "both/and" rather than "either/or." For many Caribbean authors, space is at all times a material fact and a representative image; specifically defined and generally relevant; culturally bound and open to a kind of "worlding" or "relation" beyond its immediate context; a site of culture and the problem of the individual; an opening to otherness, to the outside, and a closure into the imagined autonomy of an inside. Here we confront space as a representative image and as a specific material fact and are therefore better equipped to examine the ambiguous and persistently liminal nature of spatial analysis itself. In this sense Caribbean discourse, with its persistent focus on its own contested spatiality, opens a unique possibility for reconsidering and broadening the scope of spatial theory, whose important but often underappreciated concern has to do with the way imaginary representations of space reflect and subsequently shape the real places we inhabit. As they reflect on their region and its history, Caribbean authors and theorists address the inherent complexity of space itself—as image, concept, and experience; projection, utopia, and fact.

This constitutive ambiguity is, in my view, precisely the reason why space is such an attractive, rich, and repeatedly invoked concept: its potential meanings can never be exhausted because they are always dynamically implicated in questions of cultural identity. The complex nature of insular topography itself seems to suggest paradoxes and dualities, which fuel our generic perception of islands; they fascinate us as "surrounded yet open on all sides, disconnected yet whole," so that "in our imaginations, island ecology includes homes for dragons and elves and enchanting spirits; islands are wild and dangerous, or homey and safe, depending on our definitions. They are usually the imagined home of extraordinary and noble indigenous people. But we also keep dangerous and important prisoners on islands" (Anderson, 1). In the spirit of Robert S. Anderson's uneasy and consciously ironic passage from "enchanting spirits" to "dangerous prisoners," we should remember that the Caribbean islands are likewise torn between fact and fiction. The region is continually fictionalized as the terrestrial incarnation of the Edenic myth while remaining a factual site of brutal colonial history, conveniently obscured by tourists' quest for tropical bliss.[1] The metaphoricity and materiality of island topography in general and the Caribbean archipelago in particular draw our attention to the uneasy yet mutually constitutive relationship between how we imagine things and how they really are. We produce places as we imagine them, while the facts of that place-production become in turn crucial for our representation of their reality. Nowhere is this imagination of the world, which becomes world-reality, clearer than in Christopher Columbus's factual arrival at an "imaginary" location in the New World, where in the actual place we now know as the Caribbean he mistakenly "discovered" the continent sought after by European imperial powers. The Caribbean thus became "the West Indies" and to this day bears the name of an imaginary geography. V. S. Naipaul's sardonic recounting of this event draws into focus the complication that such materialized geographical fiction will later have for East Indian indentured laborers: "When in 1492 Columbus landed on the island of Guanahani he thought he had got to Cathay. He ought therefore to have called the people Chinese. But East was East. He called them Indians, and Indians they remained, walking Indian file through the Indian corn" ("East Indian," 39). Antonio Benítez-Rojo sees this same geographic fantasy as generative of a particularly lopsided view that the West will end up having of the Caribbean: "The West's idea of the Caribbean is a product of these and other mistakes and inventions" (*The Repeating Island*, 220). In this narrative of colonial "bungling,"[2] the moments of fiction cannot be extricated from real events, showing us that spatial reality is always produced by the complex processes of imagination and exploration, discovery and misrecognition, fascination and brutality, encounter and conquest, memory and misremembering. As Robert Harbison argues in the case of architecture and its function, "The solidest architectural facts are fictional to a degree" (7). The same can be said for the solid materiality of geographical and spatial claims: they inevitably depend upon fictions that first motivate and subsequently sustain them. My selection of spatial discourses reveals an interest in those spatial theories that foreground the imaginary and utopian dimensions of spatial practice alongside its material and embodied realities in order to show them as mutually constitutive and, at the same time, always uneasily poised against one another.

Although the Caribbean was, after Columbus's "discovery," initially conquered by the Spanish, northern Europeans started their own permanent colonies in the seventeenth century, first on the still unoccupied islands of the Eastern Caribbean and later moving west into the Greater Antilles. The rise of northern European colonial interest meant that "the islands often changed hands during wars in Europe, as local forces or naval expeditions seized control" (Rogozinski, 59).[3] Saint Lucia, for example, "probably holds the record for frequent changes of ownership" (144), passing fourteen times from the French to the British and, in that same spirit of spatial mythologization, earning the nickname "Helen of the West Indies." This history of colonial competition over "available" and exploitable space reveals the extent of European interest in the Caribbean and the phenomenal profit that the Atlantic slave trade and plantation slavery brought to the European colonial powers. According to Eric Williams, "By 1750, there was hardly a trading or manufacturing town in England which was not in some way connected with the triangular or direct colonial trade. The profits obtained provided one of the main streams of that accumulation of capital in England which financed the Industrial Revolution" (*Capitalism and Slavery*, 52).

To this day, and despite official independence (gained mostly in the 1950s and 1960s), the Caribbean islands are still claimed from the outside and exploited for tourism: the region is "in danger of being reduced to sun, sand, sex, smiles and servility by multinational capitalism and with the eager cooperation of its own local political and economic elites" (Strachan, 2–3). Recast as a worldly paradise, the region is today commodified for the world consumer despite the fact that the Edenic myth sits quite uncomfortably with the history of the Caribbean as a series of plantation colonies marked by the violence of slavery. Contested because it is in various ways perpetually claimed by an outside, either for wealth extraction or for the myths of leisure and fun, the Caribbean is a region whose critical, literary, and artistic discourses aim at resisting the danger of either being reduced to the peripheral position of the ex-colony or being governed by an increasingly miasmic global elsewhere in providing de-historicized spaces for pure consumption of pleasure. Yet, as Nick Nesbitt argues in the context of the French Caribbean (though we can treat this observation as relevant for the entire region), "Amid growing dependency on and imbrication within national . . . and now global capitalism, Antilleans have consistently offered a multifaceted critique of their self-estrangement and lack of autonomy" (4). In other words, Caribbean authors strive almost unanimously to redefine the region as a locus of diversity, rich cultural and artistic production, and a complex regional and relational identity. In Ian Gregory Strachan's words, "Caribbean discourse, then, is customarily shaped by an underlying economy: the imperialist-colonial economy of wealth extraction and exploitation and an often anti-imperialist counter-economy, one that concerns self-worth" (4).

In some of the most widely known critical assessments of Caribbean cultural history, the region appears emblematic of colonial alienation and its brutality. As Ashcroft, Griffiths, and Tiffin argue in their seminal study *The Empire Writes Back*, the almost complete extermination of the indigenous people in the West Indies and the displacement suffered by its entire contemporary population (originally from Africa, India, China, the Middle East, and Europe) means that "the West Indian situation combines all the most violent and destructive effects of the colonizing process" (25). Created by exploitative colonization (as opposed to settler colonialism), the West Indies cannot indulge in the dream of filiation to some precolonial world nor view the decolonizing process as a simple reversal or rejection of the colonial history. As a result of its complex relationship to colonialism, seen as a destructive force that nevertheless brings the contemporary Caribbean into being, the region is here defined as "the crucible of the most extensive and challenging post-colonial literary theory" (144) and as the clearest representation of the irreversible impact of colonialism, which begins with the ancestral exile of the African and continues with the present-day hegemonic pressures from Europe and the United States.

This view of Caribbean exceptionality in its experience of and response to the colonial history is already present in George Lamming's juxtaposition of African and West Indian colonial experiences: "What the West Indian shares with the African is a common political predicament: a predicament which we call colonial; but the word colonial has a deeper meaning for the West Indian than it has for the African. The African, in spite of his modernity, has never been wholly severed from the cradle of a continuous culture and tradition. . . . It is the brevity of West Indian's history and the fragmentary nature of the different cultures which have fused to make something new; it is the absolute dependence on the values implicit in that language of his colonizer which has given him a special relation to the word, colonialism. . . . Colonialism is the very base and structure of the West Indian's cultural awareness" ("The Occasion for Speaking," 34–35). The relative brevity of modern Caribbean history, its linguistic dependence on the colonizer's language and the fragmented diversity of its cultural components constitute the exceptional dimension of this region and, at the same time, give the Caribbean an exemplary status within the context of colonial history. The Caribbean is thus often propelled into an emblem of the new global diversity, itself marked by a kind of direct or indirect spatial, cultural, and linguistic displacement of all people, even those who once claimed the privilege of theorizing their "roots" and "purity."[4] According to this view, the Caribbean allows us to confront directly and without illusions the extent of displacement that colonialism and slavery, which lie at the core of contemporary capitalist development and its global reach, visited upon its victims.

Other readings of the Caribbean often give it an equally exemplary status and, while arguing Caribbean specificity, paradoxically establish something profoundly emblematic about the notion of "Caribbeanness." Regardless of the exuberant richness of this theoretical figuration, the Caribbean runs the risk of becoming a metaphor for itself. Yet if this geocultural metaphor ends up substituting for the Caribbean as a specific place and dislocates its spatiopolitical reality, the potent and suggestive discursive construct threatens to erase the material irreducibility of the location and its needs. In *The Repeating Island* (1996), Benítez-Rojo's seminal rereading of the Caribbean aesthetic and cultural history by means of chaos theory and the rhizome, the notion of Caribbeanness is extended to include people, artifacts, and performative cultural practices that are not, strictly speaking, Caribbean.[5] In Benítez-Rojo's interpretation of the Caribbean, which "comprises a rich and at times daring combination of literary criticism, theory, historicism, and creative writing" (de la Campa, 91), there is actually no such thing as "strictly speaking." Instead there is a sense that the Caribbean exists and generates things in "a certain kind of way." This suggestive formulation allows Benítez-Rojo to speak of jazz as "a kind of music that dwells within the Caribbean orbit" (*RI*, 19) or of Martin Luther King as someone who, although North American, was also able to be Caribbean: "His African ancestry, the texture of his humanism, the ancient wisdom embodied in his pronouncements and strategies, his improvisatory vocation, his ability to seduce and be seduced, and, above all, his vehement condition as a dreamer . . . and as an authentic performer make up the Caribbean side of a man unquestionably idiosyncratic in North America" (24). According to Román de la Campa, this radically open discourse emerges from a postmodern perspective that Benítez-Rojo constructs through "a string of metasignifiers such as chaos, free-play, supersyncretism, and polyrhythms, which lead ultimately to the category of performance" understood as "a Caribbean cultural disposition" (92). What it means to be Caribbean is stretched here to the point of bursting since anything and anyone sharing specific "Caribbean" features (such as, for example, a skill for performance, improvisation, dreaming) can be included in "a certain way" of being Caribbean. Although the deliberate looseness of this formulation signals a rejection of rigid discursive boundaries and definitions, especially those concerning narrow nationalism or ethnic rivalries, the stretching of the Caribbean "meta-archipelago," as Benítez-Rojo calls it, from Bombay to Gambia and from a Cantonese tavern of circa 1850 to an old Bristol pub (*RI*, 4), runs the risk of leaving us with no sense of the Caribbean at all. In being everything (across time as a "repeating island" and across space as a "meta-archipelago"), the Caribbean could easily turn into nothing in particular, just like that overused notion of "space" Lefebvre once lamented. The metaphorically spatialized Caribbean archipelago labors, in my view, under the enormous weight of having to suggest an opening beyond material geography while nevertheless preserving the sense of Caribbean specificity in historical, geographic, and cultural terms. We are thus confronted with another version of the dual structure, here in the opposition between the emblematic and the singular. This structure seems to tear at the notion of Caribbean space and often strains spatial analysis itself. So how can we think of space in general and of Caribbean space in particular as something other than an overextended metaphor for itself, as something more than just a narrowly defined regional topography for which vague notions of cultural diversity often replace a serious engagement with the Caribbean aesthetic?

Benítez-Rojo is invested in maintaining the possibility that the Caribbean can be thought about without being too narrowly defined since it is by its nature both decentered and unbound. What characterizes this unique region is then a series of spatial and other competing metaphors: it is aquatic, it is like the Milky Way, the lava, the wind, the clouds, it is chaos, fractal mathematics, the uncanny novel, and more. In exploding the metaphor, Benítez-Rojo suggests that the Caribbean "resists being captured by the cycles of clock and calendar" (*RI*, 11) associated with Europe and leads us instead to contemplate the continual paradoxes by which the Caribbean aesthetic, with its memories of colonial violence, seeks to find "territory of the absence of violence" (25). For Benítez-Rojo, the rejection of synthesis in favor of the perpetual flux between polarities also signals the rejection of exclusionary choices, which would indeed be violent if applied to the Caribbean. Insisting on unresolved bifurcations and paradoxes that, in resisting the synthetic impulse, reveal Caribbean literature to be "fugitive by nature" (25), he concludes that "a syncretic artifact is not a synthesis, but rather a signifier made of differences" (21). This position is shared by many Caribbean thinkers who strive to undo the harmonized but isolated identity constructs in favor of a more communal and diffracted sense of belonging. In Bernabé, Chamoiseau, and Confiant's "In Praise of Creolness," for example, the notion of Creole identity suggests something akin to Benítez-Rojo's "heteroclitic, fractal, baroque" (*RI*, 25) forms of expression and offers a similar resistance to synthesized and totalizing discourses: "Because of its constituent mosaic, Creoleness is an open specificity. It escapes, therefore, perceptions which are not themselves open. Expressing it is not expressing a synthesis, not just expressing a crossing or any other unicity. It is expressing a kaleidoscopic totality, that is to say: *the nontotalitarian consciousness of a preserved diversity*" ("IPC," 892, original emphasis). Far from being exhausted or explained by vague multicultural harmony, the question of the racial, cultural, and linguistic diversity of the Caribbean contests rigid centers and boundaries, leading its prominent writers to theorize nonviolence and forms of cross-cultural cooperation. In the spatiocultural context of the Caribbean there can be, according to Lamming, no simple binary between "a traditional, indigenous culture and a colonizing power" ("Caribbean Literature," 36). Instead the Caribbean is, from the very start, a region marked by "a triplicity of cultural strains—Africa, Europe, and Asia: local populations which can claim no ancestral roots in the soil that was to become their home" (36). This objective triplicity of Caribbean cultural space necessitates various imaginative theorizations of the relationship between people and their spatial context, and it finds, I argue, a very productive resonance in Lefebvre's triplicity of space and the "trialectic" approaches to human geography of the late twentieth century and early twenty-first.

In his famous presentation of "the black Atlantic," another conceptual and geographic third space meant to restructure reductive colonial binaries such as Europe versus Africa or the Old versus the New World, Paul Gilroy expresses his concern with the "continuing lure of ethnic absolutisms" and "cultural insiderism" (3) shaped by the Manichaean dynamics of race and national belonging. He favors instead "the rhizomatic, fractal structure of the transcultural, international formation" of the black Atlantic (4). This complex cultural formation serves to remind us that, although "manifestly inadequate" (15), concepts like creolization and syncretism, so prevalent in the Caribbean discourse, indicate that cultures and cultural consciousness of all the participants of Atlantic colonialism, from the European settlers to the decimated indigenous populations, from the African slaves to the indentured Asians, all participated in an inevitable and continuous cross-cultural exchange and "were not, even in situations of the most extreme brutality, sealed off hermetically from each other" (2). Revising Gilroy's complex theorization of the black Atlantic, Michaeline A. Crichlow examines Caribbean creolization in the global context by introducing the notion of a "post-creole imagination" in order to decenter "the traditional focus of Creolization discourses on the Caribbean, plantation, and in part, even the 'black Atlantic,' while being critical of those deployments of the creolization motif in contexts where power is erased" (202). While discourses of creolization are here recognized as diversely and rhizomatically rooted in the Caribbean, they are also removed from their strict localization in order to reflect upon larger processes of global economic and cultural power structures, which shape them. Crichlow investigates how the dual nature of Caribbean geocultural location offers a view of specific local practice and of a broader set of global relations while remaining alert to the possibilities and limitations of these positions. This liminality, she argues, is "vital to an understanding of creolization as embedded in a politics of place that extends beyond the black Atlantic" (204). As these important theoretical interventions clearly show, the central ideas of Caribbean discourse remain productive for rethinking binary relations between local and global, specific and general, exceptional and exemplary, material and imaginative.

Yet as Benítez-Rojo insists, despite the mutual permeability and fluid circulation of communities and cultural practices, despite syncretism, creolization, and deliberately celebrated images of "impurity," at the origin of the present Caribbean there lies an image of a transhistorical and transgeographic violation:

> Let's be realistic: the Atlantic is the Atlantic (with all its port cities) because it was once engendered by the copulation of Europe—that insatiable solar bull—with the Caribbean archipelago; the Atlantic is today the Atlantic (the navel of capitalism) because Europe, in its mercantilist laboratory, conceived the project of inseminating the Caribbean womb with the blood of Africa; the Atlantic is today the Atlantic (NATO, World Bank, New York Stock Exchange, European Economic Community, etc.) because it was the painfully delivered child of the Caribbean, whose vagina was stretched between continental clamps, between the *encomienda* of Indians and the slaveholding plantation, between the servitude of the coolie and the discrimination toward the *criollo*, between the commercial monopoly and piracy, between the runaway slave settlement and the governor's palace; all Europe pulling at the forceps to help at the birth of the Atlantic. (*RI*, 5)

Here the sea becomes, to borrow Iain Chambers's formulation, "the countersite or heterotopia of modernity" (679). Parallel to this bloody birth of an ocean, which exceeds the limits of a geographically defined body of water, the Caribbean archipelago also comes into being as "an island bridge" and a violently inseminated "womb" (*RI*, 4, 5). And it finds itself, as Benítez-Rojo repeatedly states, *between* continents, capitalist projects, class symbols, exploitative systems, and racial strictures. Always systematically in between, the Caribbean thus claims both a clear geohistorical specificity and a potent metaphorical amplification of its meaning. Paradoxically, in creating this dizzying proliferation of images, Benítez-Rojo invites us to "be realistic." The graphic depictions of this spatiohistorical rape and violence and the images that contest them are presented as equally relevant: there is no other way to speak of the Caribbean complexity. Unless we recognize the actual fact and the imaginative resonances and distortions of that fact, we cannot quite grasp that "certain way" in which the Caribbean both takes part in and overcomes the threat of political violence.

Despite the fearless exuberance and complexity of this approach, I have reservations about the ability of an expansive spatial image to account for a specific place and have to wonder when exactly the metaphor begins to obscure not just the place itself but also the problem it seeks to address. Offering an anecdote about the typical Caribbean response to despair, Benítez-Rojo writes, "In Chicago a beaten soul says:

'I can't take it anymore,' and gives himself up to drugs or to the most desperate violence. In Havana, he would say: 'The thing to do is not to die,' or perhaps: 'Here I am, fucked but happy'" (*RI*, 10). According to this description, the Caribbean is not an apocalyptic world "in pursuit of the vertical desires of ejaculation and castration" (10), where notions of all or nothing, for or against—all European ideological propositions—dictate the way of being. Instead the Caribbean is a place where one can be "fucked" and "happy" at the same time because one simply "is" and strives "not to die." What troubles me about this anecdote, despite its potent mockery of the apocalyptic politics and its dehumanizing effects, is the quick passage from despair to happiness, from dire privations and imminent death to a discourse of triumphant survivalism. The image is seductive and hopeful; it is the kind of image we like to embrace when we speak of poverty, pain, and despair probably because we wish, quite understandably, to be released from their reality into the fantasy of optimistic solutions that do not require our engagement: the triumphant and disembodied human spirit resolves material problems on its own! The question remains, however, and nags us from under the shimmering surface of the Caribbean metaphor: When speaking of centuries of exploitation and extraction of resources and capital, of the contemporary renewal of that exploitation under the guise of global capitalism, of poverty and deprivation that all Third World countries face (and many of them are in the Caribbean as well), can the image of a man who is "fucked but happy" postpone the problem of global and historically rooted inequality or resolve it? I wish I could accept this image. While I admire the utopian gesture that brings it about, I have to question what this image obscures and where it falls short of giving an adequate answer to the enduring binary violence inherited from the colonial world.

Edouard Glissant's poetic approach to the Caribbean and its spatiotemporal complexity reveals a kindred focus on the "bastard" nature of cultural exchanges triggered by the violent history of colonialism in the region.[6] His reflection on the Caribbean as a particular spatiohistorical formation reveals a familiar wavering between the emblematic and the exceptional, which characterizes many versions of the Caribbean discourse, whether it derives from the Anglophone, Francophone, or Hispanophone parts of the archipelago. At the very beginning of *Poetics of Relation*, Glissant argues that the survived horrors of the Middle Passage and the slave ship have made the African into an exception. Yet far from being something to brag about, this tragic exception arises from being "chosen" for the abyss. The Relation initiated within this void arises from the fact of its survival, not the virtue of its experience. At the same time—and paradoxically—in the spirit of most Caribbean discourse, this exceptionality of abysmal experience becomes something communicable: "For though this experience made you, original victim floating toward the sea's abysses, an exception, it became something shared and made us, the descendants, one people among others. Peoples do not live on exception. Relation is not made up of things that are foreign but of shared knowledge. This experience of the abyss can now be said to be the best element of exchange" (8). The spatial image of the ship as a literal and metaphorical vessel of such exchange, which also serves as one of Foucault's examples of heterotopia par excellence, appears as a recurring trope of Caribbean discourse.[7] In his examination of this spatial image with respect to the infamous *Zong* massacre of 1781, Ian Baucom raises the question of theoretical ambivalence that, on the one hand, insists on the Caribbean exceptionality and, on the other hand, sees it as emblematic. In the process the tragedy of colonial dislocation and dispossession in the Caribbean becomes a kind of postcolonial currency, something that, as Glissant points out, initiates the process of exchange and constitutes, according to Baucom, a move from "irreversible human damage" (65) to "a compensatory economy of postcolonial gain" (71). In examining the relationship between "the exchangeable and the singular" (63) in the black Atlantic discourse, Baucom shows that the *Zong* massacre serves as "this" particular story, a monument to the atrocity of the slave trade (exceptional, invaluable), and as one in a series of such stories, becoming thus the equivalent of the slave trade itself or, even more broadly, of modern displacement in general. Only an emblematic story can enter into the circulation of exchangeable values, while the specific story seeks to remain inexchangeable—the only one. Baucom points out that Glissant's idea of exchange with respect to the survived horrors of the slave trade serves deliberately to transform the exception into a practice of sharing, or, to be more accurate, into Relation: "*Exchange*, in this sense, once more names a form of substitution, though here what replaces exceptionality is not fungibility but relation, where *relation* is a word for an antimelancholic politics of memory, and a word for those new forms of culture, identity and solidarity that emerge from even this most violent scene of Atlantic exchange" (67). The meaning of any singular "event" is here viewed as a process of unfolding of after-events and serial transformations whose resonance surpasses the singularity of the exceptional tragedy and turns it into a metamorphic sign of cultural exchange. The image of the drowning bodies of the slaves thrown overboard becomes "an image of a body impoverished and strangely rewarded by 'exchange'" (68). The unsettling choice of the word *reward* signals the manner in which the drowning body becomes, according to Baucom, "the originary body in a genealogy of creole identity *and* a body of insurrection against the disciplinary regimes that seek to produce it (whether as a marketable 'exchange value' or as the waste matter of cross-Atlantic imperial exchange)" (68). What should have been the ending of a culture and a people thus becomes their beginning, a kind of generative matrix in the midst of colonial atrocities.[8]

In Caribbean poetics, besides the slave ship, other spatial metaphors fulfill a similar function: the sea, the archipelago (or Benítez-Rojo's "meta-archipelago"), the island topography, the plantation, the mangrove, the banyan tree,[9] the hurricane, *le morne* (the hill), the barrack yard, and the shack, all maintain their geographical specificity while being transformed into a metaphor (and subsequently an emblem) of cultural location. These spatial metaphors serve as currency and transfer meaning beyond the confines of their specific semantic origin (*metapherein*: to bear, to transfer). As Paul de Man suggests, metaphors are themselves linguistic and cultural travelers or migrants since they explain one thing in terms of another and are, in a sense, a form of translation: the word *translate*—German *übersetzen*—itself translates the Greek *metapherein.*[10] This important and widespread figurative dynamics of the Caribbean and spatial discourses opens onto another aspect of my argument: the creation of intimacy and communal sharing.

In his discussion of this topic, Ted Cohen argues that, among other things, metaphors serve to achieve intimacy: "There is a unique way in which the maker and the appreciator of a metaphor are drawn closer to one another. Three aspects are involved: (1) the speaker issues a kind of concealed invitation; (2) the hearer expends a special effort to accept the invitation; and (3) this transaction constitutes the acknowledgment of a community" (6). In creating and interpreting the metaphor, its maker and receiver engage in "the cooperative act of comprehension" (7), which entails much more than we might at first suppose: both the maker and the receiver of the metaphor make a series of assumptions, hypotheses, and inferences about each other's knowledge, beliefs, and attitudes, about the context and intention of the metaphor and about its relation to its literal meaning. Although the process of figuration, because of the complex interpretations it entails, may appear more complicated than necessary, the work of metaphor is nevertheless crucial for the creation of intimacy between distant terms that the metaphor draws into relation and also between the interlocutors who share in the creation of this proximity.[11] In generating and decoding the metaphor, the interlocutors agree to cross the boundary that separates the common expected meaning from the new metaphorical one, but they also enter into a closer relation with one another as they strive to figure out the path and goal of metaphorical expressions they have agreed to share.

Because the word *metaphor* is, as Paul Ricoeur points out, itself a metaphor of a spatial relation—it designates a displacement and transfer of meaning across space (143)—its function is of great relevance for my dialogical reading of Caribbean and spatial discourses. The metaphoricity and the ensuing emblematic nature of Caribbean discourse, particularly in its use of spatial images, suggests, above all, an attempt at creating the interpretative and readerly community drawn into close proximity with the Caribbean as a concrete geographical space but also as a network of cultural images drawn from the specific context yet capable of being shared across strict contextual boundaries. Consciously working against the notions of colonial periphery and postcolonial margin, Caribbean theorists and writers, in their use of spatial metaphors, transform Caribbean spaces into images shared in a cooperative proximity between the writer and the reader. Unlike the tourist, who is really a consumer of ready-made and prearranged meanings (equivalent to dead metaphors), the reader who engages in the notion of the Caribbean as the meta-archipelago, for example, or Caribbean culture as a mangrove, must agree to enter an uncharted territory and begin to share with the writer not only the image of these spaces but also the historical subtext of such images and their relational relevance to the cultural discourse at large. The imaginative crossing and displacement, which necessarily occur in this productive transfer of meaning—as in the sentences "The unity is submarine" or "The Sea is History"—pull even the reader unfamiliar with Caribbean history into a network of hypotheses and interpretations that require an effort of learning, understanding, and caring for the fundamentally relational structure of the metaphorical process. In this sense Glissant's use of rich poetic images in his *Poetics of Relation* is itself a gesture toward a relational process not merely between heterogeneous ideas, which are suddenly revealed to share a generic kinship, but also between the context of Caribbean writing and the broader context of non-Caribbean readership (or what, in *Malemort*, Glissant calls "lecteurs d'ailleurs"—readers from elsewhere or foreign readers). The metaphorical transfer is therefore a production of conceptual intimacy and, above all, spatial intimacy where the metaphor of space serves to bring distant geographies and cultural contexts into closer contact. This contact, in which the spatial poetic strives to "sublimate apocalypse and violence" (*RI*, 16), relies also on the abolished separation between onlooker and participant. The intimacy thus created connects the performative poetics to the poetics of location and works to overcome at one and the same time fragmentations of diversity and the violence of imposed totality.

Another dimension of metaphors and figurative speech may be relevant here. As both de Man and Ricoeur remind us, figurative language aims at giving a "face" to what otherwise does not have it: "The very expression 'figure of speech' implies that in metaphor, as in the other tropes or turns, discourse assumes the nature of a body by displaying forms and traits which usually characterize the human face, man's 'figure'; it is as though the tropes gave to discourse a quasi-bodily externalization. By providing a kind of figurability to the message, the tropes make discourse appear" (Ricoeur, 142). This fundamental embodiment of language and its gesture toward sensuous perception of an image has a particular resonance for the transatlantic postcolonial context. As many critics have pointed out, the problem of linguistic deprivation and subsequent colonial silencing of subaltern voices produced a profound and lasting concern with cultural silence. One potent example of this dislocation is the concerted effort, on the Middle Passage slave ship and beyond, to keep slaves isolated from their language group so as to limit the possibility of rebellion. The languages that the slaves subsequently spoke, either the adopted language of the colonizer or the various instantiations of New World Creole, testify to the loss of an immediate linguistic and cultural connection to Africa and to any immediate concept of origin. The region is therefore representative of colonialism at its most alienating with respect to physical location and cultural belonging and serves as a matrix from which the brutality of colonial exploitation can be grasped. The poetic images of slave ships, slaves thrown overboard and drowned, people reduced to commodity and cargo, initially deprived of dialogue and discourse in order to be cast as human tools in the structure of plantation slavery—all of these require, in response, the creation of figurative connections capable of overcoming the historical fragmentation of communities and silencing of their histories in the Caribbean. In response, the metaphor gives a "figure," a perceptible shape, to forgotten, repressed, or marginalized experiences of the Caribbean communities regardless of their origin.

At the same time, spatial representations that I am concerned with also give expression, a face, to the profound relationship between people and their immediate environment precisely because that environment is historically acquired through forced migration. As DeLoughrey et al. clearly show, the Caribbean poet must commemorate "a history that has no surviving witnesses except nature itself" (1) and reveal that "the historical and racial violence in the Caribbean is integral to understanding representations of its geography" (2). The sense of place established through spatial metaphors therefore seeks to address and challenge historiography's lacunae, cultural amnesia, and loss of origins (13–14). According to Naipaul, the connection between a community and its location is, to a large extent, a product of that community's artistic and literary tradition and depends for its validation on the work of the creative artist: "If landscapes do not start to be real until they have been interpreted by an artist, so, until they have been written about, societies appear to be without a shape and *embarrassing*" ("Jasmine," 47, original emphasis).

Yet, as Glissant points out, one of the greatest difficulties of writing in the Caribbean context is how to deal with reality. Realism as a literary theory and technique strives for a "total" representation, which Glissant describes as irritating when introduced wholesale into the Caribbean. "The misery of our lands," he writes, "is not only present, obvious. It contains a historical dimension (of not obvious history) that realism alone cannot account for" (*Caribbean Discourse*, 105). Instead he argues for the centrality of landscape and place in Caribbean literature: "The relationship with the land, one that is even more threatened because the community is alienated from land, becomes so fundamental in this discourse that landscape in the work stops being merely decorative or supportive and emerges as a full character. Describing landscape is not enough. The individual, the community, the land are inextricable in the process of creating history" (105).[12] In the writer's effort to deal with reality (a reality Glissant describes as "miserable"), direct realism is replaced by an investment in alternative ways of tackling both the observed limitations and the imagined possibilities of place.[13] One example of this alternative approach is the literary practice of *marvelous realism* in the literatures of "the Other America"; another is the sustained linking of landscape and community in these same literatures. Such relationship to landscape (and space more generally) offers, in J. Michael Dash's words, "a kind of meta-language in which a new grammar of feeling and sensation is externalized" (introduction, xxxv). Spatial metaphors are therefore a form of metalanguage in which creative imagination finds its indirect and complex ways of giving a "face," through figuration, to a specific reality in which the landscape itself preserves traces of history. We thus find in Glissant's writing an emphasis on what Dash calls "the shaping power of place" (xv). This necessary focus on space and the processes of figuration by which it becomes visible and relational clearly lies at the center of the Caribbean literary aesthetic and pulls the reader into an intimate proximity with the region that may otherwise seem distant or increasingly charted by consumer discourses of tourism.

Finally, the spatial metaphor signals a conceptual necessity of moving "beyond" the limitations of the imposed, absent, or denied location, particularly significant for the Caribbean postcolonial subject whose grounding relation to space and landscape is, as Glissant points out, undercut by the historical memory of an initial violent displacement, whether through slave trade or indentured labor. Caribbean spatioliterary rhetoric therefore relies on the spatial metaphor's gesture of transcending the shortcomings of narrow cultural insiderism or miasmic processes of globalization.

This notion of "beyond" can be found elsewhere in postcolonial discourse, where it plays the same role of suggesting a horizon beyond the usual binary oppositions but refrains from resolving them. In Bhabha's use of this term for postcolonial writers who strive to account for split minority identities and, at the same time, envisage communal solidarity from that interstitial perspective, the "beyond" suggests that one can inhabit an in-between space, a space of ambiguity between prescribed polarities, and still intervene in the present to revise it (*The Location of Culture*, 7). From Bhabha's "beyond" to Glissant's metalanguage and Benítez-Rojo's "certain kind of way," metaphorical and poetic intervention in the sociopolitical realities carries the possibility of shaping the world differently through poetic, conceptual, and imaginative practices. The migrant nature of metaphors themselves, their role in crossing conceptual distances and transferring ideas beyond established conceptual borders, participates in the displacement that Benítez-Rojo attributes to the Caribbean literary text: "Caribbean texts are fugitive by nature," as they constantly disrupt expectations of totality and strive to create and affirm the poetic space of liminality "beyond imprisonment or liberty" (*RI*, 25, 17).

Yet Glissant will also argue that the time has come to reject a "beyond" insofar as it encapsulates a constant orientation toward an elsewhere, which—in the Caribbean context—valorizes the historically imposed centrality of Europe or the counterimagination of a return to

Africa. Instead of transcendence Glissant will therefore argue for "transversality" (*Caribbean Discourse*, 66–67), which frees the Caribbean of the linear and hierarchical visions of history and offers instead a complex notion of cross-cultural convergences that constitute this region. As Dash explains, from early on in his career Glissant sought to make "an epistemological break with the poetics of erasure" practiced by an earlier generation of Caribbean authors in order to effect "a shift from the ideal of a heterocosmic point outside of time and space to the quest for a continuum within time and space—in Glissant's language, the shift from transcendence to transversality" (*The Other America*, 148). However, the kind of "beyond" that he allows for—if I may call it "beyond," despite Glissant's sustained critique of transcendence—has to do with the poetic and literary creativity, whether oral or written, "when a community whose collective existence is called into question tries to put together the reasons for its existence" (Glissant, *Caribbean Discourse*, 104). In this context literature is not an object of pleasure but serves to "dismantle the complex mechanism of frustration and the infinite forms of oppression" (107). Figurative language, as one way of disrupting expectations and calling habits into question, can certainly accomplish this dual role of opening a utopian horizon over there, while registering the shortcomings of what is available right here, thus countering mechanisms of oppression. At the same time, the substitutive gesture of metaphors, although it creates conditions for shared intimacy and alternative imagination, may also obscure the immediate concerns that motivate its initial use.

As I have already pointed out, there is reason to question the extent to which spatial metaphors substitute for concrete problems of place. It is worth considering that while metaphors travel, people often stay put and lack the freedom of motion that discourses enjoy and seem to promise. When it comes to discourses that commemorate and rethink the history of violent conquest, a crucial distinction needs to be made between the sign and its referent, the narrative and its material context. Recent studies of the spatial component in postcolonial fiction certainly emphasize this inextricable link between the fictional and material dimensions of postcolonial spatiality. In *Spaces of Fiction / Fictions of Space: Postcolonial Place and Literary DeiXis*, Russell West-Pavlov insists that although fictive descriptions construct spaces that they seek to describe, they also necessarily "draw upon the material contours of those spaces and must, in turn be informed by them" (2). West-Pavlov's chosen representation of this dialectical relationship between fiction and reality of postcolonial space is "deiXis," a linguistic means by which speakers situate their utterance in a concrete referential place of enunciation: words like *here*, *there*, *this*, and *now* are typical deictic elements of language and can be unambiguously interpreted only in a given pragmatic context. Deixis exemplifies the necessary connection between language and its spatiotemporal referent, but also between the act of describing and the act of locating that speakers always engage in. The act of interpretation is, in turn, an act of linguistic understanding but also, just as importantly, an act of contextual mapping of the utterance. Without its contextual anchor in the concrete place of enunciation, language is always at risk of being ambiguous, misleading, or simply incomprehensible. The capital X in West-Pavlov's "deiXis"—itself a provisional marker of a "third space" between the word and its material referent—points to the fact that the mutually constitutive structure of language and location also relies on the rhetorical figure of chiasmus (as in his titular pair: spaces of fiction and fictions of space), which marks the relationship of reciprocity between language and space: "Language does not merely gain purchase upon space via the instrument of deixis. Conversely, space can be said to ground, indeed, more actively, to inform or infiltrate language" (3). The reason for insisting on such reciprocity and for reading it both into and out of the literary text lies in the fact that, as many critical geographers also argue, space has been largely absent from critical inquiry, and particularly from literary criticism. West-Pavlov suggests that "there has been a long-standing elision of space in narratives of conquest. The purpose of this elision is to obscure the territorial dimensions of Europe's global expansion. Conversely, such an elision of space conceals the profound debt to space underlying territorial mastery" (104). In his critique of the dominance of historicism in critical thought, Edward Soja makes a very similar claim—that space hides consequences from us insofar as the privileged position of history tends to block from view "the critical significance of spatiality of social life" (*Postmodern Geographies*, 24).

In postcolonial studies, as West-Pavlov shows, the elision of spatial critique runs the risk of downplaying the centrality of territorial dispossession and economic exploitation of the postcolony. Exemplifying the way the linguistic-metaphorical dimension emphasizes the spatial-material dimension of the postcolonial condition, Stuart Hall's famous reminder, "I am the sugar at the bottom of the English cup of tea" (48), literalizes the metaphor of sugar: although it stands for the Caribbean people and the history of plantation slavery, it also paradoxically ceases to be a metaphor and becomes instead a reminder that the sugar-based plantation slavery is woven into the contemporary cultural and economic texture of England. Yet if we fail to pay attention to this haunting thread of literal meaning in postcolonial spatial metaphors, their creative potential for generating models of discursive exchange and poetic relationality may obscure the reality of experiences that cannot (and should not) be transcended, although they are often discursively contained within the safe confines of a powerful image. The movement of images across established boundaries, where they challenge the norm and disrupt the rules of discourse, is not equivalent to or easily mapped onto the real relations of people in a given space at a particular time. Much of our spatial experience is precisely that—a given—and is rarely available for creative rearrangements. In other words, there is often a great distance between things as they are and things as we picture them to be, but it is characteristic of the novels I analyze to draw into sharp and unresolved tension the reality of place and the attempts at the imaginary restructuring of its real shortcomings. As I argue for a cautious rereading of spatial metaphors and their triumphant yet inevitably failing answer to the experience of spatial destitution, I am above all attempting to do justice to what the literary representations of Caribbean space seem to suggest: that the emblematic and figurative celebration of space only draws into sharper focus the specific and literal absence of autonomous location. The spatially dispossessed individuals and communities that I examine attempt but ultimately cannot indulge in the luxury of metaphorical crossings. Their confinement and deprivations are—although presented within a literary text—material, literal, and often beyond representation. As such they are far from being emblematic or exchangeable. Their destitution becomes instead, to borrow Baucom's phrase, "invaluable," singular, and, paradoxically, beyond communication. And yet this dispossessed silence is precisely what needs to be expressed. Caribbean authors force us to engage in reading literary texts that claim to represent at one and the same time the mute material reality of its destitute protagonists and their unrelenting efforts to challenge and transform that reality through communal solidarity, humor, and sheer exuberance of language. But the question remains: Is exuberant and rich language a sufficient response to the paucity of material conditions? Can the mobile metaphor of space transform the actual spatial limitation?

Many postcolonial critics have repeatedly voiced their concern with the excessive circulation of postcolonial "master tropes," which instead of critiquing tend to mask the unequal global relations rooted in the history of colonialism. By contrast, in her essay "The Postcolonial: Conceptual Category or Chimera?," Benita Parry underscores precisely the conceptual possibilities opened by contemporary spatial critique for rethinking some of the more celebratory versions of postcolonial theory. Parry reminds us that David Harvey, Edward Soja, and Neil Smith, for example, have all focused on the fact that the global integration of space, which began under colonialism and was completed under imperialism, resulted in the uneven insertion of the colonies into the world economy.[14] The resulting international division of labor makes it impossible to place metropolis and colony on a level plane: "To speak, then, of metropolis and colony as inhabiting the same interstitial ground neglects that this territory was differentially occupied and that it was contested space, being the site of coercion and resistance, and not of civil negotiation between evenly placed contenders" (16). As Parry points out, the detachment of the signifying systems from the material conditions in which they are made to signify in the first place leads some postcolonial theorists away from their most pressing concern, that of addressing global patterns of uneven development under capitalism as it expresses and redefines itself through various colonial and imperial projects.[15]

What emerges here is an age-old conceptual combat between hard social materialism and fluid cultural imagination, reality and fiction, fact and utopia. What side of the question should spatial analysis occupy? Is space just a neutral container for the dynamic struggles of history and human life? Is it a concept whose very abstraction ensures, as Sara Upstone points out, a conceptual openness that resists fixed definitions (2–4)? Is it a material reality we inhabit whether or not we reflect on it, or a metaphor we resort to when we speak of our position in the world and of that world itself? My reading of this complex interplay between the material and fictional aspects of space in Caribbean postcolonial literature evinces a narrative struggle to imagine a different position and space for the postcolonial subject while persistently drawing attention to the limited and oppressive material reality of the postcolonial location and the specific historical and political conditions under which it was and is being produced. Instead of subordinating the real to the cultural and the semiotic, a conciliatory procedure Parry is right to critique (*Postcolonial Studies*, 5), I seek to elucidate the ways Caribbean fiction uses the third space of imagination, utopia, and metaphorical substitution not to resolve or neutralize the enduring legacies of the colonial conflict but rather to draw into sharper focus the shortcomings of an incomplete postcolonial autonomy and the socioeconomic inequality that continues to operate in global capitalism's posture of mutuality. What interests me here is not only the dialectical dependence of one conceptual pole on the other, but also the ways literary texts, which constitute my primary focus, challenge and undermine the binary of any such conceptual combat. This challenge to the binary opposition between, for example, the colonizer and the colonized, or between the First and Third World, does not dissolve its relevance and certainly cannot mollify its devastating effects, but it does underscore the constitutive violence of the binary structure and challenges the sociopolitical context that institutes such a binary as the only operative and lasting relation. With respect to space, we could ask a kindred question: Is space important as an actual reality or as an image, as a social fact or as an endlessly mobilized metaphor Lefebvre is right to question? If space is both, as I maintain, along with many theorists of space, then literary imagination has much to teach us about the nature and possibilities of our materiality. Literary representations of spatial practice and the spatial metaphors of identity do not merely describe or comment on what is actually perceived but project a possibility—an image of how a community could live in the space that it claims through daily use and attachment rather than ownership. In the subsequent chapters I will attempt to show how this alternative spatiality comes into being in specific literary texts.

2 A House of One's Own

Individual and Communal Spaces in the Caribbean "Yard Novel"

> Fiction is like a spider's web, attached ever so lightly perhaps, but still attached to life at all four corners. . . . But when the web is pulled askew, hooked up `at the edge, torn in the middle, one remembers that these webs are not spun in mid-air by incorporeal creatures, but are the work of suffering human beings, and are attached to grossly material things, like health and money and the houses we live in.
>
> —Virginia Woolf, *A Room of One's Own*

MANY ACCOUNTS OF SPATIALITY seek to distinguish *space* from *place*. For instance, Edward Casey's comprehensive study of the philosophical history of place, *The Fate of Place*, gives precedence to place over space, suggesting that "to be at all—to exist in any way—is to be somewhere, and to be somewhere is to be in some kind of place" (ix). Because it is so central to our existence, place is often taken for granted and subsumed by the more dominant categories of space and time. The notion of space, Casey argues, is traditionally described as universal, infinite, and ubiquitous. Place, on the other hand, has the advantage of being a more modest and more significant category for a "particular *somewhere*" (xii, original emphasis), constitutive of the way we exist in the world. Other, usually phenomenological traditions of spatial analysis introduce a similar emphasis on the category of place. For Yi-Fu Tuan, space is an abstract term that serves to organize human biological needs and social relations, while place signals a spatial engagement on a different scale, allowing affective experience and intimate attachment to determine the way a particular place emerges out of the abstract realm of space (149).

For the purpose of my argument, I follow those theorists of space who recognize the inherent complexity of spatial considerations by suggesting that the strict separation of terms may be neither necessary nor necessarily productive. In *Place and Experience: A Philosophical Topography*, Jeff Malpas suggests, for example, that the investigation of place can be pursued only in conjunction with an investigation of space

(25–26). Malpas's notion of place is relevant for my discussion insofar as it recognizes that "place *is integral to the very structure and possibility of experience*" (32, original emphasis) and that within place, subjectivity itself is established (35).[1] The social itself emerges through the interplay between self, intersubjective relations, and location (36). We do not merely observe a passive spatial world that offers itself ready-made to our gaze, nor do we simply construct that world through our psychological and social perception. Instead, in a familiar gesture of undermining the binary through a third (metaphorical) solution, Malpas likens the complexity of place to the "process of triangulation and traverse by which the topographical surveyor builds her map" (41). Similarly "the delineation of place can only be undertaken by a process that encompasses a variety of sightings from a number of conceptual 'landmarks' and that also undertakes a wide-ranging, criss-crossing set of journeys over the landscape at issue" (41).

Although he emphasizes the ontological dimension of human spatiality (13), Malpas is attentive to the interconnected dimensions of individual experience, social relations, and a specific locale. He thus shares some of Lefebvre's concerns regarding the role of space in structuring social practices. Malpas disengages, however, from Lefebvre's socially *produced* and politically inflected spatiality. Central to my reading of the Caribbean, Lefebvre's production of space allows me to emphasize the manner in which exploitative and alienating socioeconomic structures (of which colonialism is one potent example) also produce particular kinds of spatial hierarchy. In my reading of Caribbean literary texts, what emerges most powerfully is the continuous impact of socioeconomic deprivation on the self-understanding of the protagonists. This deprivation is not only socially produced but derives its structure and modes of operation from an established practice of capitalist exploitation so cogently exposed by Marx and Engels and their followers, of whom Lefebvre remains one of the most spatially perceptive. The inherently ontological nature of human spatiality remains only one facet of social space; beyond the moment of our inherent place-bound existence, we also generate space in accordance with our cultural, economic, and political understanding of the world. Our spatial existence is therefore not only given but also continually produced and reproduced and as such reveals that forms of spatial practice can be imposed upon us in a dominated space that we passively experience, just as space can be transformed through our everyday practice and active ways of conceiving it. This vital dynamic of the way space emerges in and from particular social practice and in turn shapes it leads me to consider in Caribbean literature the creative contestations of dominated space inherited from the colonial world order.

For this reason, it is useful to remember Doreen Massey's suggestion that considerations of place, important though they may be, should "not be opposed to, but rather set within, a politics of space" ("Don't Let's Counterpose Place and Space," 25). Instead of "romanticizing" the notion of place as "the sphere of the everyday, of real and valued practices, the geographical source of meaning" (Massey, *For Space*, 5), Massey insists that, "in an age of 'globalization' we need also to be able to 'ground' our international connections, to recognize responsibility at a distance, to appreciate that 'the closest in' maybe should not always be the first priority" ("Don't Let's Counterpose Place and Space," 24). In offering this amendment to theorizations of place, Massey recognizes nevertheless that "international connections" often spring from and can lead to the violent acquisition of space understood as territory and possession; her book *For Space* opens with a spatially inflected account of Hernán Cortés's arrival at Tenochtitlán and his subsequent conquest of this Aztec city. Such an opening is a valuable reminder that the history of conquest and the conquistador's perception of space relegate other places, peoples, and cultures to the role of surface phenomena deprived of their own produced histories and trajectories. In a similar vein, Massey suggests, contemporary neoliberal capitalist globalization presents itself as an inevitable project in which others are never conceived of as coeval. Their histories and alternative futures, like that of the Aztecs, are spatially obliterated because they are understood as lagging "behind" and therefore in dire need of being brought in line with Western versions of "progress."[2] The potentially valuable transnational and global connections run the risk of promoting centralized and homogenizing cultural models. They also send us back to the history of colonial conquest through which the ideological precedence of one socioeconomic model found itself spatially enacted across the globe. For these reasons, Massey's insistence on "the politics of space" as a healthy counterweight to the celebration of innocent and meaningful place has much relevance for my own reading of space. In the Caribbean literary context, the "poetics of relation" beyond local boundaries necessitates a clear recognition of the ways the Caribbean locale was itself violently inserted into global history and spatiality through colonial conquest, transatlantic slave trade, and plantation slavery. Even if we choose to define it as a meaningful place that stands apart from some notion of abstract spatiality, this meaning would always need to recognize the constitutive violence of its perpetual globalization. No account of place that I deal with in this book can therefore overlook the politics of space in which the interpretations of place are necessarily embedded. Although I never treat place and space as interchangeable, I do keep them in a perpetual relation and use them, in the context of Caribbean literature, as diversely inflected facets of the same phenomenon of spatiohistorical awareness and self-perception.

There is nevertheless one important way my project focuses its more general spatial concerns and offers a localized analysis of Caribbean spatiality. In order to read not only the overall metaphorical and material meaning of spatial imagination in the Caribbean but also its concrete embodiments, I focus on the house and housing conditions as one spatio-architectural element that exemplifies and informs my theoretical concerns. The figure of the house serves to draw attention to marginalized people's struggle for a place of their own. Yet it also draws attention to the absence of such a place and the failure to obtain access to it precisely because of the spatial politics generated by colonial socioeconomic relations. The insistence on the acquisition and possession of a house is therefore also a form of resistance to the imposed structures of the administered and dominated spatial practice.

The house, of course, has a long history and significance of its own both in its actual quotidian existence and in its various theoretical and imaginative usages. Like the concepts of space and home, the house is as metaphorical as it is concrete, as rich as it is reductive, as suggestive as it is banal, a locus of everything from the recent housing market crash to the gothic narrative. Yet in the Caribbean context, the house, more than any other type of space, allows me to address the intertwined questions of private and communal space, ownership and dispossession, and material destitution and its utopian substitutes.

Above all, however, my focus on the house recognizes Caribbean authors' explicit interest in using the house as a symbol of legitimate autonomous place and as a concrete reminder of its material absence. Through the figure of the house, I explore the centrality of space in Caribbean literature, which, at its historical core, grapples with displacement and claims to place. Given the profound geographic discrimination produced by colonial occupation and administration of territory, the etymologically understood concept of destitution allows me to examine the problematic of spatial exclusion of the individuals and communities represented in V. S. Naipaul's *A House for Mr. Biswas* (1961), Patrick

Chamoiseau's *Texaco* (1992), Beryl Gilroy's *Frangipani House* (1986), and Raphaël Confiant's *L'Hôtel du Bon Plaisir* (2009). Focusing on the etymological sense of the word *destitution* (to be put away or placed outside), I question the paradox of "the insider's outsideness" (Bhabha, *The Location of Culture*, 14) within a dominant power structure. The destitute in these novels are thus defined by their spatial identities, produced in their struggle to reclaim their denied location (a house, a self) in both material and imaginative terms.

Houses often become the site of convergence for the external and internal preoccupations of a culture and are seen as the symbolic manifestation of its real historicopolitical concerns. In *The Architectural Uncanny*, for example, Anthony Vidler relies on the architectural elements of the Freudian uncanny to focus on the house as a significant, albeit ambiguous, topos of the nineteenth-century uncanny narrative. Vidler's study is important for establishing a complex and rarely examined link between spatial reality, literary imagination, and psychological experience of those spaces, such as houses, that are at one and the same time most familiar and most threatening to us and that simultaneously evoke our tangible reality and our fictional departures from it. By exploring a series of ambiguities and contradictions that haunt architecture and endow it at the same time with an immense figurative power, Vidler shows that the enclosed house spaces can signify safety while paradoxically threatening us with entombment. The house therefore stages a physical encounter between our utopian certainties and our heterotopian dread and shows that architectural spaces can reveal the very manner in which unresolved contradictions are played out: "Space, in contemporary discourse, as in lived experience, has taken on an almost palpable existence. Its contours, boundaries, and geographies are called upon to stand in for all the contested realms of identity, from the national to the ethnic; its hollows and voids are occupied by bodies that replicate internally the external conditions of political and social struggle, and are likewise assumed to stand for, and identify, the sites of such struggle" (167). Our focus on spatially produced social meaning therefore partakes of the twofold nature of spatial experience in which space exists as a palpable reality and "stand[s] for" (as Vidler puts it) or "substitutes for" (in my terms) the contested domains of identity. The complex interplay between identity and its spatial production can be read from the contradictory and fluctuating aspects of social space. What is particularly uncanny in this social space is, Vidler argues, the fear that haunts the imaginations of the privileged classes, which have carefully demarcated the safe spaces of their ownership: "Space as threat, as harbinger of the unseen, operates as medical and psychical metaphor for all the possible erosions of bourgeois bodily and social being" (167). The threat of uncanny space is therefore expressed through the fear of being suddenly dispossessed of the objects, territories, and signs of class belonging that define the privilege of ownership as a form of identity.

Taking up this bourgeois phobia of threats to domestic safety—a phobia based on an implicit recognition that bourgeois comfort is itself founded on capitalist exploitation and colonial conquest that can come back to haunt it—Bhabha presents a similar concern with the metaphorical house in which space is haunted by the "unhomely" return of specific historical events and their transhistorical ramifications. This idea informs his influential discussion of "the house of fiction" ("The World and the Home," 141), where the unhomely appears as the invasion of domestic space by history itself. The consequence of such haunting is a blurred boundary between home and world. The moment of postcolonial writing results, for Bhabha, from the forced (colonial) encounter with alien cultural practices and produces, in turn, the recognition of self through the projection of otherness. The task of the critic must therefore consist in fully realizing and taking responsibility for "the un-spoken, unrepresented pasts that haunt the historical present." At the same time, Bhabha is particularly concerned with "the metaphoricity of the houses of racial memory," which he finds in various postcolonial writings, particularly those of Nadine Gordimer and Toni Morrison, although his entire discussion begins with the dwelling failure of Mr. Biswas (147). In this sense Bhabha shows "the world forcibly entering the house of fiction in order to invade, alarm, divide, dispossess," while at the same time insisting on the way "literature haunts history's more public face, forcing it to reflect on itself in the displacing, distorting image of Art" (152). This particular use of spatial images, notably that of the house, to signify the locus of encounter between realms of social practice (private and public) and cognition (self and other) and also between art and material facts of history allows Bhabha to argue for a postcolonial aesthetic that admits other temporalities and historical memories into our reading of social reality. In this way the metaphorical use of space—or space understood as the site of material and signifying practices—allows us to read history and space in conjunction and to view the fictional representations of space as so many attempts to construct historical identity from and into the concrete spatial experience of daily life.

In my view the centrality of space in Caribbean fiction can be detected in the wealth of literary examples that deal with dwelling and in the significant attempts to recognize and emphasize this inherent spatiality in the theoretical approaches to Caribbean literary tradition. In his essay "Houses in West Indian Novel," Edward Kamau Brathwaite insists that West Indian novels, although concerned with spatial living conditions of their protagonists, "*all take place outside the four walls of traditional houses*" (115, original emphasis). Drawing attention to this fact, which includes the genre of the "yard novel," Brathwaite raises the question of houses and their role in Caribbean fiction: "One of the main problems facing the West Indian writer is how to write a novel about houses. A house suggests clearly defined boundaries: physical, emotional, traditional" (111). Confirming that "the house has always been a privileged locale in Caribbean writing," Maeve McCusker argues that for Brathwaite, it also represents "a more ambivalent, fragile, and contested site than in the traditional European novel" and that, for this reason, Brathwaite refuses "any notion of ontological security or of a firmly established identity, sedimented over time." In the Caribbean context, the house is instead "a space which has had to be wrested, both physically and ideologically, from the hands of the ruling classes" (44). Although he emphasizes the significance of Jean Rhys, Edgar Mittelholzer, and John Hearne for their depiction of houses, Brathwaite singles out Naipaul's *A House for Mr. Biswas* as the first instance of a house achieving symbolic stature in West Indian fiction. Given its role of rigidly upholding the sense of East Indian tradition, Naipaul's Hanuman House satisfies the criterion of marking clear boundaries, necessary in Brathwaite's view for the genuine symbolic significance of the house. This particular kind of house (discussed further in chapter 3) constitutes a kind of "sanctuary" (*HMB*, 180) in which the family may focus, without the intrusion of strangers, on its own hierarchy and self-preservation. Within its walls, Hanuman House contains a world of elaborate relations that also serve to maintain an enduring connection to ancestral India and its half-remembered rules and rituals. By contrast, Brathwaite argues, "the great mass of West Indian novels—concerned mainly with the black population of the island—are about people without this sense of sanctuary; they are about people without 'houses' in the John Hearne/Vidia Naipaul sense" (113). The absence of houses signals the lack of social structure that houses arise from and serve to maintain. Despite their focus on dwelling, yard novels all take place outside, beyond the boundaries of a house. "Yet the *structure* of these novels . . . [is] not significantly different from that of *Mr. Biswas* or the novels of Hearne, though their emphases are. Their concerns, to put it another way, are substitutes for houses, not alternatives" (115, original emphasis). Brathwaite associates the "alternative" with the work of writers like Wilson Harris and George Lamming, whose approach to space gives rise to "a genre entirely alternative to 'the house,' structurally wall-less in a hierarchical sense but corresponding to our Caribbean sense of community. This will be the *literature of the yard*" (119, original emphasis). The wall-less nature of the yard novel contests the hierarchical and rigidly structured spaces of the house, moving the focus from enclosed interiority to the open and fluid sense of communal exchange. All yard novels certainly emphasize spatial relations of the collective and its ability to foster and determine identity. In other words, the identity described in the yard novel, which takes place outside, is the identity arising not from an internally experienced self but from a set of external relations between individuals within a group. As Rhonda Cobham aptly puts it, a typical barrack-yard story "lacks a central dominating consciousness and takes its unity instead from the spatial confines of its yard setting" (ix).

In an attempt to define a typical West Indian literary genre, which nevertheless "also illustrates the unity which undergirds the much vaunted diversity of the Caribbean" (104), Robert D. Hamner, in his essay "The Measure of the 'Yard Novel': From Mendes to Lovelace," surveys a series of novels whose action focuses on this particular kind of space: the yard and its shacks and barracks. The yard novel concerns itself with "the yards and streets of lower class, urban West Indian neighborhoods" (99) and finds its instantiation in *Black Fauns* (1935) by Alfred Mendes, *Minty Alley* (1936) by C. L. R. James, *The Hills Were Joyful Together* (1953) by Roger Mais, *Miguel Street* (1959) by Naipaul, and *The Dragon Can't Dance* (1979) by Earl Lovelace, to name but a few instances of this genre in Caribbean fiction. We could add to this list the famous Francophone example (although Hamner himself does not mention it), Joseph Zobel's *Black Shack Alley* (1950).[3] The number of novels dealing with the barrack yard signals an emerging pattern, which is, Hamner insists, "not confined to one author, one nation or one time period" (99). At the same time, this kind of writing can be considered original to the Caribbean and not an extension of the European literary tradition. Seeking to describe this properly Caribbean generic contribution while placing it in a comparative relation to the European canon, Hamner suggest that the yard novel can be productively compared to the picaresque novel insofar as they are both episodic, focused on low-class rogues and socially marginal characters, full of satirical social commentary, and almost brutal in their attention to quotidian detail (99). Yet the two genres also differ in that "the Yard novel progresses by shifting among the adventures of a group of central figures rather than concentrating on the career of a single protagonist" (100).

Does this mean that in the typical yard novel interiority does not matter at all since its alternative has been offered through communal spaces and interactions? Since I am interested in investigating the failing "substitutes" for the house and not its "alternatives," to borrow Brathwaite's language, I propose that the problem of interiority and autonomy in relation to the collective remains central in the novels that I analyze as well as in the typical yard novel itself. In Lovelace's *The Dragon Can't Dance*, for example, the titular dragon, Aldrick Prospect, gradually experiences a sense of detachment from the yard and its collective identity when he confronts the rigid communal patterns of behavior that he cannot embrace. Racial discrimination is the case in point. When the yard judges, rejects, and ultimately assaults its only East Indian dweller, misreading his efforts at being integrated as signs of vanity and ostentation, Aldrick suddenly feels distant from the collective yard identity and faces the profound need of carving his own path within his close-knit but rapidly changing community. This example clearly shows that communal and open-space identity does not resolve or eliminate the question of individual autonomy. Instead the two can only be read as dialectically related. To wrest the notion of interiority from community is, in my view, a path to creating a false and ultimately untenable dichotomy between structural elements that cannot be read in isolation. The same holds true of space: the house is certainly not a site of pure autonomy or isolation, nor is open space a site of pure and boundless circulation. Invisible boundaries crisscross seemingly open spaces, while enclosed spaces can offer an unexpected sense of vastness and movement.[4] Although in Mendes's *Black Fauns*, one of the yard dwellers, Miriam, bemoans the lack of unity among black people in Trinidad—"Nigger people haven't got no unity. If they did have unity, look what happen in this island, my child!" (10), the refrain of Lovelace's yard novel, "All o' we is one" (149), invites us to reconsider the vast potential and necessary limitations of any form of communal identity. As much as "All o' we is one" sounds like a triumphant recognition of commonality, it also carries—as Lovelace is careful to note—the risk of imposed normative identification that ensures a level of safe homogeneity within the group. In this sense the yard novel, with its complex examinations of individual and communal identity, from its early days in the 1930s novels of James and

Mendes to its later incarnations in Lovelace's *The Dragon Can't Dance* and Chamoiseau's *Texaco*, interrogates precisely the "paradoxical connotations of community and claustrophobia" (Cobham, x) that emerge from the spatial structure of the yard. At the same time, the yard novel successfully challenges the role of the educated middle-class spectator whose sympathy for the common people is undermined by his sense of superiority and the judgments produced by his class affiliation. This kind of yard dweller, from James's Mr. Haynes to Naipaul's Mr. Biswas and Raphaël Confiant's Auguste Dorimont, constantly asserts the need for individuality within the group. Such yard dwellers recognize the limitations and contradictions of separate individuality, which always relies on the existence of a community as a definitional backdrop only to deny its formative impact.

With respect to my discussion of spatial destitution in the Caribbean postcolonial context and the spatial metaphors that seek to contest it, the yard novels offer a couple of important narrative procedures that shed light on the genealogy of the spatially oriented Caribbean fiction. First of all, the yard novel's concern with the patterns of collective life and its impact on the individual fate of a single protagonist prefigures the particular kind of spatial representation of social practice that emerges in the later, properly postcolonial novels I analyze. This emergence of the "collective protagonist" emphasizes the communal nature of underprivileged housing and its ambiguous impact on the single protagonist, a person struggling for a clear sense of individuality within a group. When it provides a relevant context and affirmation of one's relational identity, the community is enabling and sheltering, but it is crippling and oppressive when it encroaches on one's sense of autonomy and need for change beyond established patterns of behavior. Second, the yard novel allows us to examine the role of poor housing conditions as they simultaneously impede and stoke the dream of self-possession and autonomy, material ownership, or ultimate escape: "Whether in Georgetown, Kingston or Port-of-Spain, there is the same picture; each brought to life, however, with fresh personalities entrapped in the same predicament. Herein may be traced one of the common thematic threads which appear in different forms in each of the novels. It seems that a desire to escape pervades them all" (Hamner, "The Measure of the 'Yard Novel,'" 103). In many yard novels the protagonists struggle to acquire more money, either through hard work, theft, or sexual relations of convenience; they fight for better education that may take them away from the squalid yard, and they ultimately see various forms of possession—of money, house, or education—as means of establishing and maintaining self-possession and autonomy. The struggle within and outside of the yard is therefore a struggle for a different kind of individuality through which the authors of yard novels nevertheless recognize and seek to chronicle the centrality of collective experience and its cultural value in the Caribbean urban context.

One of the earliest examples of the yard narrative, James's short story "Triumph" (1929), offers the first fictionalized glimpse of yard life, which will subsequently permeate the entire genre of the yard novel: "Where people in England and America say slums, Trinidadians say barrack-yards. Probably the word is a relic of the days when England relied as much on garrisons of soldiers as on her fleet to protect her valuable sugar-producing colonies. Every street in Port-of-Spain proper could show you numerous examples of the type: a narrow gateway leading into a fairly big yard, on either side of which run long, low buildings, consisting of anything from four to eighteen rooms, each about twelve feet square. In these lived the porters, the prostitutes, cartermen, washerwomen and domestic servants of the city" (35). James's story, published during his years of association with *Trinidad* and the *Beacon*—two short-lived but influential journals appearing in the 1920s and early 1930s that anticipated the independence movement in Trinidad—signals a shift from the turn-of-the-century focus on middle-class Creole manners and values to the depiction of the underprivileged majority. According to Stewart Brown, the representation of the yard and its community reveals an increased concern with "issues of pride and dignity among people who have little material wealth or social status" (xx). In order to situate them, James immediately establishes a comparative context in which the barrack yard is a slum, that is, a transnational sign of poverty (it exists in the United States and Britain as much as in Trinidad), but it is also a specifically Trinidadian version of outcast dwelling. The very space of the yard is a relic of wartime, when England was diligently protecting its "valuable sugar producing colonies." This reminder of the material value of the colony to its metropolitan ruler emphasizes all the more starkly the relatively insignificant status of the colonial working population, whose labor sustains the wealth of the European center and at the same time marks the ordinary worker as a reject of that distant world. James lists the details: the size of the gate, the yard, and the rooms as well as the professions of those who are relegated to inhabiting them. In this image of the yard, the imperial military spaces are repurposed to house another kind of war: the war for survival and self-reliance of the forgotten urban infantry, from prostitutes to domestic servants.

We will encounter this yard, this slum, many times. In James's *Minty Alley*, for example, the same context reappears to present us with yard inhabitants facing two competing problems: the constant struggle against the precariousness of their material means and the desperate need to perform that struggle in full view of their neighbors so that the tragedy of their condition will not remain invisible or unacknowledged. In this sense the yard novel exemplifies the performative dimension that, according to Benítez-Rojo, distinguishes the properly Caribbean aesthetic. The specific significance of this performativity arises, in this case, from the protagonists' indirect plea for visibility and witness that the otherwise outcast and forgotten people must claim for themselves. The yard becomes a communal stage on which many of the smaller quotidian and bigger life tragedies are performed, observed, and resolved. From his cramped room Haynes, the educated narrator and lodger, observes all the other protagonists of Minty Alley as they repeatedly rush out into the yard to talk, fight, cry, scream, flirt, or make speeches. The emotions exceed the confines of tiny rooms and spill into the yard to be lived in full view of the neighbors, who play their shifting roles of spectators, participants, jury, and council. As space, the yard is a theater of impoverished living:

> The surroundings were nothing the eye would dwell on without reason. The yard was reddish dirt and bits of stone, but much more dirt than stone, so that on rainy days it would be a mass of slippery mud, treacherous to shoe and slipper, and needing care even from naked feet. Opposite his room was the kitchen, long, low and concrete-floored, with two doors that opened on to the yard and two windows that looked into the alley. As is usual in the tropics, all windows and doors were wide open and he could see straight into it. Joined to the kitchen was the bathroom, and in front of the bathroom but to one side was a pipe with a sink. For the rest there was nothing else to see but the encircling hedge and the upper portions of the neighboring buildings. A dull enough prospect. But if the surroundings were drab, the inhabitants were busy. (28)

James emphasizes here the contrast between "nothing to see" with respect to the qualities of space, its drabness and lack of distinction (something one would not look at without reason) and the "busy" vivid nature of the human drama that unfolds within. The insignificance of location only highlights the complexity of the life it shelters and allows us to focus on watching, through open windows and doors and, in Haynes's case, even through a carefully enlarged peephole in the wall, the yard as the dramatic stage. Nevertheless James treats the lodgers' regular outbursts with humor, giving us the vision of the yard through Haynes's eyes. As a middle-class scholar and bookworm, he enjoys observing the real life of ordinary people while retaining the privilege of leaving it behind any time he chooses. From his perspective, much of what goes on in the yard is excessive, overdramatized, and even grotesque. Occasionally Haynes is deeply moved by the scenes he witnesses; they prompt him to participate or intervene. Yet, as Kenneth Ramchand observes, "one of the novel's concerns is the mutually impoverishing alienation of the educated West Indian from the people" (13). Despite the fact that their vividness is "one expression of life's triumph over narrow surroundings" (12), these people remain prisoners of the yard, locked in its patterns of hope and failure.

This imprisonment by poverty and the absence of future prospects leads Hamner to emphasize escape as a constant obsession of the yard novel. In Mais's *The Hills Were Joyful Together*, for example, one of the main characters, Surjue, attempts to secure his escape from the squalor of the yard by committing robbery. When he is betrayed by his accomplice, Flitters, and caught, Surjue finds himself in a bleak Jamaican prison and is ultimately killed by a prison warden as he tries to escape. "It is Mais's allegory of the fact that his people are entrapped by poverty on the one hand and by the iron grip of overwhelming authority on the other" (Hamner, "The Measure of the 'Yard Novel,'" 100). Surjue comes from the yard in which a familiar drama of intersecting human destinies is performed daily, but, unlike James, Mais makes no appeal to humor to lighten the tragedies in this theater of poverty. Instead he poses a question to which the simultaneously solitary and interlocked destinies of his protagonists serve as an answer: "What happens to people when their lives are constricted and dwarfed and girdled with poverty . . . things like that and that and that come out of it . . . moral deformity, degradation, disease" (197). The extent of material deprivation is here contained in the spatial and spiritual confinement of the yard itself. What is most striking about Mais's yard novel is the fact that the genuine sense of community seems to be hindered precisely by destitute communal living. The inhabitants of the yard share the same living conditions and all of their neighbors' twists of fate, but their concern is first and foremost for their own well-being and survival. Although Mais's purpose may well be "to present a community caught in a deadlock of poverty, hopelessness, and inevitable crime, from which there is no escape" (Maes-Jelinek, 130), most of the yard dwellers do not have the luxury of excessive fellow feeling or generosity. They can participate and help in small doses, for brief periods of time; they can offer their presence and understanding of all the tragedies that the yard contains, but they cannot engage in any sympathy that would tear at the scabs of their own wounds. And because those wounds are constant and many, the community of Mais's yard is always only partially communal. Within it also lies a fierce need for independence, self-reliance, and privacy—precisely those features of human life that destitute living systematically precludes.

On one occasion, however, Mais's yard dwellers come together. By the gratuitous generosity of fate, one of the lodgers, Ras, finds a great quantity of fish, which had mysteriously washed up on the shore. The report from the Fisheries Department later clarifies that the fish had died of suffocation because the recent heavy rains triggered the excessive decomposition of microscopic life responsible for the maintenance of oxygen in the water. Unable to sell it all, Ras organizes a large fish fry in the yard, and all the tenants, exhilarated that they "got fish fo' nothin'," come out to participate: "That evening they built a big fire and set big stones about it in the middle of the yard, and they sat around on chairs and benches and stools and upturned boxes and anything they could sit on, and the women fried fish and Johnny-cakes, and the big fire lit up the darkness and sent up showers of sparks, and they sang songs and told stories and cracked jokes and forgot their worries and their fears and their jealousies and their suspicions and the occasion took on all the aspects of a picnic, and they were like children again" (39). The image of the dark and dreary yard suddenly illuminated by a big fire creates a sense of festive connection among people who are otherwise constantly forced to calculate, incur debt, or repay for everything they ever wanted or needed in life.[5] The unexpected gratuity of the communal fish fry transforms the yard dwellers into children again, suggesting that their adulthood and wisdom are above all the result of accumulated fears and disappointments, a bleak knowledge that only poverty, struggle, and death are guaranteed to them. Everything else feels like a miracle: "And they all laughed, and bright tears stood in the eyes of some, to witness that they still understood the meaning of miracles" (52). In this fleeting image of the spontaneous celebration and unexpected bounty, Mais's narrative shows us that even a sense of community depends on some minimal level of well-being and material security, which would in turn ensure that people have something to give one another in the context of mutual trust and sharing. But for those with nothing, there is nothing to offer with generosity or receive with dignity. The material deprivation thus becomes a source of frustration, insecurity, and ultimate violence. Yard dwellers like Surjue end up wanting to steal or wrestle out of life things they do not have and thus, through any kind of agency, even a criminal one, recapture some personal autonomy with respect to an overwhelming sense of doom. Fish without oxygen, which constitutes their feast, is an apt image for precisely the kind of people who live in the yard, gradually suffocating in the flood of misery. The fish fry is therefore not only a joyous feast but also a prefiguring of death, which seems to be the only viable escape from poverty: "Like flotsam in a turbulent sea, the yard-dwellers are depicted as being tossed about by indifferent waves over which they seem to have no control" (Morris, xiii).

The fish fry nevertheless confirms the bond that connects all the yard dwellers; their sense of identity and mutual recognition is based on their shared spatial existence, and although they rarely enter into one another's lives except by virtue of being thrown together within the same limited space, they nevertheless share the knowledge of the yard itself. In this sense the yard is the measure of their commonality; even if they know nothing else of each other, they know what it means to be defined and confined by the poverty of the yard. While this shared spatial identity helps them recognize and respect their neighbors, it also sets them apart from those who belong elsewhere and whose social and human possibilities are not circumscribed by their living conditions.

At the same time, through one of the secondary characters, Flitters, we gradually discover that the yard, for all its dreariness, is not even the worst of living conditions for the Jamaican poor. Flitters is desperately running through Kingston in an attempt to escape his killers, two men who are set on avenging Flitters's betrayal of Surjue. In the course of his mad and ultimately unsuccessful flight, certain areas of Kingston emerge as gathering grounds for people lost to the world and even to themselves. Around the Ward Theatre, for example, Flitters tries to blend into a group of homeless sleeping on the pavement: "rows of dirty human bundles, looking like cast-up flotsam on a lonely beach" (224). When they later awake to the cries of an elderly woman who was robbed and Flitters, as an alien to the group, is suspected of the theft, they are described as a "hideous bunch" and remind Flitters of "a colony of lepers" (227); people who initially looked like bundles of old clothes on the pavement now reveal themselves to be covered in running sores and disfigured by syphilis. Flitters's horror at this group is palpable, and he fights to escape them as desperately as he runs from his killers. In the nightmarish sequence of his flight, all that we encounter—from the homeless cripples to the neighborhoods of indescribable poverty—acquires the status of murderous agency. Flitters is trying to run from everything that surrounds him, and his killers, who are constantly reemerging from the shadows of the city, are merely an incarnation of all the forces of death and despair that Kingston unleashes upon its dwellers. In the last moments of his mad flight across the city, Flitters ends up in a slum:

> He was walking through back streets and alleys of gloomy, interminable slums.
>
> Stark old tumbledown two- and three-storey houses rose up out of the palpable shuddering greyness, seemed to totter together in a nightmarish huddle above the narrow, evilly-leering, gutted streets. (228)

In contrast to this anthropomorphized "leering" habitation whose evil seems to emanate from the houses themselves, Flitters bitterly remembers that there are people in the world who find slums interesting precisely because they do not have to live in them. This "slumming" mentality of the privileged classes is here exposed with unforgiving irony, suggesting that only the wealthy can find poverty quaint or romantic. For the poor, destitution is a daily threat of being gradually dehumanized in a struggle for basic survival: "There were nice people who thought, ain't old slums awfully quaint-looking and romantic, and in their own way beautiful? . . . people who had nice manners sitting in restaurants eating, and smelt of expensive toilet water, and spent the afternoon, by appointment, at the hairdresser, or sitting smoking cigarettes and reading the latest Book-of-the-Month selection steaming their pores in hot scented baths" (228). The dominant feature of this passage is its focus on agreeable scents that the wealthy and educated people can enjoy; they are perfumed, groomed, soaked, and scrubbed by appointment. Meanwhile the homeless covered in putrid sores pick themselves up from the dirty pavement while the wind blows across "the carelessly swept-up heaps of untended roadside garbage where dogs, scuffling, snarling, fighting, had been before" (228). The pleasant scents of the upper classes are contrasted with the stench of garbage heaps in the slums. The two types of spatial identity, marked here by the type of smell that surrounds them, evoke the stark contrast between the housing conditions and determine the kind of morality available to them. Mais indirectly links the poor, who fight desperate and merciless battles, to the snarling dogs on garbage heaps, while he describes the privileged as those who can afford aesthetic appreciation of the world and of themselves. In *The Hills Were Joyful Together* the kinds of space available to people determine the scope of their human interaction and the possibilities of their identity. The privilege of not being defined by one's spatial existence is reserved for those whose spaces are clean, open, and multiple. In other words, economically privileged people are spatially and socially mobile and enjoy the luxury of not being restricted by their spatial identity. This class-conscious and critical dimension of Mais's writing leads Brathwaite to conclude that his commitment to the underprivileged black majority led Mais in search of a "nativist aesthetic" ("The Unborn Body of the Life of Fiction," 31). In his depictions of the yard and its quotidian chipping away at the dwellers' basic humanity, Mais is more of a social realist than any of his fellow writers and could be productively compared to Dickens or Dostoyevsky with respect to the unflinching honesty of his realism. It is particularly his refusal to offer communal living and shared suffering as answers to material deprivation that sets him apart from other authors of yard novels, whose humorous and festive depiction of the collective allow us a different and much more hopeful view of the yard.

In Lovelace's *The Dragon Can't Dance*, for example, the initial image of the dire living conditions yields room to a warm and fairly optimistic representation of the profound connections between yard dwellers. There is, despite their poverty, a sense of pride and strong neighborhood identity that permeates Port of Spain's Calvary Hill and its inhabitants and is further marked by their keen preparations for Carnival. Nevertheless, for all of its ambiguity of tone, the novel's opening image of destitution and its consequences cannot be overlooked: "This is the hill, Calvary Hill, where the sun set on starvation and rise on potholed roads, thrones for stray dogs that you could play banjo on their rib bones, holding garbage piled high like a cathedral spire, sparkling with flies buzzing like torpedoes; and if you want to pass from your yard to the road you have to be a high-jumper to jump over the gutter full up with dirty water, and hold your nose. Is noise whole day. Laughter is not laughter; it is a groan coming from the bosom of these houses—no—not houses, shacks that leap out of the red dirt and stone, thin like smoke, fragile like kite paper, balancing on their rickety pillars as broomsticks on the edge of a juggler's nose" (9). Lovelace describes the same hungry dogs, heaps of garbage, putrid stench, mud, and noise that Mais also seeks to expose, but his tone is different. Is he trying to make us smile as we take in the subtle humor of the image of playing banjo on the starved dog's ribs or high-jumping over the gutter of dirty water while holding one's nose? The language is humorous, extravagant, and bold: garbage is as high (and awe-inspiring?) as a cathedral spire, flies are sparkling (like diamonds?) and buzz like torpedoes, and shacks balance on their rickety pillars like brooms on a juggler's nose. Poor living is saturated with images, from athletic feats to circus performances, with banjos, torpedoes, and kites woven into the unruly mix. We might laugh at the festive excess and deliberate incoherence of the tropes. But we are also soberly reminded that "laughter is not laughter" here but rather a "groan" coming from the shacks. If we ever wanted to smile at the acrobatics one needs to master in order to survive poverty, we are immediately stopped in our tracks. Are we really finding humorous the unsanitary conditions Lovelace is describing even as he tempts us, with that same humor, to confront our desire not to take poverty very seriously? He describes children "lean and hard like whips, their wise yellowed eyes filled with malnutrition and too early knowing" and reminds us that, from such early age until the end of their lives, the yard dwellers hold "their poverty as a possession" (10), almost like jewelry or a magic charm, which they inherit from their ancestors and carry as a sign of their history. In Lovelace's series of irreconcilable paradoxes, the yard dwellers are described as the aristocrats of destitution, who hold on to their poverty like "a charmed medallion whose magic invested them with a mysterious purity, made them the blue-bloods of a resistance lived by their ancestors all through slavery, carried on in their unceasing escape—as Maroons, as Runaways, as Bush Negroes, as Rebels: and when they could not perform in space that escape that would take them away from the scene of their brutalization they took a stand in the very guts of the slave plantation, among tobacco and coffee and cotton and canes, asserting their humanness in the most wonderful acts of sabotage they could imagine and perform" (10). By tracing the history of rebellion and escape emphasized in Hamner's analysis of the yard novel, Lovelace reveals to the reader that particular kinds of spaces like the yard and the shack owe their existence to the history of slavery and the brutalization suffered by the enslaved and indentured people in the Caribbean. Their daily experience of destitution goes hand in hand with their unwavering resistance, defiance, and sabotage through which they confirm their "humanness." Their laughter is not meant to make light of the reality of deprivation but to defy any expectation that these conditions succeed in stripping people of their selfhood and dignity. Instead Lovelace's poor are acrobats and wizards of survival, though the acrobatics and wizardry do not lighten the tragedy of colonial history, which brought these people from the plantation to the yard in search of better living. Lovelace shows Carnival, laughter, and communal living as elements of "the miracle of their surviving" (40) in a world that measures humanity on the basis of ownership. In response his protagonists fight to matter by "surviving on nothing and standing up still on your own two feet" (41).

The brief period of Carnival and the meticulous preparations for it allow the struggling inhabitants of the yards and shacks of Port of Spain to recapture, however fleetingly, not only their own creative power but also their ancestral lineage from Africa to the New World as well as their potential to metamorphose from the ordinary poor into the masqueraders with magic powers conferred upon them by their costumes, masks, and rituals. The tin drums awake the Hill, announcing the masqueraders' arrival "that goes back centuries for its beginnings, back across the Middle Passage, back to Mali and to Guinea and Dahomey and Congo, back to Africa when Maskers were sacred and revered, the keepers of poisons and heads of secret societies" (120). Carnival thus offers a brief moment when one can choose and build one's identity instead of passively inhabiting an imposed identity position. Such positions are, as Lovelace continually emphasizes, fixed by poverty in a world where static possession of objects rather than fluid creation of self determines the scope of social mobility. Yet, since the yard dwellers live "the reality of non-possession as a way of life" (105), Carnival and other forms of art allow them to claim their right to selfhood. As the main protagonist, Aldrick, insists, "All we thinking about is to show this city, this island, this world, that we is people, not because we own anything, not because we have things, but because we is. We are because we is. You know what I mean?" (111). Through Aldrick's impassioned speech, Lovelace strives to separate being from ownership and rescue the idea of identity from its connection to the hierarchy of social positioning. The marginal space represented by the yard can therefore never capture or exhaust the meaning and potential of the people who inhabit it; although the yard dwellers are constantly hindered by their spatial and material confinement, they also always strive to overcome and escape it, transforming groans into laughter and despair into celebration. How successfully Carnival, calypso, steel band warfare, ancestral memory, and simple laughter defy the conditions of material deprivation we are left to judge for ourselves, keeping in mind, however, that Lovelace's central point revolves around the need to understand and honor history while moving forward and overcoming its negative legacy. The people of Port of Spain, Trinidad, and even the Caribbean as a whole have to learn to "hold in their minds the two contradictory ideas—their resistance and surviving, their rebellion and their decency" (164). The simultaneity of such contradictory notions is manifested in the very space of the yard, where the initial squalor and misery yield the story of a complex and resilient community. The yard itself is Lovelace's site of contradiction, where the metaphorical and creative potential of a people clashes against its material limitations. The spatial configuration of the yard novel is thus revealed to be a necessary meeting ground not only for the variety of protagonists and stories but also for more abstract ideas: the Lefebvrian idea of *perceived space* and its historically imposed social restrictions and the idea of *lived space*, where the inhabitants themselves reconceive of their social practice, struggling to recapture their communal and personal meaning.

The formation of personal identity and its dependence on the spatial context in which it develops is further emphasized by those yard novels that focus on the autobiographical dimension of their author-narrator's spatial memory. Naipaul's *Miguel Street* and Zobel's *Black Shack Alley* both trace the coming of age of their child narrator through the spaces he inhabits, loves, and slowly recognizes as the most significant part of his identity. Both novels are a testament to the memory of childhood spaces where, in retrospect, the narrator locates the roots of his life story and, implicitly, his subsequent desire to write.

Naipaul's novel is not, strictly speaking, a "yard" novel but focuses instead on a single street in St. James, the predominantly Indian neighborhood in Port of Spain. Nevertheless it follows the same structure as the more typical yard novel: within the same frame narrative, *Miguel Street* offers a series of smaller stories, which bring each inhabitant of the street into the spotlight while giving him a dominant characteristic by which he will be remembered. "Man-man was mad; George was stupid; Big Foot was a bully; Hat was an adventurer; Popo was a philosopher; and Morgan was our comedian" (63). In this manner, just as in the yard novels already discussed, Naipaul reveals the street to be the composite of characters and stories, which, although fleeting and episodic, create a strong sense of community. This community is defined by the protagonists who shape a collective world; just as Morgan was "our" comedian, all the other characters simply belong to the neighborhood, which owes its communal identity to the presence of the familiar (nicknamed) figures like Popo, Hat, and Man-man. As they become privy to the stories, readers are also drawn into this community: the pronoun *our* extends to include us so that we slowly become intimate with the inhabitants of Miguel Street and share in their particular "we."

Miguel Street opens with two characters, Hat and Bogart, calling out to one another: "What happening there, Bogart?" "What happening there, Hat?" As these voices echo through the neighborhood, they create the texture of aural connections and draw the reader, along with the narrator, into a world where everything is overheard, witnessed, and known. As in other yard novels, individual identity emerges only in relation to others—neighbors, friends, memorable freaks, and street "extras," who are not just people we get to know but also human landmarks orienting us within Naipaul's childhood spaces. Their arrivals and departures, professions, habits, love stories, downfalls, and fantasies shape the boy who observes them and, although he will (like Naipaul himself) ultimately leave this world behind, it is this space that provides his most genuine sense of belonging.

If we compare *Miguel Street* to Naipaul's English novel of space and dwelling, *The Enigma of Arrival* (1987), it becomes clear that the warmth of community in Port of Spain has been replaced in England by the contemplative distances between manors, isolated houses, and people perceived from afar. Sounds and voices no longer travel. *The Enigma* is instead a narrative of vision where the eye strains to take in and comprehend the world that is no longer audible and has certainly lost its taste and smell. Although he learns how to look at the English countryside near Stonehenge, which gives him the sense of ancient history, Naipaul calls his life in England "savorless" (101), resulting in the "distortion of [his] personality from the very day [he] had left home" (157). This lack of savor and the distortion of personality characterize, in Naipaul's view, the life of a migrant. He can observe and ultimately understand his surroundings, but he is also forever marked by the memories of childhood wonder in relation to his Trinidadian past, captured in *Miguel Street* and lost in *The Enigma*. Although in *The Enigma* we witness a striving to overcome, as Susheila Nasta argues, "the dialectics of a metaphor of place" (95) revolving around images of belonging or unbelonging and to develop instead "the ambidextrous vision of both a colonial and postcolonial consciousness" (96), the spatiality of loss remains the focus of this novel. It is only in the form of ruins that personal and communal histories can be excavated from the spatial configurations of one's surroundings so that the moments of belonging are always paradoxically the moments of unbelonging because one always belongs, belatedly, to the past. By contrast, Miguel Street is a place known deeply and directly through freshness of emotion and immediate engagement with the surroundings. The superficial impression that Miguel Street is a slum cannot really hold; its apparent material poverty is, as in all yard novels, replaced with an incredible narrative wealth: "A stranger could drive through Miguel Street and just say 'Slum!' because he could see no more. But we, who lived there, saw our street as a world, where everybody was quite different from everybody else" (63). Here the imagined perceptions of a "stranger," who sees the neighborhood only as a slum, are contrasted to what "we," the street dwellers, see in our environment. For a stranger who is zipping by in his car, Miguel Street will be no more than an image of poverty, exactly as in *The Enigma* the English manor will for Naipaul-the-stranger initially be no more than an image of imperial grandeur and its decay. The contrast between the stranger's and the dweller's vision lies in the dweller's ability to discern the minute relevance of any one detail in relation to the place as a physical and emotional totality. This relevance of one life or story for all other lives and stories requires the knowledge of space in time, that is, not as a briefly glimpsed image framed by a car window but as a lived and felt daily reality that unfolds in time. For this reason Naipaul's narrator insists on the fact that what to an outsider appears as a slum, to an insider has the magnitude of a world.[6] In this sense the confinement of the slum and the limited spaces of Miguel Street cannot be reduced to their material and visible components. Instead the variety and greatness of stories we read emphasize the vastness of lived experience through which space becomes charged with its own implicit poetics.

In *Black Shack Alley*, Zobel explores the same coming-of-age view of his immediate environment, recording the wealth of experiences and impressions that are generated even by the most modest or downright impoverished living conditions. His story begins in the hills around Fort-de-France in Martinique, notably Petit-Morne, where the narrator, José Hassam, grows up with his grandmother, M'man Tine, who works on the nearby sugarcane plantation. It is in this early childhood that José witnesses the unrelenting hardship of the villagers who toil on the plantation and live in dire poverty on the street Cases-Nègres. The street is described as a set of barracks at the foot of a hill; around them are endless fields of sugarcane: "Black Shack Alley comprised some three dozen ramshackle wooden huts, covered with galvanize, standing at regular intervals at the side of the hill" (11). The plantation workers can barely make ends meet. Their children run around dressed in rags, which are easily torn or simply fall apart during play. Hunger is one of the boy's recurring experiences, and Zobel depicts it in unforgiving detail. Yet José perceives this world as rich and endlessly exciting: the games are those of discovery, and the stories he overhears constantly expand his sense of the world. However, unlike other yard novels, Zobel's depiction of childhood focuses on M'man Tine as the central figure of the narrative and a foundation for the life of its young protagonist. She is also his source of gradual realization of the historical and racial structure of poverty and exploitation in Martinique. Despite her hardships, however, the grandmother represents a kind of home for the boy as she is the only solid, reliable, and safe context he knows. When she falls seriously ill and is taken to the hospital, José experiences the house they live in as a darkened prison with no warmth or hope. In this sense Zobel's depiction of dwelling is focused on the emotional value of space from the perspective of a child. M'man Tine is also a connection to everything that, almost unconsciously, the boy understands to be his history; she is the force of ancestral memory, and it is her faith and loyalty, her firm knowledge of custom and traditions, that guide him from the poverty of the hill to a successful education. M'man Tine's main motivation in all the hard work she does is to see the boy free of the necessity of working for the white plantation owner, even well after independence from slavery has been achieved. Although herself unschooled, she sees in scholarly success the only opportunity for the black boy to escape the destiny of continued but disguised servitude.

M'man Tine's strength and dignity permeate the novel and suggest another view of dwelling, whereby a particular person and her emotional fortitude substitute for the dire reality of destitute living. For as long as his grandmother is around, José is certain that he is safe and sheltered. No house or material comfort can replace her, while her presence, by contrast, continually erases the limitations of poverty. Nevertheless, in his frustration with the poverty and material suffering of those he loves, José occasionally dreams of wealth. Yet he stipulates, even in his daydream, that his property will not be reliant on sugarcane (except the little he needs to chew on for dessert!): "As for me, I'd have a large property, as big as the whole countryside around us. I wouldn't plant any sugar cane, except a few stalks for my dessert. But I'd have many people cultivating vegetables and fruits along with me, rearing hens, rabbits, but even to go to work, they'd put on trousers and shirts that were not torn, they'd wear fine suits on Sundays, and their children would all go to school" (101). José's vision of a better future consists of a large property where people work in collaboration for everyone's benefit rather than working for the owner, in servitude. The workers he imagines are all well-dressed, dignified, and content, and their children are educated. Sugarcane is not a deadly crop of exploitation but simply a dessert. In José's imaginary world of ownership, to own is a means of giving to others and lessening their hardships. His friend Jojo reminds him that only "béké," the white man, has access to such a life: "But your workers, then, they'll be almost as well fed and lodged as the *békés*! Then there'll be no more niggers; and what are the *békés* going to do!" (101). Jojo's reminder implicitly emphasizes that race is a matter of social and economic status: if everyone is well fed and well dressed and has access to education, there will be no more "white" and "black." These categories ultimately designate wealth and poverty rather than any physical characteristic. In this manner Zobel underscores the role of economic marginalization in the creation and maintenance of racial discrimination. "Béké" and "nègre" are, for the two boys, categories that signal economic opportunity in a particular social structure, and this understanding of race carries with it the full weight of the history of slavery. More sinister and more humorous still is Jojo's final question: If there are no more "nègres," what would the "béké" do? This question, as if it were a simplified version of Hegel's famous master-slave dialectic, suggests that the privileged postslavery plantation owner owes the meaning of his existence to those he can exploit. Without them, in the boys' view, he would cease to exist. The exploited plantation workers, on the other hand, continue to live their daily hopes and struggles with unwavering dignity and self-possession.

Their perseverance is represented through the figure of the storyteller, M. Médouze, whom José considers his best friend despite the enormous age difference. The old man reveals to the boy the traditional structure of oral storytelling, drawing him into the world of proverbs, riddles, and tales. Most important, however, M. Médouze reveals to José the importance of spatial coordinates of Martinican culture. In the course of his storytelling, the old man teaches the boy about the triangular relation between Martinique, France, and "la Guinée." La Guinée is a magical final destination in Africa from which everything came and to which everything will return. And although José remarks that, unlike other elders, M. Médouze never gives him any objects or treats, what he receives from M. Médouze's stories is an experience of how a world of objects becomes animate and how in turn the animate creatures can become things (30). This magic of narrative transformations attests to Zobel's belief in metaphorical spaces' power to challenge the confinement of the socially and economically prescribed space.

From *Miguel Street* and *Black Shack Alley* as examples of autobiographical yard fiction to Lovelace's, Mais's, and James's biographies of yards, yard novels exemplify an attempt to show space as constitutive of identity, produced and contested through quotidian battles of their inhabitants to redefine the fixed coordinates of class, race, age, and gender. In Caribbean fiction and beyond, the yard novel is an excellent instance of the literary representation of spatial practice in which the questions of material and symbolic production of space are inextricably related. In many ways these novels serve as literary precursors and generic parameters for reading the more contemporary versions of spatially inflected Caribbean fiction. The images of destitute houses and yards, the marginal nature of ramshackle compounds and slum neighborhoods require us to take a closer look at the role of the house itself in determining the scope of personal and communal freedom in the context of spatially defined material deprivation. Already in the yard novel, houses and yards turn out to be more than physical containers for a particular population and certainly more than just a setting to the story. They allow us to give serious consideration to the spatial intersections of material and metaphorical concerns through which a literary representation seeks to challenge the perceived limitations of real spaces. These are spaces of confinement and spaces of freedom, spaces of gathering and spaces of fragmentation. As Lovelace aptly observes in *The Dragon Can't Dance*, such contradictions must remain in constant dialectical relation despite the fact that many of the yard novels may ultimately strive to resolve them through the act of storytelling itself; in all these texts the telling of the story is itself a space—a powerful literary space—that can hold such contradictions together while constantly reminding us of the looming dangers of their embattled existence. At the same time, the notion of literary space is itself an often contested metaphor that seems to crumble easily when juxtaposed to real spaces: slums, yards, shacks, and all places of material destitution. Such spaces are certainly not only the source material for fiction but also, and more important, the daily social reality of the Caribbean and many other places around the world.

As a matter of fact, the reality of insalubrious and slum living is, as many sociologists argue, an increasing pattern of contemporary global capitalism and its attendant overurbanization. It is therefore important to question what literary texts concerned with spatial deprivation and poverty have to say with respect to the reality of such problems. How does the imaginary engage with and respond to the daily spatial practice in spaces dominated by global economic growth that persistently produces the paucity of public spaces, affordable housing, and opportunities for "nonmanaged" communal life? Literary discourse on houses and spaces is as valuable as any firsthand participant observation of spatial practice and offers that dimension of symbolic engagement with real space that Lefebvre valued so highly. More important still, and this is a point to which I will keep returning in subsequent chapters, the literary engagement with real conditions of living and housing creates images of potential life, a sort of utopia, for a specific community and its members. In this sense the literary representations of spatial practice and the spatial metaphors of identity and belonging do not merely describe or comment on what is actually perceived (this would fall under the category of Glissant's "irritating" realism discussed in chapter 1) but project a possibility—an image of how a community could live in the space that it claims through daily use and attachment rather than ownership. Although the literary image has its obvious shortcomings—it is just an image and cannot offer itself as a practical solution to a concrete problem—its potential lies in the fact that it recognizes the human dimension of what might, at first, appear as a mere question of economic and spatial destitution. The literary substitute, like the image of a yard or house in the Caribbean novel, reveals what has always been there: the presence and persistence of "humanness" (as Lovelace would put it) behind the brutal reality of deprivation. The substitute is, I insist, both deeply insufficient and absolutely necessary. It is, at one and the same time, the most powerless and the most urgent answer not only to the actual material lack but also to any material reductionist approach that would turn such a lack into the only lens for the perception and interpretation of a particular place and its people.

The house is here a site of accommodation, a place claimed in response to various forms of material deprivation. Yet this accommodation, when interpreted materially, signals the need to resolve serious material problems and also a reduction of the concept of ownership to mean only property instead of self-possession.[7] In the yard novel and subsequent texts that follow and expand this Caribbean literary tradition, there is nevertheless a sustained attempt to remind the reader of the alternative dimensions of ownership—understood primarily as cultural identity and its spatial practice—as a powerful answer to the bourgeois narrative of individual economic progress.

Spatial gentrification, which goes hand in hand with such progress, threatens to eradicate the fluid life of underprivileged communities, which move freely between interior and exterior spaces, crossing and thus undoing the boundaries between private and public space. In the case of James's *Minty Alley*, the yard community is slowly replaced by the enclosed middle-class household, which no longer connects to the street and the yard. The novel ends with an image that expresses regret about the gradual gentrification of the yard. When all the yard inhabitants, defeated by their broken love stories and unsuccessful financial ventures, finally move away, Mr. Haynes passes by the old place one evening and peeks into the house: "One night . . . he was walking along Victoria Street and almost instinctively came to a halt when he reached Minty Alley. The front door and windows were open, and from the street he could see into the drawing-room. Husband and wife and three children lived there and one of the children was sitting at the piano playing a familiar tune from Hemy's music-book. Over and over she played it, while he stood outside, looking in at the window and thinking of old times" (244). The sight still suggests a kind of a theater, but it is no longer the high drama of the yard, where the protagonists run out to enact their soaring emotions and life battles in full view of their neighbors. Now the direction of Haynes's gaze is reversed: he is no longer spying from the seclusion of his room onto the rich life outside but is instead watching from the street the window-framed scenes of the nuclear family's daily rituals. James designates the family members by their function—"husband," "wife," "three children"—removing their specificity and distinctiveness, which was, by contrast, the central appeal of the former yard dwellers. We now have a set of general familial categories that de-specify the house, suggesting that the scene Haynes is witnessing could very well be unfolding somewhere else in a similar fashion; that is, any husband, wife, and three children could look like this, seen through the window.

Their upward mobility is signaled not only by the neat structure of a family unit, with its definite membership and clear roles, but also by the change in sound. The former world of gossip, conversation, and communal cooking and eating is replaced by the repetitive sound of piano practice, where the regularity of finger exercises and the presence of one of the most static musical instruments, the piano, announce the tedium of rules and heaviness of possessions in a very settled world. In response Haynes is thinking of "the old times," and along with him the reader feels the same nostalgia for the unpredictable drama of the former yard, where life always burst out in the open and could not be contained. In comparison, the view through the window into a neat home filled with repetitive piano music seems strangely sedate. The image Haynes observes feels like a still life, and the interior of the house is its proper frame.

With a similar sense of apprehension, Lovelace describes the gradual "improvement" in the living conditions on Calvary Hill. Tired of their endless rebellion and strife, the dwellers of the Hill are slowly entering into a kind of contract with the larger world and with themselves, concerned with getting and keeping jobs, acquiring possessions, and generally reaching a higher social status than was previously available to them. This change in the life of the Hill is particularly visible in the transformation of the steel band: what used to be an unrestrained and warrior-like expression of each neighborhood's distinctive identity through which slave history, rebellion, and the people's enduring links to Africa were regularly reenacted now becomes a sponsored event. The masks that used to disturb are becoming pretty. The destiny of Carnival and the steel band is thus the first sign of compromise between identity and possession. As he observes this change, Aldrick Prospect realizes that he does not want to sign away his freedom so that he can become a quiet participant in a daily struggle for material acquisitions. When, with a group of fellow "hooligans" from the Hill, he steals a police jeep, abducts a policeman, and drives around the city yelling for the people of shanty towns to take power, this short-lived rebellion leads him to realize that "even when we acting we ain't the actor" (188). His sudden insight is that life cannot be lived only for a couple of days during Carnival, that it must be pursued with equal passion and courage all the rest of the time, with a clear sense that one's own being cannot be measured according to someone else's value system. As he returns from jail after this unsuccessful uprising, he notices that Calvary Hill is becoming the "Hill of accommodation" (193). Nevertheless he refuses to be conquered by this change and concludes instead, "Each man . . . had responsibility for his own living, had the responsibility for the world he lived in, and to claim himself and to grow and to grow and to grow" (204). Lovelace advances here the same principle we encountered earlier: the precedence of ordinary human life and self-ownership over any other form of possession or identification. Through the dual connotation of the word *accommodation*, meaning both "a place of dwelling" and "a compromise," Lovelace shows how the quest for spatial possession can easily lead to a loss of spatial identity. Thus the quest for proper housing transforms Calvary Hill into the "Hill of accommodation," where the acquisition of a better house also results in a slow capitulation to the forces of gentrification and compromise. This dual nature of accommodation emphasizes the crucial dimension of my overall argument, that the house as a site of material and symbolic belonging represents the most obvious step toward autonomy but is also paradoxically an obstacle to achieving it. Spatial identity is, in the early yard novels and their later postcolonial incarnations, constantly stranded between the materiality of spatial problems and their metaphorical significance. In the Caribbean novels I analyze, human identity, whether communal or individual, finds itself perpetually torn between these two extremes. Yet the notion of daily human life and its intrinsic value, so forcefully represented and defended by all of the novelists I discuss, goes hand in hand with the notion of *lived space* in Lefebvre's sense: there is here a vital connection between being and space or between human identity and its spatial manifestations. Lived daily life, with its various performances of personal independence and communal bonding, gives meaning and value to the neutral or even negative space by transforming it into a dynamic alternative space whose symbolic significance ultimately exceeds its material limitations. The metaphorical value of even those impoverished yard spaces is captured primarily through narrative representation, emphasizing the importance of the aesthetic response to the material facts of daily spatial practice. In subsequent chapters I will therefore elaborate on the way literary texts offer themselves as the "third space" in which the extremes of material poverty and linguistic wealth, despair and resistance, possession and being, dwelling and compromise are recognized and challenged but never quite overcome.

3 "No Admittance"

V. S. Naipaul's *A House for Mr. Biswas*

Whoever has no house now, will never have one.
Whoever is alone will stay alone.

—Rainer Maria Rilke, "Autumn Day"

THE APPROACH TO IDENTITY as an outcome of spatial practice constitutes one of the most important aspects of V. S. Naipaul's semi-autobiographical novel *A House for Mr. Biswas* (1961). This novel is a prime example of the correlation between spatial theory and Caribbean postcolonial discourse and draws into sharper focus a number of questions that I have been raising. The novel consists of a central triad—space, self, and writing—that, in its triple orientation, allows me to examine the material significance of the house, its impact on identity, and its symbolic relevance in the protagonist's quest for autonomy and authorship. This intimate connection between space and identity allows Naipaul to question the process by which spatial dispossession deprives the protagonist of a sense of self. In response Mr. Biswas seeks to reclaim his individual autonomy by struggling to acquire a house of his own, but when this quest repeatedly fails, his only remedy for the indignities of material deprivation resides in repetitive and frustrated attempts at writing. Naipaul's narrative of spatial dispossession is thus inextricably woven into a gradual crumbling of the self and shows that, in the end, the absence of location (physical and psychological) can only be contested through authorship. Nevertheless the attempt to resolve material destitution narratively turns out to be an inadequate substitution, which only emphasizes the absence at the heart of the story.

In this chapter I address the triplicity of *A House for Mr. Biswas* (space, self, and writing) by relying on Lefebvre's theory of appropriation of repressive spaces through imaginative spatial practice. Naipaul's novel certainly offers a rich literary instantiation of Lefebvre's *lived space* in which the ordinary user strives to reclaim through daily symbolic practice those abstract spaces that embody various structures of power. We know, often implicitly, that "the built environment mediates, constructs and reproduces power relations" (Dovey, 1) but are less clear on how such relations can be contested and transformed. In order to elucidate the role of imagination in this process of spatial appropriation, I will also refer to Gaston Bachelard's "topoanalysis," which seeks to understand space as the dialectical interplay between the material and imaginative dimensions of daily human activity. *A House for Mr. Biswas* is, in my view, a compelling example of the individual engagement with material spatial limitation, which metaphorical spaces seek to challenge. The production of an alternative kind of space, even when that space is imaginary, represents Mr. Biswas's attempt at contesting and transforming the already produced spaces in which his autonomy and freedom are denied.

Naipaul's tragicomic protagonist, Mohun Biswas, is an Indo-Trinidadian depicted primarily in relation to the spatial configurations of his unaccommodated existence. Despite the fact that Mr. Biswas is housed throughout the novel, he continues to think of himself as destitute. This is because his dwelling, no matter how squalid or cramped, is always provided for him by his wife Shama's family, the matriarchal Tulsi clan, who owns property and houses throughout Trinidad and treats Mr. Biswas as a rather contemptible, although inevitable, tenant. The quest for the house in *A House for Mr. Biswas* is therefore not just a matter of physical shelter but, more important, a dream of ownership through which Mr. Biswas wishes to assert his independence and dignity in relation to any form of authority. The wealthy in-laws' spatial handouts, instead of helping, only confirm Mr. Biswas's position as a perpetual dependant. Consequently we find that the individual and the space he inhabits become interchangeable. This equation of identity with its spatial setting suggests that, like many other Caribbean authors, Naipaul turns to spatial images to explore the questions of geographic limitation and denied autonomy, which lie at the core of the colonial predicament. Mr. Biswas's sense of marginality arises from his economically driven spatial dispossession, suggesting that any form of autonomy, whether personal or political, depends on the acquisition or recovery of the place of one's own.

The physical places described in *A House for Mr. Biswas* crystallize the protagonist's ambiguous relationship to the New World, where, through the practice of indentured servitude, his ancestors faced the loss of their geographic, cultural, and linguistic grounding. As an inheritor of this aspect of Trinidadian history, Mr. Biswas strives to define his identity in this diasporic location. Incomplete memories, inadequate homes, and partial self-understanding threaten to turn his sense of self into either a pure fiction or an ossified token of some historically frustrated "original" existence. The immediate experience of this condition is reflected in Naipaul's focus on the house as a utopian dream, which nevertheless defies the reality of destitution and asserts the identity of the destitute. Mr. Biswas's spatioeconomic confinement thus evokes the consequences of colonial exploitation of labor and territory and their impact on the struggle for postcolonial independence.[1] Moreover the postcolonial concern of linking spatial autonomy to personal and cultural identity allows me to treat identity itself as location: a place one chooses or is assigned, the site where one exists, is situated, or remains destitute. Etymologically these words share the same root: the Indo-European *sta*, which designates standing, an act whose symbolic relevance animates much of (post)colonial literature. The hope for a people "unforeseenly standing" permeates, for example, the anticolonial protest expressed in Aimé Césaire's *Notebook of a Return to My Native Land*. Césaire contrasts the humiliations of colonialism with the intrepid response of the downtrodden, defiantly "standing and free" (131). In a related image of a man fighting to stand on his own, Naipaul's novel encapsulates the ideal of autonomy and the right to self-determination, which depend on being housed in the place of one's own choosing. Standing upright thus becomes a symbolic and literal gesture of resistance to destitution and external domination. This is a fundamental concern of *A House for Mr. Biswas* as well. Because accommodation ultimately depends on Mr. Biswas's—and, by extension, Naipaul's—ability to create a fictional space of his own, I argue that language and narrative resistance become the central, although always inadequate, response to material destitution. As Glissant points out in *Caribbean Discourse*, this sense of inadequacy always haunts the attempts at imaginative appropriation of space and self: "Just as a community can constitute an independent state and nevertheless experience a profound form of cultural alienation, so an individual can proclaim that he wishes to regain his identity and yet suffer from a terminal inadequacy even in the way in which his cry is expressed" (105). In Mr. Biswas's case, the "terminal inadequacy" of his housing and writing quest is nevertheless challenged by the humorous persistence of his "cry," and in this unrelenting challenge we find Naipaul's key response to destitution.

With respect to the postcolonial discourse more broadly, Bhabha's notion of "the house of fiction" (*The Location of Culture*, 12) seeks to capture precisely this link between spatial reality, literary image, and identity. Such a "house of fiction" allows us to examine how postcolonial literature confronts disjunctive colonial history with unhomely returns. For Bhabha, the recurring housing metaphor in postcolonial texts signals the experience of a deep historical displacement and draws into focus the same question Naipaul also seeks to explore: how a literary house, in the absence of an actual one, becomes a symbol of (and a literary substitute for) the experience of the diasporic subject who seeks “accommodation” for himself and his history (12). This subject belongs to the “culture of survival,” rooted in specific histories of cultural displacement from the Middle Passage of slavery and indenture to the colonialist civilizing mission and the postwar Third World migrations (Bhabha, “Freedom's Basis,” 47). In Bhabha's analysis, the historically ruptured experience of postcolonial cultural space generates a split in both identity and narrative and produces an interstitial location from which the postcolonial subject must confront, in the absence of privileged historical continuity, the position of “the insider's outsideness” (*The Location of Culture*, 14).

Focusing on Naipaul's struggle to create textual alternatives to predetermined colonial and postcolonial binaries (such as colonial mimicry vs. postcolonial authenticity), Nasta argues in *Home Truths* that Naipaul's ambiguous position as part of the English literary canon and as its outsider leads him to approach the process of writing itself as “a performative act of intervention and survival” (94). He is a writer concerned with forging “a language by which to redefine the colonial past, to develop a way of seeing and reading the world free from the dialectics of a metaphor of place that stressed above all the need either for a culture of ‘belonging,’ or its shadow, a space of ‘unbelonging’” (95). Although I adopt Nasta's notion of writing as a performative act that challenges the limitations of an inherited marginality, I also argue that Naipaul's crucial literary intervention consists in showing that writing, for all its audacity and irreverent assaults on established interpretations, actually fails to remedy the problem of symbolic and material dispossession. Instead the spatial representation of identity in *A House for Mr. Biswas* brings into focus the tense relationship between fiction and materiality in postcolonial literature, where the triumphant literary solution always appears inadequate in the end. Despite the fact that, in this novel, identity and location become inextricable, I propose that we must ultimately question this tendency to resolve the material through the imaginary. Although I am drawn to Naipaul's idea that for the writer “the revolution takes place in the mind” (“East Indian,” 43), I also argue that such a revolution remains a matter of imagination and words, which are more often than not swept away by the stark realities of spatial and economic exclusion.[2]

Like Naipaul himself, Mr. Biswas belongs to a historically displaced culture of indentured Indian laborers in Trinidad and reflects—through the frustrated quest for a house—the unaccommodated existence of a larger postcolonial community. Naipaul describes the Hindu community of Trinidad, seen through his immediate and extended family, as no longer quite whole or in tune with the Hindu traditions it sought to preserve. As Edward Said observes in another context, Naipaul's subject is "extraterritoriality—the state of being neither here nor there, but rather in-between things" ("Bitter Dispatches from the Third World," 99). In Trinidad Naipaul's (and Biswas's) Hindu community is separated from the certainty of its past rituals and beliefs, becoming, as Bhabha puts it, "eternally out of place between the African slave and the British master" ("Naipaul's Vernacular Cosmopolitans"). Mr. Biswas is thus a grotesque and always tragic reflection of the split between imaginary rootedness and daily destitution. The fictional house clearly cannot resolve the problem of material privations depicted in the novel but, on the contrary, makes them more visible by underscoring the absence of place for the destitute. Their most potent response, as Mr. Biswas's story shows, consists in demanding the "right to signify" (Bhabha, "Freedom's Basis," 50).

Following Lefebvre's lead, I approach Mr. Biswas's story as a struggle for symbolic reappropriation of historically expropriated spaces of colonial domination and its legacies.[3] In Lefebvre's analysis, the everyday struggle to repossess dominated space involves a constant interplay between "*fictitious* solutions, superimposed on the *real* solutions when these are, or seem to be, *impossible.* Thus problems and the search for solutions overstep the frontier of make-believe, 'projections' unobtrusively fill the gap between experience and make-believe and people project their desires onto one group of objects or another: the home, the flat, furnishing, cooking, going away on holiday, 'nature', etc. Such projections invest the object with a double existence, real and imaginary" (*Everyday Life in the Modern World*, 88). Following Lefebvre's cue, we could say that Mr. Biswas's object of frustrated desire is the house he wishes to own. This house becomes, throughout the novel, not only an obsessive quest, but also, and more important, the projection of make-believe through which Mr. Biswas both recognizes and seeks to undo the insurmountable conflict between poverty and autonomy. The house, as both a material and an imaginary object, thus turns into a constant reminder of Mr. Biswas's frustrations, namely the personal independence he is deprived of because he cannot afford the luxury of shutting his door on the world. The privacy afforded by such a gesture is implicit in the privilege of ownership. The barring of entry to the outside world symbolizes for Mr. Biswas the luxury of having an autonomous self, distinct from others. Such interiority is provided by the existence of the house. Unable to accomplish full ownership, he dies in the end in a heavily mortgaged house whose very existence awes him: "And now at the end he found himself in his own house, on his own half-lot of land, his own portion of the earth. That he should have been responsible for this seemed to him, in these last months, stupendous" (*HMB*, 6). The house embodies Mr. Biswas's claim to his "portion of the earth," his right to exist on his own terms and make choices he can back up by virtue of solid ownership. It is not just the house but the "audacity" (as Naipaul puts it) of having a self at all that stupefies Mr. Biswas. His triumph is, of course, partial and tragic: the mortgaged house is no more than the final resting place of a dying man. He enjoys his independence for a couple of years only and recognizes, in the last months of his life, something that would have been truly terrible: "to have lived without even attempting to lay claim to one's own portion of the earth, to have lived and died as one had been born, unnecessary and unaccommodated" (11). Naipaul establishes here the intimate connection between denied space and a crumbling self. A destitute man like Mr. Biswas, who is always out of place, both spatially and socially, requires various substitutes or, as Lefebvre puts it, projections of the "make-believe": his dream house and his writing. Through this continuous engagement with the imaginary, Mr. Biswas serves to illustrate a Lefebvrian conflict between property and appropriation.

According to Lefebvre's Marxist approach, the kind of space that prevails in the contemporary capitalist world is the *abstract space* ruled by the dominant classes. This space is both alienating and repressive to its everyday users, whose desires, spontaneous activities, sensuous experiences, and bodies are effectively controlled by the limits of such space. The central meaning conveyed by *abstract space* is prohibition, marked by "gates and railings, ditches and other material barriers," which act as signs that "protect the spaces of elites—rich neighborhoods or 'select' spots—from intruders. Prohibition is the reverse side and the carapace of property, of the negative appropriation of space under the reign of private property" (*PS*, 319). Lefebvre's response to this repressive abstraction of space consists in advocating for a different, positive kind of reappropriation against the inherently prohibitive structure of private property. This kind of relationship to space inaugurates a different, artistic and symbolic use of space for counterculture. The result is *counterspace*—festivals and fairs, ludic spaces, spaces of art and leisure, subjective spaces, which embody a utopian alternative to real space (349). In this alternative reappropriation of space, the body puts up resistance to rationalized cycles of production and consumption, to hierarchy and its own marginalization within it. Instead the ordinary human being, with his or her ordinary sensuous experience and unstructured desires, seeks to reappropriate and "achieve dominion over domination, as the imaginary and the utopian incorporate (or are incorporated into) the real" (348). The struggle for reappropriation of *abstract space* thus happens through *lived space*, with its quotidian unpredictability and its qualitative use of dreams, symbols, and desires in contesting the reductive nature of repressive spaces.

Considered from this perspective, *A House for Mr. Biswas* is a novel that explores the contestation of *abstract space* through the irreverent utopia of *lived space* and its figurative incarnations. Since Mr. Biswas belongs to the underprivileged class of simple users of space whose lives have no particular impact on the organization and distribution of material means (the Tulsi family represents this power of production, property, and social status), he often appears precisely as the "intruder" that Lefebvre refers to in illustrating the nature of prohibitive space. The very fact that Mr. Biswas is a perpetual tenant suggests that his position is always temporary and has to be authorized by someone else. He is always reminded of his insignificance, even superfluity, in the world of successful members of a productive society. In the Tulsi world—and Tulsis merely strive, against all odds of the colonial system, to be well-integrated and upwardly mobile participants in a capitalist economy—productivity signifies the acquisition of money, property, and status, none of which belong to Mr. Biswas. With no material possessions to endow him with social meaning, his existence is embarrassing, burdensome, and unjustified. We are therefore not surprised to discover that his struggle throughout the novel consists in dreaming of ownership that would anchor him and in deliberately violating all the established signs of prohibition and authority. In order to show his resistance, Mr. Biswas engages in clownish behavior whose purpose is to assert his individuality by disrespecting the hierarchies he is forced to inhabit. Secretly, however, under the sad layers of slapstick comedy, he cherishes his dream of a house, a modest space whose simple beauty might protect him from destitution.

Drawing on the conceptual ambiguity of the house, which I discussed in chapter 2, I would like to emphasize that Mr. Biswas's house, for all its utopian significance, remains an inherently dual space, which serves to comfort and shelter but can also isolate and imprison. To be held within such confined space is, for him, a source of both comfort and anxiety. On the one hand, "he knew that as soon as he stepped out of the yard he returned to nonentity" (*HMB*, 181); on the other hand, to remain fixed in one place fills him with dread. An image of a solitary boy glimpsed from the bus window illustrates this fear of confinement, through which the utopia of the house is subtly undermined: "The sun fell; and in the short dusk they passed a lonely hut set in a clearing far back from the road. Smoke came from under the rugged thatched eaves: the evening meal was being prepared. And, in the gloom, a boy was leaning against the hut, his hands behind him, staring at the road. He wore a vest and nothing more. The vest glowed white. In an instant the bus went by, noisy in the dark, through bush and level sugarcane fields. Mr. Biswas could not remember where the hut stood, but the picture remained: a boy leaning against an earth house that had no reason for being there, under the dark falling sky, a boy who didn't know where the road, and that bus, went" (182). This episode testifies to the ambivalence with which Mr. Biswas invests both the nomadic (the bus) and settled (the hut) spaces. From the shut-in security of the bus he looks out on the sugarcane fields in the early dusk and feels comforted by the predetermined trajectory of the ride. From his perspective, the lonely boy is somehow deprived of purpose because the larger world, evoked by the bus and the road, escapes him. The boy's "rugged" home is situated "far back from the road" and belongs to the margin, from which Mr. Biswas comes and tries to flee. At the same time, the boy's white shirt literally gleams in the dusk, almost as if it were a source of light against the growing darkness. There is a kind of powerful autonomy in the boy's glowing figure, silhouetted against the "falling sky." Behind him the smoke comes from the hut as the evening meal is being prepared. There is a sense of warmth, maybe a family. Mr. Biswas's perception of the hut seems filled with wistful longing to be part of the evening meal by the fire. Although he feels sorry for the solitary boy, we know that he himself is much lonelier. In the confined and unsettled space of the bus, he has no access to any meaningful interiority, either spatially or personally. His passing pity for the boy is based on the boy's ignorance of the larger world, an ignorance that, in Mr. Biswas's eyes, confirms the futility of the boy's existence. And yet Mr. Biswas seems to recognize himself in the boy's solitude, which uncannily reflects his own. We imagine Mr. Biswas momentarily framed in the bus window, as purposeless and transitory as the boy. They mirror one another, both forgotten by the larger world, ignorant of it, and metaphorically left by the side of the road. The world passes them by while they persist in their loneliness and find "no reason for being there." Yet it remains unclear in this passage who is inside and who is out—Mr. Biswas or the boy—and whether the shelter is to be found on the road or in the hut. In context the distant larger world is some undefined space (wherever the bus is headed) of broad possibilities and even bigger threats, which surrounds Mr. Biswas and hinders his acquisition of a house. It appears, in the end, that he is alternately imprisoned outside and exiled inside. This structural circularity of inside and outside, represented by various spatial images in the novel, makes it all the more necessary to situate Mr. Biswas in order to understand Naipaul's vision of the destitute person's crumbling interiority, its alienating effects, and its demand for expression.

In his "Foreword to *A House for Mr Biswas*," Naipaul describes his early experience in London as marked by material precariousness and a haunting fear "to have found no talent, to have written no book, to be null and unprotected in the busy world. It is that anxiety—the fear of destitution in all its forms, the vision of the abyss—that lies below the comedy of the present book" (130). This "fear of destitution in all its forms" comes to define Mr. Biswas as well. As I noted in previous chapters, the etymology of *destitution* is revealing: to be destitute means to be put away, placed outside, and forsaken. The etymology is relevant here because it links the absence of choice and the fear it generates to the notion of denied and then forcibly reassigned location. In its original meaning, to be destitute is to be displaced, yet this process of spatial expropriation also signifies being marginalized and alone. Poverty, which the word *destitution* now commonly designates, is thus intimately connected to spatial and psychological dispossession. Naipaul's novel explores precisely these multiple facets of being "null and unprotected in the busy world" by integrating spatial, emotional, and economic concerns.

Mr. Biswas's sense of destitution also arises from his inability to inscribe his presence onto the world, to leave behind a trace by which he may be remembered. Homelessness is linked for him to an existence where nothing is built and nothing remains. Imagining that houses have their own memory, the kind of memory he himself is often unable to conjure, Mr. Biswas realizes that the spatial void he fears may be the vacant spot where he, and not the house, should have been standing: "Suppose, Mr. Biswas thought in the long room, suppose that at one word I could just disappear from this room, what would remain to speak of me? A few clothes a few books. . . . He had lived in many houses. And how easy it was to think of those houses without him! . . . In none of these places he was being missed because in none of these places had he ever been more than a visitor, an upsetter of routine" (*HMB*, 125). His birth house in the swamplands is, he imagines, already razed: "The world carried no witness to Mr. Biswas's birth and early years" (40). The real problem is not so much in remembering as in being remembered. We thus discover another meaning of houses: they represent places of memory by which individual life is inscribed onto the world. This inscription serves to transform chaos into order—into a kind of personal cosmos.[4] In the absence of place, owned and marked, everything in Mr. Biswas's experience turns back into the void: "There was nothing to speak of him" (125).

Bachelard's phenomenological reading of the "protected intimacy" (3) of the house in *The Poetics of Space* emphasizes precisely this issue: that the value of a house arises not merely from its function of providing a shelter but, more important, from the fact that the house is lived in and marked by that life. Traces of the past, legible in the space we consider our home, deepen the experience of that space, which would otherwise be no more than a physical container: "The house is not experienced from day to day only, on the thread of a narrative, or in the telling of our own story. Through dreams, the various dwelling-places in our lives co-penetrate and retain the treasures of former days" (5). The complexity of the house as a privileged kind of space arises from its being a site of superimposed images that simultaneously inhabit the house, animating it with past and potential meanings. In Bachelard's discussion of topo-analysis, which he defines as "the systematic psychological study of the sites of our intimate lives" (8), memory is described as "motionless" (9) because it needs to be localized in order to have intimate significance: "To localize a memory in time is merely a matter for the biographer and only corresponds to a sort of external history, for external use, to be communicated to others. . . . For a knowledge of intimacy, localization in the spaces of our intimacy is more urgent than determination of dates" (9). According to this view, the experience of space and the spatial image determine the very possibility for our intimate memories, which—if they are not localized—amount to no more than an impersonal series of dates and biographical data. Yet biography is not life: Mr. Biswas's desire to be remembered attests to his craving for personal, intimate, and autonomous space, which would bear witness to his existence and allow him continuity in his experience of self. When they imagine the impact of owning a house, Mr. Biswas and his family (infected by his housing fantasies) imagine that "from now on their lives would be ordered, their memories coherent" (*HMB*, 556). Yet without such a space, Mr. Biswas becomes a fragmented series of random biographical facts, which, abstracted from his day-to-day living, never amount to a story.

In his foreword to *A House for Mr. Biswas*, Naipaul focuses on anxiety born of destitution, drawing our attention to the dependence of individuality on location. If to be destitute is to be forced outside of some legible and legitimizing structure of relations, then the question remains what kind of existence and self can be built in the state of psychological and material nowhereness. Mr. Biswas experiences two opposite but complementary tendencies: the disappearance into a sweeping, anonymous, and unifying multitude of people, where he would be one of many and feel safety in finding affinities, even similarities, with others; and separation, differentiation, and absolute autonomy of identity defined against the crowd that now becomes a threatening backdrop. This dual positioning of the protagonist—between blending in and standing out, between assimilation and autonomy—becomes particularly clear in his relationship to his wife's ever-proliferating family, the matriarchal Tulsi clan. On the one hand, the dream of independence from Tulsi control motivates most of his emotions and deeds: he longs to become his own person, separate and clearly distinguishable from any group and its tradition. In the context of the close-knit Tulsi hierarchy against which he rebels only to return to it, shamefully aware that he has nowhere else to go, he quickly realizes that "he mattered little to the house. His status there was now fixed. He was troublesome and disloyal, and could not be trusted. He was weak and therefore contemptible" (*HMB*, 97). His position is, yet again, predetermined and quite beyond his control, suggesting that the only form of identity available to him consists in being labeled in a cursory but permanent way. On the other hand, the separation from the Tulsi crowd brings home all the fear of independence and its isolating potential. In his moments of psychological disintegration, Mr. Biswas feels paradoxically "secure to be only a part of Hanuman House, an organism that possessed a life and power to comfort which was quite separate from the individuals who composed it" (289). Even the Tulsis' Hanuman House sometimes appears as a comforting place and exceeds its status as a built structure or commodity: it is instead an organism that shields Mr. Biswas whenever he feels like a detached particle, pulling him back into the familial system with "authority's power to rescue and assist where there was need, authority's impersonal power to forgive" (282).[5] In this sense, whenever Mr. Biswas's claims to autonomous space fail, they give way to a childlike craving to be sheltered by a pseudo-parental authority in a large family house. This family house is an encompassing system that can protect him while denying him any form of independence. In Mr. Biswas's case, the very notion of identity is dual: Does identity designate grounded and balanced action that connects fully formed and creative individuals—in paradoxical terms, authors of their fate? Or is it a frightening and unproductive separation of an isolated particle from the rest of its environment? The threat of exteriority is bound to and inadequately resolved though the construction of interiority. Mr. Biswas's ever-failing dream of self-possession reflects his vexed and clownish status in the Tulsi clan and also shows him as permanently alienated—made exterior—to himself. Naipaul leads us to acknowledge that the impossibility of self-possession arises from an imposed economic and social exteriority. Since Mr. Biswas is, in historical terms, already a displaced colonial subject and is, moreover, deprived of a decent place to live in, he cannot be present to himself but instead becomes his own fiction.

In reading *A House for Mr. Biswas* most critics inevitably waver between looking at the specificity of this novel and substituting this specificity for broader historical or political questions. Naipaul invites us to do so: his protagonist and story are always stranded between the literal and symbolic but persist in questioning and mocking this condition. The long history of the novel's critical reception bears witness to the tendency of reading Mr. Biswas's house as a symbol and Mr. Biswas as a type. According to R. H. Lee, for example, the house is "the primary symbol in the novel, and represents the hero's furthest success in turning the traditional passivity of his religion and society into some purposive activity" (75). Although Gordon Rohlehr warns, in contrast, against the "danger of regarding Biswas as a figure representative of the Caribbean predicament" ("Character and Rebellion in *A House for Mr. Biswas*," 92), he also sees Mr. Biswas as a figure that brings out "bare humanity" beneath one man's history of underprivilege ("The Ironic Approach," 193). My own spatial analysis of Naipaul's novel supports Rohlehr's observation that *A House for Mr. Biswas* possesses a liminal quality and mobilizes a number of binary oppositions (local/universal in this case) without resolving them. Yet, despite his desire to resist an easy postcolonial typology, Rohlehr, along with a number of other critics, succumbs to the tendency of explaining Mr. Biswas's house as primarily symbolic. Hamner also presents Mr. Biswas as both a particular and a universal figure, representative of and isolated from the world in which he resides (introduction to *Critical Perspectives on V. S. Naipaul*). Mr. Biswas's house presumably sends us deeper into the complexities of the postcolonial condition, of which Naipaul himself is sometimes seen as a skilled reporter and sometimes as a symptomatic example.[6] His self-selected role of an observer who examines the particular in terms of its broader "universal" meanings has earned him Bhabha's uneasy critique for being "today's global writer" ("Naipaul's Vernacular Cosmopolitans").[7] I say "uneasy" because no one is quite certain where to place Naipaul, what words to hold him responsible for and when generously to exempt him. Self-consciously stuck in between, Naipaul leaves his readers similarly stranded.

"To be colonial," Naipaul writes, "is to be a little ridiculous and unlikely" ("East Indian," 38). The interpretations of his novel indeed appear to follow a prevalent view of Naipaul himself: he is a type, a "global writer" (Bhabha, "Naipaul's Vernacular Cosmopolitans") trapped in his "jaundiced views" (Panwar, 14), seeking refuge in "castrated" easy satire (Lamming, *The Pleasures of Exile*, 225). In short, a self-appointed reporter on the Third World, whose universalism is just another disguise for bitter colonial mimicry. As Said suggests, Naipaul is a scavenger in the ruins of postcolonial history (100): someone who profits from the vestiges of the colonial world only to side, in the end, with the enemy. These views place Naipaul in a position quite similar to that of his protagonist Mr. Biswas and suggest that Naipaul is indeed, as Nasta points out, a privileged outsider on the inside of the postcolonial canon and remains to this day a fitting incarnation of the inadmissible.

Paradoxically this inadmissible aspect of Naipaul's writing seems to make him, in turn, most typical. Reflecting on Naipaul's place in the enduring spatial problematic of the Caribbean context where, "for the exile or migrant, 'landscape' consists in the formation or (re)formation of connections with the adopted place" (199), Helen Tiffin briefly turns to *A House for Mr. Biswas*, suggesting that this novel offers "a (qualified) 'progression' from an 'unaccommodated' man to an identifiably Trinidadian way of being" (211). Tiffin's focus on the importedness and translocation of most Caribbean dwellers requires this particular counterpoint, some "identifiable Trinidadian way of being" in the specific case of Naipaul's protagonist. Since this opposition between transplantation and rootedness shapes many discussions of Naipaul and his work, he is persistently defined by his embattled position between these two poles: not quite Indian, not quite Trinidadian, and English only through an act of unforgivable assimilation.[8] Like many postcolonial writers, he is examined biographically and tested for his geographical loyalty. Wiltshire, England? Naipaul's chosen location is itself perceived as the symbol of colonial assimilation, with its tasteless admiration for the colonial center, or rather as a sign of the outsider's dream to be let inside.

Naipaul's infamous view of "West Indian futility," which leads him to claim that "nothing was created in the West Indies" (*The Middle Passage*, 20), has made him into a controversial author whose attitude allegedly exemplifies an intellectual complicity with colonialism and merely echoes the weathered interpretation of former colonies as underdeveloped and in need of being "civilized." It is by now almost a cliché to focus on Naipaul's dismissive reading of postcolonial "smallness" in favor of an imaginary grandeur of the former empire.

In his 2001 article "Naipaul's Vernacular Cosmopolitans," Homi Bhabha describes glimpsing Naipaul in an Indian restaurant, where he overhears him delivering one tell-tale word, "civili . . . zayshun," in "a polished Oxford voice, a touch maudlin, with the merest trace of a Trinidadian lilt." Over the plate of authenticating curries, Bhabha concludes that "of all the stray words that one might accidentally catch from the private conversation of this most elusive and aloof of English writers, none could be more appropriate than this somewhat nostalgic, anxious, call to 'civilization.'" Yet despite this dangerously quick summary of a person, Bhabha does not fail to recognize the power of Naipaul's unadorned language, able to shift "a whole cultural landscape, to change the entire meaning of life." According to Bhabha, Naipaul is often guilty of "large-scale civilizational arguments," which destroy "the resonance of detail and dialogue that is the fingerprint of his remarkable gift." However, when Naipaul's "themes and character unsettle the sober propriety of moral and metropolitan 'centers,' they reveal an unsurpassable spirit of vernacular cosmopolitanism contained in the art of narrative itself." Bhabha focuses here on the paradoxical relationship between Naipaul's dubious "Oxford voice" and his ability to disrupt the politically correct centers of judgment.

"Civili . . . zayshun," however, rests on the English language one can speak either badly or too well. Depending on the expectation, one may be accused and found guilty of either one of these accomplishments.[9] Naipaul, for example, abandons his "authentic" Indo-Trinidadian self in favor of its bland Oxbridge incarnation; he says "civili . . . zayshun" and fails to rebel against the Empire. This infamous Nobel laureate can always be criticized for his inauthenticity or his lack of postcolonial affiliations. In his assessment of *The Enigma of Arrival*, Derek Walcott interprets Naipaul's focus on the English landscape as a self-aggrandizing attempt to achieve "the final mimicry" into the English countryside and into the tradition of the English pastoral. He sees Naipaul as inscribing himself in what Walcott cleverly calls "the squirearchy" of club and manor, showing "virulent contempt toward the island of his origin" (28). In this same review Walcott accuses Naipaul of featuring no love in his books. Caryl Phillips, reviewing Naipaul's more offensive interviews, deplores his "sardonic, often bitter tone" and his avoidance of "the region of the heart" (190, 187). Thanks to *The World Is What It Is* (2008), Naipaul's authorized biography by Patrick French, readers may finally plunge into the writer's all-too-expected monstrosity, which brings us back to the weathered contrast between barbarity and "civili . . . zayshun." Naipaul thus remains, according to Paul Theroux, "the ultimate Caliban with a college degree." As a celebrated outsider to the postcolonial canon, the author is now alarmingly close to his protagonist, whose main tragedy lies in his comical and unconvincing attempts to enter a world of legitimacy, which on some level remains shut to Naipaul-the-writer as much as to Mr. Biswas–the-protagonist.

In view of so many unfavorable and mutually reinforced readings of Naipaul's personality, there is less room for fresh readings of his work itself.[10] And yet it is Naipaul's own long-standing literary strategy of blending the world and the text, the person and the story, history and fiction that makes these confusions unavoidable. In making them, the critic merely echoes Naipaul's own textual concerns: if the real and the fictional merge inextricably in the critics' approach to Naipaul's work it is because they appear to be one in the way Naipaul structures his own writing. Yet because of this weaving of historical and (auto)biographical reality into literature, Naipaul's writing calls upon the critic to observe and then resist a hasty slippage: the power of the literary is here mobilized to comment on and critique the real, not to reflect it unproblematically. In order to preserve the critical power of the literary, one has to recognize that Naipaul's texts employ such confusion as a strategy and reveal our inability to perceive the line that separates fiction from reality. No doubt some would argue that such lines do not exist and that we would be hard-pressed to mark them accurately, but it is the tremendous contribution of Naipaul's work to draw attention to the indiscriminate and dangerous blurring between the two.[11] It is then no wonder that the reading of Naipaul's work and personality are also subject to such confusion and invite us to reexamine our notion of the literary and its function. Ironically, in the critical commentary on Naipaul we sense again that "if there was a place for him, it was one that had already been hollowed out by time, by everything he had lived through, however imperfect, makeshift and cheating" (*HMB*, 303). Somewhat uncannily, Naipaul has already described the strategies with which he will be read; he depicts the shape-giving void of predetermined meanings that will end up constructing both the celebratory and the critical discourses about his fiction. Moreover, in accord with my readings of the inside and outside, the inside of the novel is repeatedly colonized by the external readings of its author, while the author is, conversely but rather unsurprisingly, made to echo his own protagonists. The distinction between fiction and reality, between the novel and the world, is thus perpetually broken, and we are again reminded that this distinction itself may be no more than a convention, which always fails to fulfill its promise of neatness.

While fiction and reality blur, often unwittingly, in Naipaul criticism, sacrificing significant narrative details to the logic of a vast discourse, they are made deliberately inextricable within the structure of his novel. In the frustrated struggle against his squalid reality, Mr. Biswas fabricates a dream house, signaling a curious nostalgia for something he has never had: "He thought deeply about this house, and knew exactly what he wanted. He wanted, in the first place, a real house, made with real materials. . . . He would walk up concrete steps into a small verandah; through doors with coloured panes into a small drawingroom; from there into a small bedroom, then another small bedroom, then back into the small verandah. . . . And his house would be painted. The roof would be red, the outside walls ochre with chocolate facings, and the windows white" (*HMB*, 201–2). Despite his imaginative requirement that the house be "real," its description has the compact neatness of a child's drawing. He imagines himself walking through such a space proprietarily, from room to room, as if surveying his little domain. In the small, solid, and colorfully cozy world of Mr. Biswas's house, there is a child-like wonder at the existence, even at the mere possibility of ordinary things that can ground the one who claims them. Instead of pointing outward to some allegorical or symbolic reference beyond the text, this utopian house only underscores the absence within it. As a miniature, Mr. Biswas's house inspires and, in its smallness, contains the vast discourse on homelessness and alienation. But it also remains a detail;

a diminutive, even selfish concern; a child-like dream of a shelter that speaks to the most profound tragedy in the novel: the impossibility of the seemingly obvious.

The miniature representation of a house, when it finally appears as part of the plot, connects quite literally the architectural figure to the human body. As a Christmas gift, Mr. Biswas buys a dollhouse for his daughter Savi. Since an unhoused Christmas becomes a parody of itself and is reduced to "a series of anticipations" (*HMB*, 206), he attempts to make up for this emptiness by purchasing something of its splendor and promise at a reduced price:

> The following day Mr. Biswas cycled from Green Vale to Arwacas. When he turned into the High Street the sight of the stores, open again and carelessly displaying Christmas goods at bargain prices, reminded him of the presents he had forgotten. He got off his bicycle and leaned it against the kerb. . . . Mr. Biswas disappeared into the shop. Not many minutes later Mr. Biswas and the shopman reappeared. They were both smoking and excited. A boy came out of the shop partly hidden by the large doll's house he was carrying. The doll's house was placed on the handlebar of Mr. Biswas's cycle and, with Mr. Biswas on one side and the boy on the other, wheeled down the High Street.
>
> Every room of the doll's house was daintily furnished. The kitchen had a stove such as Mr. Biswas had never seen in real life, a safe and a sink. (206)

As we contemplate this scene, we realize that the narrator's eye remains, like a fixed camera, outside the store. We don't know how or why Mr. Biswas chooses this miniature house, but we are not surprised that he buys it. It has all the household wonders and riches that he has never enjoyed in real life and is thus a tiny image of a vast ideal. However, as Naipaul's narration clearly shows, we remain on the outside of this desire and this dream. We only watch Mr. Biswas from the street as he disappears into the store and reappears with the dainty dollhouse. His dream is otherwise closed to us. Yet as we read "The kitchen had a stove such as Mr. Biswas had never seen in real life," we share some of the pain of his poverty.

After Savi's dollhouse is broken to pieces in Hanuman House so as not to inspire jealousy of other children, it is described as a wounded body: "And there, below the almost bare branches of the almond tree that grew in the next yard, he saw it, thrown against a dusty leaning fence made of wood and tin and corrugated iron. A broken door, a ruined window, a staved-in wall or even roof—he had expected that. But not this. The doll's house did not exist. He saw only a bundle of firewood. None of its parts was whole. Its delicate joints were exposed and useless. Below the torn skin of paint, still bright and still in parts imitating brick-work, the hacked and splintered wood was white and raw" (*HMB*, 209). The merciless obliteration of Savi's dollhouse astonishes Mr. Biswas—not because the house is "broken" but because it no longer "exists." The insides of the house are exposed by means of Naipaul's language; we are made to perceive the miniature as a flayed body, turned inside out, whose interior organs are revealed by an act of annihilation. We become aware that this house is, at the same time, a miniature of Mr. Biswas himself, his body and dreams exposed and made irrelevant: "the skin of paint," the "delicate joints," the "raw" flesh under the skin. Yet Naipaul does not resort to similes; we are not reading a comparative account in which the broken dollhouse is "like" Biswas's body. Instead the passage uses literal images (joints of a little structure, raw wood, skin of paint) to suggest, somewhere on the periphery of our perception, that the miniature house is Mr. Biswas, or that Mr. Biswas is this and any other ruined house. As he runs back inside to find the culprit of this act of demolition, Mr. Biswas is similarly hurt: "The edge of a wall scraped against his shoulder, tearing his shirt and tearing the skin below" (209). This is clearly more than a mere conceptual substitution based on some essential similarity, as would be the case with literary figures; we encounter instead the most disturbing form of identity between Mr. Biswas and the house.

This emphasis on the corporeal identity of the subject and object by which the would-be dweller and the house are equated and made interchangeable suggests that in Naipaul's novel the body serves as a disruptive and uncontainable element capable of challenging, often unconsciously, the abstract logic of any system. This is precisely Lefebvre's approach to the potential of lived spaces and the shelter they offer to the sensuous and bodily dimensions of daily human existence. In Lefebvre's analysis the body is an enigma "at once banal and profound" (*PS*, 395), capable of producing differences, of behaving as a "differential field" (384) that challenges the limits and habits of any imposed system, asserting itself as that which exceeds boundaries and definitions. When, in Mr. Biswas's case, the body of the man and the body of the house become one, we are made to realize the proximity between subject and object, even their identity, which contests that instrumental and alienating separation we most often impose on these categories. In the case of Naipaul's protagonist, and quite in keeping with Lefebvre's theory of the "total body" (384), we are invited to consider the dialectical interplay between physical and ideal forms of existence while recognizing that any form of separation between them constitutes an act of violence. In this episode the house is temporarily transformed from a commodity into an extension of Mr. Biswas's sensuous and imaginative being. The meaning of space is therefore reattached to the living human being and his bodily existence and thus rescued, however provisionally, from the abstractions of ownership, wealth, social status, and power.

In her discussion of size and scale as forms of "longing" in the world of narrative representation, Susan Stewart focuses on "metaphors that arise whenever we talk about the relation of language to experience or, more specifically, whenever we talk about the relation of narrative to its objects" (ix). In Stewart's account, the miniature is considered a "metaphor for the interior space and time of the bourgeois subject. Analogously, the gigantic is understood as a metaphor for the abstract authority of the state and the collective, public, life" (xii). Her discussion of an exemplary miniature object, the dollhouse, helps illuminate Naipaul's use of that same object in the passages I discuss here. According to Stewart, "the dollhouse has two dominant motifs: wealth and nostalgia. It presents a myriad of perfect objects that are, as signifiers, often affordable, whereas the signified is not" (61). In the case of Mr. Biswas, however, and more broadly in the colonial and postcolonial contexts, neither the material object nor its metaphorical representation are really "affordable," to use Stewart's term. Instead Mr. Biswas's longing for a house and the purchase of a dollhouse that quickly becomes firewood only signal the devastating absence behind the nostalgia for something that has never existed in the first place: a space of his own. In this sense the dream house, with its various miniature representations throughout the novel, is not a representation of the interior space of a "bourgeois" subject but a reflection on the fact that such a subject cannot even come into being in the context of colonial displacement and postcolonial destitution, the conditions that Bhabha designates as "one of history's stiffest sentences" ("Naipaul's Vernacular Cosmopolitans"). Interiority and subjectivity are themselves, in Mr. Biswas's case, a utopian image, that is, a fiction of a self that fails to materialize precisely because there are no material conditions for selfhood.

Regarding the dollhouse as a paradigmatic object of miniature representation, Stewart emphasizes its capacity to transform use value into "display value," making the dollhouse into something that is "consumed by the eye" (62). Its visual perfection is meant to create the illusion of a complete and hermetic world. And yet the world of the dollhouse cannot be experienced sensually; it is unavailable to the body and thus remains, in a way, the most abstract of miniature forms. The illusion of wholeness and perfection represented by the miniature dollhouse stands in stark contrast to the incomplete and progressively deteriorating sense of the world and self that characterize Mr. Biswas. Unable to inhabit a perfect house, he must settle instead for an uninhabitable miniature representation of that desire. At the same time, this miniature house, whose only purpose is to offer an image of ideal dwelling instead of an actual living space, is paradoxically equated with Mr. Biswas's body in Naipaul's subtle correlation of scrapes and injuries they both suffer. Finally, the dollhouse is an ideal space for dolls, suggesting with cruel irony that, in the world oriented toward acquisition of wealth as the measure of personhood, objects are accommodated more easily than people. From the perspective of a historically denied and repeatedly failing quest for interiority and its socially legitimate status, Naipaul's miniature house, precisely because of its abstracted smallness and illusory perfection, underscores the gigantic problem contained in the geopolitical hierarchy of the capitalist world from which Mr. Biswas, and many like him, are quietly excluded. Clashing with that world, the miniature dollhouse ends up as firewood: its display value is again transformed into use value. Moreover this transformation entails the reduction of a dream into a concrete material need. Naipaul's powerful critique of displacement and destitution produced by colonialism suggests that they operate, among other ways, through the violent reduction of the imaginary and conceptual life to the barest material necessity: dollhouse to firewood. Both are miniature concerns of gigantic proportions. From Lefebvre's perspective, this is also a clash between "needs" and "desires": "Each need finds satisfaction in its object, in the consumption of that object, yet such satisfaction eliminates the need only temporarily, for a need is repetitive in character and after being satisfied will arise again and again, stronger and more urgent, until it reaches a saturation point or is extinguished" (*PS*, 393–94). In Mr. Biswas's case, the house is indeed such a need, although never satisfied, saturated, or extinguished. Nevertheless this need for space fixates on the house as its ultimate object of satisfaction and pursues it with the repetitive fervor that Lefebvre describes. However, the house is also Mr. Biswas's desire, defined by Lefebvre as "the energies available to the living being, energies that tend to be discharged explosively, with no definite object, in violent and destructive or self-destructive ways" (394). In his paradoxical relationship to the house as both a need and a desire, as an object of possession and an object of dreams, Mr. Biswas strives to acquire his ideal living space and at the same time always participates in its undoing. Because the house is thus a space that is vitally needed and yet persistently out of reach, we gradually realize that the house in this book cannot really be owned as a commodity because it is equated with Mr. Biswas, containing the fundamental elements of his corporeal and imaginative existence. Ownership of the house as if it were just an object external to Mr. Biswas is therefore impossible. The house is not merely the satisfaction of a material need, nor can it be reduced to a lofty object of perpetual desire. Emphasizing the vital connection between the user and his spatial practice, the house becomes a manifestation of daily life and not just a mere sign of abstract material possession. Viewing Mr. Biswas's house from a Lefebvrian perspective, we would have to recognize it as something more than an acquirable commodity: as an element of spatial *practice*, it signals its relevance to *lived space*, invested at one and the same time with material and imaginative value. When the miniature house reappears, it is a distant vision from the window of a moving bus that takes Mr. Biswas to Port of Spain: "He fixed his eyes on a house, as small and as neat as a doll's house, on the distant hills of the Northern Range; and as the bus moved north, he allowed himself to be puzzled that the house didn't grow any bigger, and to wonder, as a child might, whether the bus would eventually come to that house" (*HMB*, 296). Although this image echoes the earlier hut glimpsed from the bus, this time around Mr. Biswas is puzzled that the image never comes any closer to him. The permanent smallness of the house in the distance, at which Mr. Biswas wonders "as a child might," clearly reasserts the dominance of a small unattainable dream of sheltered life that can never be reached and remains on that horizon he cannot approach.

So how does Mr. Biswas respond to the empty space opened up by the absent house? He initially does so by deliberately constructing pointless descriptions of his condition. The emphasis falls on "complete sentences" by which he seeks linguistic control over psychological void and material limitations that trigger it: "Slowly and carefully, like his actions the night before, his thoughts came, and he framed each thought in a complete sentence. He thought: 'The bed is a mess. Therefore I slept badly. I must have been afraid all through the night. Therefore the fear is still with me'" (*HMB*, 255). The completeness of his sentences signals his desperate attempt to give shape and logic to the overwhelming panic that threatens to destroy him. His response to destitution is thus, throughout the novel, countered by structures of language and writing. Whether in the fragmented form exemplified above or in the more complete journalistic narratives, we gradually discover Naipaul's "third space" meant to accommodate Mr. Biswas: it is located in the deliberate buffoonery of his writing, which defies the limitation of his living conditions. Mr. Biswas's fictional responses to deprivation ultimately serve to challenge its ability to limit, confine, or reduce him.

Material scarcity and its humiliations are, of course, not just Mr. Biswas's personal experience; they are the lot of many destitute who surround him and seem to consider him, because he is literate and employed, implicitly above destitution.[12] When he finally gets a job in Port of Spain as a journalist with the *Sentinel*, he excels in writing much appreciated, sensational stories and is finally able to give expression "to the facetiousness that came to him as soon as he put pen to paper" (*HMB*, 310). His exaggerated or completely invented "news" gives voice to the fantasy, his one means of detaching himself from his unbearable reality. The increased sales of the *Sentinel* attest to the popularity of his darkly humorous reports about the Bonny Baby Competition (about a dead white baby found on the rubbish dump) or the U.S. explorer's last journey on ice, entitled "Daddy Comes Home in a Coffin." When the editorial leadership of the *Sentinel* is purged in a prudish effort to replace sensationalist reporting with serious news, Mr. Biswas is appointed investigator for the Deserving Destitutes Fund, which is meant to boost the journal's suddenly dropping sales. His duty is to "read the applications from destitutes, reject the undeserving, visit the others to see how deserving or desperate they were, and then, if circumstances warranted it, to write harrowing accounts of their plight, harrowing enough to encourage contributions for the fund. He had to find one deserving destitute a day" (423). In this "beauty pageant" for the poor, Mr. Biswas faces all the chilling irony of his condition; although he can barely make ends meet, he appears to the poor contestants as a member of an elite invested with power to evaluate whether their poverty is noteworthy. In reality he is one of them: "'Deserving Destitute number one,' he told Shama. 'M. Biswas. Occupation: investigator of Deserving Destitutes'" (424). In order to diminish the dread that abject poverty inspires in him, Mr. Biswas calls his destitute "Destees." This irreverent transformation of the word emphasizes the recipient relationship implicit in the condition of dispossession. If there are "Destees" who *receive* poverty as their status, we can imagine their counterpoint in the world of "Destitutors" who *provide* poverty in the same way that an advisor would give guidance to his advisee. Unfortunately Mr. Biswas is excluded from both of these roles: he is neither destitute enough to receive nor privileged enough to provide and thus vanishes between the cracks, "null and unprotected" yet again. Nevertheless we discover in this episode that, in Mr. Biswas's world, even poverty is something to be measured, rated, sold, and invested in; it is ultimately a commodity the poor need in order to be seen, while the privileged rely on it to channel their hierarchical compassion. Mr. Biswas's horror at playing the arbiter of destitution comes from the fact that he is no longer allowed to mock the tragedy; in asking him to report on poverty in "harrowing" terms, the editors deprive him of his irreverent humor as his only weapon in countering his own and other Destees' misery. By providing "harrowing accounts," Mr. Biswas ultimately capitulates to selling deprivation as a commodity. He therefore loses his subjecthood by becoming the object in an uneven exchange, selling destitute stories to the smug elite. His role of special investigator endows him with sudden status, but it also leads him to relinquish his opposition to the establishment and incur instead the distrust of the poor to whom he used to belong. His only claim to real autonomy comes, in the end, from those moments when he dreams up circumstances and interpretations that expose the "battle of possessions" (441) and challenge the context in which possessions are a sign of personhood.

The "privilege" of ranking poverty offers Mr. Biswas no respite from accumulating images of squalor and hopelessness. His impression of the destitute focuses on their living conditions: the confined and forgotten spaces of their slimy yards, airless rooms, and hopeless debasement. Their children are described as animals in "litters" (424), while their houses are filled with stench and illness. In this context the destitute are clearly those who are forgotten, left to survive or die on their own. Even in the birth of destitute children Mr. Biswas recognizes "haste and disgust," as if, from the very start, these children were selected for exclusion and left unaccommodated. In their circumstances Mr. Biswas recognizes his own predicament even though it is entirely hidden by his make-believe position of power.

During this time U.S. military bases are established in Trinidad, "something called Coca-Cola" (321) arrives with them, and the sense of a larger, more prosperous world (despite or thanks to World War II) imposes a strange and shifting hierarchy on the island. Mr. Biswas threatens Shama that he will become "a labourer with the Americans" (421), an occupation that seems to him more appealing than being a local journalist. What emerges is a terrible hierarchy, not only among ordinary people who compete to be either at the top or bottom of the ladder (even if it's just poverty they excel in) but also among nations whose relative power dictates their position in a similar kind of global competition. On any established grid, however, Mr. Biswas always loses; he does not make enough money to be independent, nor has he sunk so low as to impress the charity donor on whose behalf he conducts his investigations. The paradox is disturbing: a destitute man does not qualify to be "rewarded" for his poverty unless his destitution is successfully performed.

Over time Mr. Biswas learns to distinguish between real and make-believe Destees and acquires, he thinks, a flair for genuine poverty. He knows, however, that the *Sentinel* will honor only the applications of those poor who will receive the award with "groveling gratitude" (425); defiant destitutes do not qualify. In other words, as he parades around the slum judging people's misery or running for his life in fear that the poor might take revenge on him, Mr. Biswas becomes conscious of the ways poverty is performed, ignored, or abused. It is not certain which is worse: the poor who stalk and threaten him in order to get a coin or two, or the privileged who wish to remedy their own sense of guilt or make money from the pageant of the poor. When in the end Mr. Biswas has to deal with his deaf relative's claim to the prize and sits in a dark, squalid room diagnosing his own family's right to being destitute in a deserving way, he experiences the terror of abject poverty. And horrified by its reality, he runs back to his house to destroy his attempts at fiction writing: "He took the stories to the lavatory in the yard and stayed there for some time, creating a din of his own, pulling the chain again and again" (435). Confronted with the daily misery of people he can neither help nor ignore, Mr. Biswas turns against his own fiction, flushing it down the toilet like excrement. In the incommensurable oscillation between the actual and the imagined, his world suffers from too much reality. In its excess this reality threatens to annul the power of the imaginary to restore some meaning to his quotidian frustrations. We realize that Mr. Biswas will really be defeated by his circumstances when he loses "the vision of the house" (474) and the ability to poke fun at daily tragedies, as he used to do in his sensational newspaper reports. But for as long as he can visualize and narrate his fictions, he is still living. His defiantly humorous stories and his unrelenting dream house seem to be his only anchor.

In his autobiographical essay "Prologue: Reading and Writing, a Personal Account," Naipaul addresses the intimate connection between material destitution and writing. He explains that the idea of becoming a writer was to him "less a true ambition than a form of self-esteem, a dream of release, an idea of nobility. My life, and the life of our section of our extended family, had always been unsettled. My father, though not an orphan, had been a kind of waif since his childhood; and we had always been half dependent. As a journalist my father was poorly paid, and for some years we had been quite wretched, with no proper place to live. At school I was a bright boy; on the street, where we still held ourselves apart, I felt ashamed of our condition. Even after that bad time had passed, and we had moved, I was eaten up with anxiety. It was the emotion I felt I had always known" (12). Connecting his own experience of poverty with his father's circumstances, Naipaul reflects on the state of separation from others induced by a profound feeling of shame and anxiety born of destitution. To this he opposes the "nobility" of writing, which promises a form of liberation from the confinement and humiliation of poverty. A writer's calling with its dream of handling and controlling the imaginary serves as a response to the material limitations of daily life. It is an escape, reminiscent of Mr. Biswas's unfinished "Escape" stories.

Against the certainty of a looming breakdown and in order to situate himself, Mr. Biswas covers the walls of his shack with newspapers in which he finds reassuring bits of someone else's reported reality. His room is thus made of words, and he derives some comfort from structured narratives, which—by promising meaning—counter the pointlessness of his circumstances. In a windowless room, the newspapers plastered on the wall literally become Mr. Biswas's connection with the outside world. From his four-poster bed he reads and soon memorizes all of the stories. Two lines in particular hold his attention: "Amazing scenes were witnessed yesterday when" and "Passers-by stopped and stared yesterday when." The rest of the sentences seems to have been sacrificed to the practical logic of the wallpaper.

When he eventually moves to the capital, Port of Spain, Mr. Biswas looks for a job as a journalist. With a vague idea that he can write, and remembering his two memorized journalistic clichés, he walks into the offices of the *Sentinel*. What follows is one of the most hilarious scenes in the novel, in which Naipaul's dark laughter reaches its peak by blurring, yet again, the narrative reality with the moments of rebellious fiction within and against that reality:

> He said to the man behind the high caged desk, "I want to see the editor."
> *Amazing scenes were witnessed in St Vincent Street yesterday when Mohun Biswas, 31 . . .*
> "You got an appointment?"
> *. . . assaulted a receptionist.*
> "No," Mr Biswas said irritably.
> *In an interview with our reporter . . . In an interview with our special correspondent late last night Mr Biswas said . . .*
> "The editor is busy. You better go and see Mr Woodward." (306–7, original emphasis)

In his fear of the bustling big city and the newspaper, Mr. Biswas—still "ridiculous and unlikely"—fictionalizes his pending meeting with the editor. By juxtaposing his exaggerated fictive responses (in italics) to the humiliating experience of asking for a job, he endows this experience with the grandeur of an event. Imagining a bold and dramatic response to the receptionist's coldness, he establishes a form of control and authorship over the alienating circumstances. If nothing else, he at least has the power to imagine a mocking sensational alternative to the real event. Moreover he later fictionalizes himself as both a gun-slinging assailant of the newspaper office and as the "special correspondent" who will obtain an exclusive interview with that very same assailant. In this double role Mr. Biswas is placed inside his own fiction, as its hero, and outside of it, as its creator. Naipaul thus underscores the necessary relation between these two positions, with respect to "real" life and also in writing. Mr. Biswas's narrative "quest for form" (Derrick, 201) comes to remedy the absence of legitimate position until, in the end, it is Naipaul's novel itself that becomes Mr. Biswas's house. A house *for* Mr. Biswas is indeed the novel with the same title; it is an offering of a narrative substitute for the house Mr. Biswas cannot own.

The standard language of the news report allows Mr. Biswas to disrupt the situation in which he is made to feel inferior. He thus appropriates, if only silently, a linguistic weapon and its power to establish one's social position. As in the standardized romantic plots in his "Escape" stories, Mr. Biswas composes his stance of defiance and protest by adopting and then pushing to the extreme precisely the most commonplace forms of expression. It is by overdoing the norm that he symbolically gains access to the news building. The receptionist cannot guard it against Mr. Biswas's sensational intervention of turning the cliché into a humorous weapon. Like Naipaul, Mr. Biswas pushes against the limits of what is admitted and normalized. Naipaul's own writing, in turn, often assaults the receptionist, who is guarding, as my initial quotes from his reviewers show, the standards of propriety.

Reflecting on the genuine predicament of Naipaul's position as a (post)colonial writer, Bhabha points out that, in response to "one of history's stiffest sentences," Naipaul's protagonists "serve their time" with wit and style, using language to resist and defy their anxieties and alienations: "Noisy with stories, garrulous with grotesquerie, gossip, humor, aspirations, fantasies—these are figures who signify a culture of survival that emerges strongly from the darker side of the colonial condition" ("Naipaul's Vernacular Cosmopolitans"). From this "culture of survival," as Bhabha puts it, one should not expect polite norms of language, laughter, or opinion. Instead, in the carnivalesque Mr. Biswas—and in Naipaul himself—there is provocative defiance; in exaggerating the statement, these figures confront and interrogate structures of authority and their standards of conduct.

Instead of being admitted as a journalist, Mr. Biswas initially gets a job as a sign painter. His first assignment is to paint No Admittance to Wheeled Vehicles, No Entry, Watch out for Vans, No Hands Wanted. Ironically he is commissioned to paint signs that would warn off from the newspaper building precisely men like himself. But once again he counters the reality of his circumstances through italicized, that is, lopsided fiction: "*Amazing scenes were witnessed yesterday when Mohun Biswas, 31, a sign-painter, set to work on the offices of the TRINIDAD SENTINEL. Passers-by stopped and stared as Biswas, father of four, covered the walls with obscene phrases. . . . . . interviewed late last night, Biswas . . . Mr Biswas said, "The ordinary man cannot be expected to know the meaning of 'No Admittance'*" (*HMB*, 309, original emphasis). In the spirit of self-assertion, Mr. Biswas corrects his fictional news report by swiftly adding "Mr." to "Biswas." By claiming this title and its dignity, he implicitly challenges other people's assumed entitlement to push or keep him out of various social hierarchies. This is why, throughout the novel, Mohun Biswas remains Mr. Biswas—a man who must be addressed respectfully, even when he is ridiculed.

Mr. Biswas's remark that "the ordinary man cannot be expected to know the meaning of 'No Admittance'" echoes Naipaul's similar refusal to write literature that can be quickly classified or easily approved of. Instead the writer, like his protagonist, celebrates writing by allowing it to create and follow its own norms, landscapes, and allegiances. If such writing is only partially admitted, or not at all, both the fictional and the real writer refuse to admit it and continue to demand, through writing, to be accommodated in the house of fiction.

4 Squatters in the Cathedral of the Written Word

Patrick Chamoiseau's *Texaco*

Spatial images are the dreams of society. Wherever the hieroglyphics of any spatial image are deciphered, there the basis of social reality presents itself.

—Siegfried Kracauer, "On Employment Agencies: The Construction of a Space"

Patrick Chamoiseau's *Texaco* (1992) chronicles the squatter community of Texaco, a slum located at the edge of Martinique's capital, Fort-de-France. As an underprivileged and illegitimate space, the slum reflects and shapes the lives of its inhabitants. The abandoned lot of the Texaco petroleum company is gradually settled by former slaves who, fleeing the plantation, arrive in the city in search of employment. The squatters' occupation of the abandoned site signals the spontaneous cultural potential of "an open community grounded not on identity but on strategic alliance" (Lincoln, 3), while also reflecting, in spatial terms, the historical deprivation of the Martinican slave population and its struggles to acquire full social recognition after the abolition of slavery. The slum community also raises the broader question of exclusionary urban politics and its zoning regulations. Given *Texaco*'s focus on the inherent urban conflict between authorized and unauthorized spaces, I approach the question of spatial appropriation in this novel through two related spatial concepts: *terrain vague* and heterotopia. The slum of Texaco represents both of these conceptual categories, allowing us a closer examination of the dialectical relationship between space and counterspace of Chamoiseau's "Creole city." While terrains vagues designate derelict postindustrial "urban sites that have lost their original function" and are now "open to unplanned activities and unofficial communities" (Doron, 208, 207) like Texaco, heterotopia is Foucault's way of accounting for spaces that are outside of our "normal" space and serve to contain or contest the social phenomena we will not accommodate. With respect to my reflection on Caribbean postcolonial space and its relationship to contemporary spatial theory, Foucault's emphasis on the complementary relationship between real social space and its imaginary (utopia) or actual (heterotopia) contestations is of central importance. *Texaco* resorts to two parallel types of spatial reflection: in one, the slum is a heterotopia, a space situated on the outskirts of the city from which it is excluded, revealing that city's normative structure inherited from the colonial world;[1] in the other, the slum is paradoxically a utopian ideal constructed around an impoverished but tightly knit Creole community whose survival depends on the oral narration of its spatial history. In this way the heterotopian reality of the slum and its utopian twin reveal and defy the normative colonial structure in which a destitute Creole citizen is treated as a sign of deviation or crisis to be contained and overcome. As Foucault points out, the nature of utopia/heterotopia is to be outside the accepted and normalized social space, but its outside status actually reveals the principles of inclusion and exclusion that regulate a particular social context. Both heterotopian and utopian spaces have the curious role of denouncing normative spaces by contesting or compensating for their strict regulations. Yet, for the purpose of my analysis, it is also important to remember that these two types of spaces constitute a kind of complementary binary: what heterotopia attempts to do in reality, utopia strives to achieve in imagination. The actual space of heterotopian contestation (the struggle for a place of one's own in a slum or a dilapidated house) continually clashes against the utopian visions of an ideal space, which fails to materialize and is ultimately created by means of narrative fiction itself.[2] Between the two poles—an inadequate heterotopian space and its unavailable utopian solution—the novels resort to a "third space," the space of narration and storytelling itself in order to respond to the limitations of spatial reality. In this way fiction becomes an alternative metaphorical space rather than a vehicle of realistic spatial depiction.

The two types of space I rely on in my reading of *Texaco*—terrain vague and heterotopia—share the character of exteriority and transgression insofar as they are first excluded and then perceived as threatening to the urban authority. From Lefebvre's perspective, both spaces constitute forms of appropriation of prohibitive and dominated spaces through simple daily repossession of "empty" space in the margins of the official city and signal the transformative social potential of counterspaces. In Chamoiseau's case, the official city is a colonial city where the traces of colonial order continue to shape social life while the slums on the outskirts of Fort-de-France shelter the dynamic communities of former slaves who are slowly entering the social fabric of the island and seek accommodation for their newly found freedom. In Texaco this struggle takes place through spatial occupation of the terrain vague and contestation of private ownership. In response the slum community establishes its land claim by simply being there, with its history, personal and collective narratives, and acts of storytelling. In this reclaimed space "the liminal community now constitutes a new internal frontier, a site of transgression and growth" (Dash, *The Other America*, 147). The battle for spatial legitimacy is thus reflected not only in material spatial terms but also through various modes of representation by which a particular community appropriates its *lived space*. The Creole city that originates in the slum is also a city of oral tradition and storytelling, which contests the dominated colonial city space and its official written character. The two types of space—one *lived*, the other *conceived*—are thus reflected in two types of narrative representation: the representation of oral storytelling and the representation of the written record.[3] In Lefebvrian terms, the *lived* and therefore *differential* spaces, by being fundamentally historical, seek to contest *abstract* administered space and bring memory back into daily spatial practice. Spatial narrative becomes a form of rereading of personal and communal history on a smaller scale. The slum and its orality are therefore transgressive: they seek to infiltrate and gradually transform the prohibitive spaces of the colonial city and its authorities, acting as a parasitic rhizome in relation to the established and enduring system of colonial relations. This rhizomatic nature of the slum and its community, which testifies to its vitality and will to survive, is also reflected in Chamoiseau's topographical arrangement of the novel, where the marginal (footnoted) text and various narrative digressions constantly interrupt the linear flow of the narrative. The novel that emerges is therefore a complex structure of spatial and textual appropriations that seek to give legitimacy to an alternative form of habitation and living. Chamoiseau's heterotopia seeks to reenter and transform the "normal" urban space just as the oral dimension of the narrative with its Creole tradition seeks to contest the normative presence of the written narrative and its official French language.

The novel opens with the arrival of the urban planner nicknamed Christ, sent by the city authorities to inspect the neighborhood of Texaco and pronounce it insalubrious. This fictional character is based on a real-life urban planner and politician, Serge Letchimy, currently serving as president of the Martinican Progressive Party and deputy to the French National Assembly. Letchimy was, with Césaire's support, responsible for the rehabilitation of Texaco. In *De l'habitat précaire à la ville: L'exemple Martiniquais*, he addresses the vital role of "insalubrious" neighborhoods like Texaco within the "urban ecosystem." Chamoiseau's fictional representation of this real political figure is an homage to Letchimy and also a broader urban critique cognizant of the tremendous efforts necessary for safeguarding the spirit while improving the material conditions of the island's informal habitations. At the end of the novel Chamoiseau recognizes Letchimy with the following acknowledgment: "To Mr. Serge Letchimy, whose work in urban planning and whose thoughts have fed these stories—with all my esteem and admiration" (391).

In Chamoiseau's fictional treatment of the real Texaco's plight, we discover the plan to relocate the inhabitants and raze the slum. In the interest of progress, a new road, ironically named "La Pénétrante Ouest," will replace the impoverished neighborhood. However, as soon as he sets foot in the slum, Christ is hit in the head with a stone, falls down half-conscious, and is taken to Marie-Sophie Laborieux, the novel's central protagonist and storyteller. As Texaco's founder, she faces the task of convincing Christ not to endorse the demolition plan. Following in the tradition of *One Thousand and One Nights*, Marie-Sophie changes Christ's mind and turns him into an ally by telling him the story of Texaco's genesis. Chamoiseau explores here "the structuring force of language in the face of extinction" (Dash, *The Other America*, 144), while self-consciously ironizing the filiations and sequencing of world history (including the literary). He rewrites the world-changing historical shifts (the Stone, Iron, and Bronze ages) and the rise of "Western civilization," marked by its various systems of writing, by placing Texaco at the center of this familiar periodizing narrative. The alternative historical sequence, or "an anthropological chronology of history" (Knepper, *Patrick Chamoiseau*, 113), is thus based on the revolution in Texaco's building materials from the Age of Straw and Crate Wood to the Age of Asbestos and Concrete. Not only is the history of the world thus transformed depending on where one identifies its center, but the large world-changing events are replaced by "small" shifts in the life of the squatter community. By rewriting world history from the perspective of a slum community, Chamoiseau critiques the structure of selective inclusions and systematic exclusions that have traditionally silenced the "small" local concerns of marginalized communities in favor of the grand historical narratives of progress, civilization, and conquest. Chamoiseau's novel explores, in Nick Nesbitt's words, yet another facet of "the imaginative capacity of individuals to act within yet think beyond the historically preformed society that complexly determines them" (4).

In *Lettres créoles*, Chamoiseau and Confiant insist, following Glissant's lead (*Poetics of Relation*, 68–69), on the intimate link between the spoken word and the spaces of plantation slavery, which suppress and, paradoxically, generate the new Creole aesthetic: "Creole oraliture is born in the plantation system, simultaneously in and against slavery, in a questioning dynamic, which accepts and refuses" (57, my translation). This paradox of acceptance-refusal remains crucial for Chamoiseau's work, marking a dual movement in which the counterculture, as it resists, also acknowledges and honors its origins in bondage and servitude. Marie-Sophie's slum of Texaco is itself an echo of the plantation: it is precarious space that generates, despite its limitations, a rich Creole counterculture in the living zone of the slum. According to J. Michael Dash, "Chamoiseau projects a liminal urban culture as paradigmatic for the modern Caribbean" (*The Other America*, 147). The destitution of Texaco is thus shown to result from a long history of colonial domination, which is, in the course of the novel, acknowledged, contested, and overcome by the narrative act.

Although Texaco is a slum—a site of poverty and deprivation—it is nonetheless impossible to call its community destitute. What the slum lacks in material means, it makes up for in the richly interwoven acts of storytelling. If *destitution* literally means to be placed outside and forsaken, then Chamoiseau's novel deals with protagonists who manage to own their story even as they remain disowned and illegitimate on the territory that they occupy. Placing *Texaco* in a broader context of urban poverty and squatting in the cities of the global South, Ashley Dawson points out that "*Texaco*'s picaresque narrative records a paradigmatic experience for the many millions experiencing urbanization in the global South: displacement" (18). Arguing that Chamoiseau is primarily interested in the practice of racially motivated exclusion from wealth and citizenship in the postcolonial city, Dawson emphasizes that "Chamoiseau's depiction of zones such as Texaco that inhabit the interstices of *l'En-ville* thus articulates the long history of subversion, resistance, and revolution through which subaltern groups have transformed colonial and postcolonial cities" (23). My approach to *Texaco* shares with Dawson's the interest in this transformative potential of the "illegitimate" urban communities and their quest for spatial reform.

Material *spatial* destitution is here confronted and reconfigured by the claim to rich *narrative* belonging. Is *Texaco* thus substituting linguistic wealth for social marginality? Is this substitution adequate or even conceivable? As I proceed to examine the uneasy tension between material deprivation and narrative abundance, I trace Chamoiseau's spatial critique of binary oppositions and his attempt to dissolve them by constructing an alternative reading of the cultural and class struggle in the postcolonial context. In an intrinsically dual structure of poverty and privilege, *Texaco* settles for neither pole. Instead, by examining the mutually constitutive relationship between community and location, Chamoiseau offers a vision of a "third space"—the space of the narrative itself—to encompass, but not resolve, the very real problems of cultural and economic inclusion and exclusion created by the history of colonialism. Arguing precisely for this utopian and imaginative power of literature envisaged in *Texaco*, Sarah L. Lincoln points out that "the task of representation, both politically and aesthetically, becomes . . . a perpetual project that always, necessarily, falls short and opens up, in that very failure, new prospects, new challenges, and new opportunities for conquest" (20). As a result Texaco's spatiality is always dependent upon the threads of storytelling and reflects the patchwork structure of Marie-Sophie's and her father Esternome's narration. Conversely the slum is built of many huts that lean into one another, connected and discontinuous at the same time. The shape of the story is thus also the shape of the settlement, or, as Dash puts it, the text is itself "an edifice of heterogeneous materials" (*The Other America*, 144).

As he reinterprets the history of Martinique and translates Marie-Sophie's story into new urban knowledge, Christ-the-urban-planner learns to make a clear distinction between the City and the Creole city; the old normative and colonial city has to be forgotten, he realizes, in favor of the Creole city, built painstakingly in the interstices of the preexisting order, which offered no space for the liberated slave population and was unwilling to cede it. For this reason the Creole city is, in its very essence, as transformative and fluctuating as the story that records its contestatory genesis. Christ concludes that what the Creole city teaches him is "Creole urbanism," which requires not just renovation or restructuring of space but also "*a mutation of the spirit*" (*T*, 234, original emphasis). This is the moment in which the third space of *Texaco* takes shape: the material concerns of urban planning and the narrative concerns of transmitting memory merge into a third space of spiritual transformation, which is both concrete and ideal. In *Texaco* it is impossible to separate the story and space since geography itself appears to be narrative and the narration always inherently spatial. The recognition of their necessary merging and mutual dependence may be precisely what the urban planner means by "the mutation of the spirit."

This imbrication of communal meaning and spatial practice characterizes terrain vague—the urban concept and phenomenon through which I read the specificity of Texaco's transgressive spatiality—as a particular kind of urban space where alternative forms of habitation and spatial behavior can unfold. Terrain vague is an abandoned urban area, like Texaco, where the vestiges of derelict industrial production are slowly overtaken by vegetation and repurposed by alternative communities exiled from normative city spaces. As Gil Doron points out, most terrains vagues have been populated by marginalized communities. At the same time, they also "present history (rather than represent it), foster creativity and nourish the aesthetics of ruins" (204). Provisionally devoid of sovereign administration, Texaco as terrain vague offers a chance to the homeless and dispossessed liberated slaves to establish their spontaneous and self-sustaining community. Texaco thus becomes a compelling example of the urban alterity offered by the terrains vagues: "Unincorporated margins, interior islands void of activity, oversights, these areas are simply *un-inhabited*, *un-safe*, *un-productive*. In short, they are foreign to the urban system, mentally exterior in the physical interior of the city, its negative image, as much a critique as a possible alternative" (Solà-Morales, 120, original emphasis). Texaco's terrain vague is an urban heterotopia, internal to the city and simultaneously excluded from its signifying structures. The arrival of the urban planner represents the moment when contemporary architecture and urban planning threaten to become, in relation to terrain vague, "an instrument of power and abstract reason" (123), seeking a violent transformation of spontaneous spatial practice into a regulated one. In response the inhabitants of the slum use their oral history to anchor them in the space they can own only through daily spatial practice. Their diverse communal living and its myriad stories are the only alternative to the domination of the spatial mechanisms of power and regulations of private ownership. Texaco is the city's unaccepted other; it shelters those populations and forms of living that the regulatory colonial city refuses to accommodate. To the extent that it is *excluded* rather than exclusionary, it shares some essential features of Foucault's heterotopian space.[4] In its struggle over excluded difference, the shantytown also illustrates Lefebvre's approach to heterotopia: "Differences endure or arise on the margins of the homogenized realm, either in the form of resistances or in the form of externalities (lateral, heterotopical, heterological). What is different is, to begin with, what is *excluded*: the edges of the city, shanty towns, the spaces of forbidden games, of guerrilla war, or war. Sooner or later, however, the existing centre and the forces of homogenization must seek to absorb all such differences, and they will succeed if these retain a defensive posture and no counterattack is mounted from their side. In the latter event, centrality and normality will be tested as to the limits of their power to integrate, to recuperate, or to destroy whatever has transgressed" (*PS*, 373). From the beginning of *Texaco*, the slum mounts the opposition that Lefebvre describes, hurling a stone at Christ-the-urban-planner and thus ironically signaling its refusal to be recuperated by the forces of urban homogenization. Marie-Sophie and the slum community struggle and succeed in preserving the autonomy of their spatial and cultural difference, claiming their exteriority as status. The mosaic structure of Creole Texaco challenges the monolithic and monolingual notion of urban order and, by extension, any order bent on regulating and silencing the concrete chaos of living.[5]

Concerned with the encounter between the imaginary and the real—"how rubbing the real with the magical . . . has added to the ways of apprehending human truths" (*T*, 324–25)[6]—Chamoiseau suggests that the real spaces we live in can be read as a narrative and then preserved in it. According to *Texaco*'s main premise, the significance of a location lies in its legibility: the specific place is marked by the lives and languages it holds and which in turn shape it.[7] To read a specific place is to engage in reading the history of a people and its collective memory, which unfolds in and is inscribed onto space. The disordered life of the Creole language is inscribed in the pulsating chaos of the slum huts and represents, as Christine Chivallon remarks, one of the "major thesis" of *Texaco*—the representation of *créolité* as chaos: "Not any random chaos of dehumanized disorder, but the chaos of mobility and lightness, where nothing is fixed or rigid, but exists as trace, as salient lines" (89, my translation). Ultimately the slum and the story echo one another as manifestations of creative disorder, which strives to embody and honor life itself. We thus encounter an attempt to speak the material world into existence and to build, in turn, a neighborhood in language. The movement is double: on the one hand, the life of a community etches itself onto inhabited space so that one can read the location and "decipher," as my epigraph suggests, social reality from the spatial image; on the other hand, when a voice like Marie-Sophie's offers an oral history of a place, spatial reality is invested with communal memory actively spoken back into existence.

Considered spatially the slum of Texaco looms on the margins of the city, while the city derives its centrality from the existence and resistance of this margin.[8] The slum is an illegal, squatted area, which ironically appropriates the name and former territory of a petroleum company, transforming it into the heart of suburban opposition to the capital, l'En-ville. By referencing this name as "a symptom of the international language of modernization," Chamoiseau's novel "reterritorializes the extraterritorial trademark Texaco within the mangrove space of Martinique" (Dash, *The Other America*, 146). Yet, true to the principle of broken binaries, Marie-Sophie also describes l'En-ville as a dream of liberation from the countryside marked by plantation slavery and slave owners. L'En-ville thus remains a utopia of genuine freedom: Marie-Sophie's father, Esternome, a carpenter and master builder, along with many former slaves emancipated in 1848, immediately abandons the plantation-ridden countryside for the promise of autonomy and opportunity in l'En-ville. Yet the enchantment of freedom is revealed to contain a grain of future misery: the liberated slaves are now in search of employment, working in factories, discovering the trap of their economic dependence. Although they are no longer property, their lives are now ruled by the logic of wage labor and job opportunities and thus still mortgaged to the "békés," the former slave owners. In other words, the abolition of slavery is not the abolition of economic servitude: "lestravay" of plantation slavery is now replaced by the poorly remunerated work in the factory. The pyramidal power structure of the plantation, with the békés on top,[9] continues to shape postabolition Martinique. Descending from the hills ("les mornes") around Saint-Pierre, the former slaves and maroons discover that they are being replaced by a new workforce, brought from elsewhere—the Chinese, Indians (koulis), and Africans (congos)—as the békés send abroad "for other models of slave" (*T*, 138). Meanwhile the former slaves face a new kind of threat—poverty—in a land they still cannot own despite the fact that they have first made it prosperous through their labor and are now officially free to claim it: "Sure, one survived, sure, one was free, but the aftertaste of misery was rising quickly. It was the bitterness of a land whose promises fly away" (139). Freedom, as Esternome realizes, does not equal inclusion or equality.

When Esternome moves to Fort-de-France, his life unfolds in a neighborhood appropriately named Quartier des Misérables. Circulating between the impressively modern and prosperous l'En-ville and his impoverished Quarter of the Wretched, Esternome discovers, and bequeaths to Marie-Sophie, the love of two contradictory-complementary faces of the Creole city composed of the orderly center and the chaotic halo of slums. These two aspects of urban composition she in turn reveals to the urban planner, teaching him to "reread" the city from the perspective of her community's collective memory and experience (*T*, 170). From Christ's newly transformed understanding of the city, it emerges that Marie-Sophie's Texaco is not only a way of materializing the dream of spatial belonging, which she inherits from her father, but is also a site of linguistic diversity, a space composed according to the logic of the Creole language: like Creole, it is unofficial, resilient, humorous, communal, and ultimately dependent for its survival upon the acts of storytelling. The neighborhood is defined linguistically, while the Creole language is reflected in the logic of its architectural design. In weaving the unofficial status of the slum with the equally unofficial nature of its language, Chamoiseau connects the urban environment with the language that it speaks, making them interchangeable. The Creole language and the slum of Texaco are profoundly connected in their opposition to the official, mostly written French language and l'En-ville as the seat of its power.

The urban and the linguistic come together as soon as the narrator, Marie-Sophie, begins to tell the long and fascinating oral history of her family and community in Texaco. This story is told at least twice: to Christ-the-urban-planner and to the writer/ethnographer, "Oiseau de Cham." As a result the fragmented and often broken flow of narration reveals a triangular relationship between Marie-Sophie, Christ, and the writer, who all intervene in shaping the tale of the slum. The writer/ethnographer, referred to as "Marqueur de paroles" (Word Scratcher), must trace on the blank sheets of paper an entire history of the spoken word as well as map the place where it is spoken. The "contrepétrie" of his name, Oiseau de Cham, reveals Chamoiseau himself as the diligent transcriber of the spoken word. Instead of blindly following the prescriptive (literally: already written) interpretation of the slum, the planner and the writer both learn—thanks to the improvisatory whims of Texaco's orality—to revise their understanding and judgment of communal space. The encounter with the self-regulating force of linguistic and architectural improvisation, both of which define Texaco, undermines the principles of normative narration or building. For example, in the indented and separate sections, which periodically interrupt the flow of Marie-Sophie's story, Christ shapes, in the notes addressed to the Word Scratcher, the episodes of her memory into an urban manifesto where he formulates a new understanding of social organization: "In the center, an occidental urban logic, all lined up, ordered, strong like the French language. On the other side, Creole's open profusion according to Texaco's logic. Mingling these two tongues, dreaming of all tongues, the Creole city speaks a new language in secret and no longer fears Babel" (*T*, 220). In *Texaco* the impoverished Creole community fights against the housing dictates that arrive, with apocalyptic force, from the cultural and historical "elsewhere" represented by the city authorities. Christ, as their envoy, encounters for the first time, face-to-face, the entire community of Texaco and the labyrinth of its hutches, which the city has pronounced literally "unhealthy" (insalubrious). What plagues the city is the parasitical nature of unauthorized life. It seems to develop and proliferate without proper system or purpose and thus automatically jeopardizes the planned nature of the city. But in the place of binary oppositions, opened by this initial juxtaposition between the *conceived space* of the city and the *lived space* of the slum, to use Lefebvre's useful terminology, we encounter instead various attempts to reverse the accepted notions of place ("lieu") and territory on the one hand, and narration and language on the other.

Instead of settling for binaries divided by an interpretive abyss in need of bridging, Chamoiseau—inspired by Deleuze and Guattari via Glissant—opts for the strategy of infiltration. He allows each notion, image, or historical relation to be multidirectional and radically polysemic, evoking in the course of the novel precisely that stubborn diversity glorified in *Eloge*. The result is a celebration of squatting: an illegal yet productive and continuous reappropriation of spaces—linguistic, geographical, and cultural—which deeply challenges the structures of legitimacy and authority. By collapsing the neatness of opposites (slum/city, place/territory, Creole/French, spoken/written, slave/owner, etc.), Chamoiseau follows the triumphant but often unpredictable logic of rhizomatic growth with no conclusive or settled approach to either space or identity. While Christ learns how to conceive of a different kind of a city, in which diversity of the "chaos-monde" will be embraced rather than suppressed, so must the Word Scratcher (Chamoiseau) attempt to write a text—the novel of Texaco—in which spoken Creole's playful resistance to norms continues to animate the traditional regularity of the written page. The slum's disruption of the neat city is mirrored by the linguistic irruption of the spoken into the written, so that the urban planner and the writer/ethnographer face the task of translating, without betraying, the slum into the city and the spoken word into a book.

The Creole language is a dynamic outcome of the plantation system, in which it served as a medium of "acceptances and denials, resignations and assertions": "Orality is our intelligence; it is our reading of this world, the experimentation, still blind, of our complexity. Creole orality, even repressed in its aesthetic expression, contains a whole system of countervalues, a counterculture; it witnesses ordinary genius applied to resistance, devoted to survival" ("IPC," 95). In this passage from "In Praise of Creoleness," Chamoiseau affirms the centrality of oral tradition in the definition of Creole culture and its ability to accomplish two other crucial tasks: to resist the imposed aesthetic and other forms of authority and to bring the potential of a quotidian "ordinary genius" into the struggle for cultural survival. Chamoiseau follows in the footsteps of Glissant, who in *Caribbean Discourse* examined the complexity of this oral/written dynamic of his own work: "I am from a country in which the transition is being made from a traditional oral literature, under constraint, to a written nontraditional literature, also equally constrained. My language attempts to take shape at the edge of writing and speech; to indicate this transition" (147). The precarious life of Texaco and its oral tradition are distinguished by their localized particularity and neither claim nor admit any existing "ism" of the French tradition, even when they admire it. In numerous "French" episodes where we encounter the glory of the French literary tradition and its legacy, Chamoiseau shows his protagonists awed by and yet distant from the abstraction of the high cultural imperative even when it is meant to support or remedy their own hardships.

In the final section of the novel, entitled "Résurrection," which marks the revival of Texaco, Chamoiseau describes his reasons for "collecting" the spoken word and weaving it into the novel. His method sounds like that of a reluctant ethnographer who resents his "bastard of a tape recorder" (*T*, 387) but also recognizes the inability of any record to do justice to the reality it records. Reflecting on the reductiveness of the linear record and the treachery of the archival future, Chamoiseau expresses in this last section the fear of treason embedded in the attempt at preserving the living presence of the word, whose preservation can be accomplished only at the cost of its life: "I did my best to write down this mythic Texaco, realizing how much my writing betrayed the real, revealing nothing of my Source's breath, nor even the density of her legend" (390). The Word Scratcher fears that the written word can save very little of what once was a vibrant life and runs the risk of conserving Marie-Sophie in a reduced form, or rather in form only: the written story threatens to empty out the body—of a person, town, community—and leave nothing but its hollow shell. Every time a memory of life and place strives to become a historical record of that life and place, there is a chance that empty structures, like vacated buildings, will replace the texture of a lived present.

The commemorative and epitaphic quality gives Chamoiseau's novel precisely that tinge of loss that accompanies any triumph. In the case of *Texaco* the highly staged and ironic snaring of the spoken word only serves as a reminder of its loss. Chamoiseau is fully aware of the irony of his position and quest: to be writing, often in "a French more French than that of the French" (see Ti-Cirique's epigraph to "Annonciation") a story of the triumph of the spoken word—a triumph belied, in the end, even by the Prix Goncourt that *Texaco* was awarded in 1992. The literary success of *Texaco* marks, as a matter of fact, the victory of the written word and of the writer/ethnographer, not of his speaking Source, her fast-dissolving oral culture, or her slum.[10] Chamoiseau's profound awareness of this historical change is already visible in his 1988 novel, *Solibo Magnifique*, a quasi-detective novel meant to elucidate the death of a great storyteller only to conclude that the "conteur" was killed by the spoken word itself. Already in this earlier novel Chamoiseau imagines that only language can kill or revive language; with *Texaco* he engages in the struggle to infiltrate his own "grand-grec" (educated) writing with the unruly vibrancy of Creole. As we know from his more theoretical and manifesto writings, this attention to inserting Creole into the written form is a deliberate literary and cultural project, which along with his cowriters he calls "Créolité."

In *Texaco* the visual layout of the printed page reflects the battle between Creole and French and the battle between the slum and the city center. Drawing attention to this topographical dimension, Serge Dominique Ménager examines the relationship between language and space of the "mise en page." We perceive that the footnote—the actual margin of the page—contains those parts of the narrative that cannot be accommodated in the main text. The story is overflowing and expands beyond the boundaries of the printed text, in a way analogous to the uncontrollable overflow of Texaco with respect to the city of Fort-de-France. Ménager calls these textual supplements and intrusions "infra-texte": a text that is simultaneously disruptive, minor, and exiled from the main text and yet, to a large extent, modifies or limits this "main" text. Through the "topographical" ordering of the page and story, both visually and narratively, Chamoiseau draws attention to those aspects of life, culture, history, or identity that cannot be contained or erased by the dominant political forces. As readers, we are invited, if not forced, to accommodate offshoots and digressions from the main story that do not contribute to its final outcome but rather to the manner of its gradual unfolding.

The small concerns of the narrative detours appear in the short titled segments of the novel; each one carries its own name, plot, and purpose. They are obviously an inseparable part of the novel and yet appear as intrusions in it. By introducing this short-story structure into a vast historical novel, Chamoiseau creates, on the level of the text itself, a feeling of multitude, of a crowded tight space, like the slum of Texaco, where one person, house, or story leans on its neighbor and draws its meaning from the agglomerated whole. The text appears as a visual replica of the plot: the multiplicity of stories is, among other things, a visual reconstruction of the slum. When she describes the construction of Texaco, for example, Marie-Sophie focuses on the magnetic power of her pioneer hutch to attract other settlers, who gradually become a community when they learn to perceive one another as connected by their common goal and mutually dependent in the task of accomplishing it: "My hutch attracted other hutches. Word about the place blew about like the wind. Since every day brought with it a flood of would-be City people, it was soon known that there was room by Texaco. . . . Hanging on to mine were already two dozen hutches in different stages of development. They were built on Sundays or at night. The newcomer appeared, closed off an area, and came back with the moon to take root in the soil. Soon, there was no need to get any help from outside. The very people on the slope lent a helping hand, gave advice, helped, shouldered each other. . . . In a few months we had become autonomous" (*T*, 300). The network of other hutches grows around her initially improvised but persistently rebuilt house: "The locale of the house is imagined in communal terms, a space of solidarity rather than of solitariness" (McCusker, 47). This neighborly solidarity constitutes the first and lasting seed of a community, which will defend the name Texaco.

As Chamoiseau explains in an interview with Maeve McCusker, he is interested in exploring the relationship between story and place ("lieu") rather than between history and territory. In the absence of a founding myth and its relation to place, what the Caribbean claims is a founding story by which a multiplicity of histories comes into being and is preserved: "If one were to search for a foundational language of the Creole-American peoples, it would be the story. And the story means diversity."

Chamoiseau concludes that a storyteller's view of history dislodges the notion of a single History in order to reconstitute it as a braid of histories, "une *tresse* d'histoires."[11] The story emphasizes the specificity of a place, but it also sets in motion its irreducible cultural diversity.

Chamoiseau's approach to Antillean history might at first appear paradoxical: the particularity (even singularity) of a location is drawn from an absolute multiplicity of histories that come to inhabit this location. The unique aspects of culture are, as Chamoiseau suggests, a consequence of multiplicity and not of lonely exceptionalism. The "unicity" ("l'unicité"; McCusker and Chamoiseau, 725) of the territorial and historical imagination, which Chamoiseau clearly rejects, would amount to sacrificing a particular place to an ideal universal (i.e., placeless) narrative.[12] Chamoiseau's "lieu" strives to reflect the indissoluble link between a geographical location and the stories that make it significant. In other words, a mere location becomes a significant place ("lieu") only if and when it is recognized as a repository of stories. Aware of the dangers of disembodied spatiohistorical narratives, Chamoiseau insists on the distinction, crucial for his work, between the standardizing "universalism" and the multilingual and multicultural "diversalism" (McCusker and Chamoiseau, 727). It is this second concept, diversalism, that allows for and brings into being a complex and relational notion of "place," simultaneously autonomous from and dependent upon the larger world. Since such diversalism results from a continuous interweaving of histories, Chamoiseau creates a necessary bridge between location and narrative: they cannot exist one without the other.

From the first moments of Antillean colonial history, through plantation slavery with its resentment of the master's Big House, through the illegal shantytown and its battle with the City, to the irreverent attitude of Creole to French, and finally even in the use of the topographical infratext, Chamoiseau interrogates the notions of settlement, conquest, and illegal acquisition of space. In various and unexpected ways, he offers a glimpse of what it means to be a squatter on a piece of property owned by another, in a language reserved for another, on the edge of a city hospitable only to some. The hierarchy of places, languages, and people is constructed around the concepts of entitlement and law. As Randolph Hezekiah points out, the historical experience of slavery and the current political status of Martinique and Guadeloupe inform this literature: "Long after the abolition of slavery by the French in 1848, the descendants of African slaves, uprooted from their homeland and deprived of their religion and language, continue a desperate search for selfhood" (379). The subsequent transformation of these colonies into overseas departments (DOM) in 1946 led to a new form of dependence: "In practice, the new system of exploitation was put in place whereby the DOM became increasingly dependent on France for basic commodities (food and clothing, for example) at prices far in excess of French prices; this tended to discourage local entrepreneurship. French Caribbean intellectuals have not been insensitive to the realities of the true relationship between metropolitan France and its Caribbean territories, and it is the Caribbean writer's perception of this relationship, reaction to it, and attempts to come to terms with it that informs their writing" (379). As we have seen, this literary reconceptualization of the spatial and cultural center-margin relationship is essential to *Texaco* as well. The ironic historical reversal, in which the former slaves reconquer the spaces of their former masters, is traced in a detailed chronology that precedes the beginning of the narrative proper. While the former slaves, who are granted their freedom but are kept economically dispossessed, descend upon the cities to claim their portion of the island, we are forced to contemplate the legitimacy not only of the plantation owner but also of economic and cultural privilege in general.

The colonizer is, originally and etymologically, a tiller of the land and also a squatter on the land of another. Over time, however, as the Caribs and Arawaks are decimated in the Caribbean, the colonizer transforms his theft of land into a law and then, through his own legal and political systems, defends the robbery and massacre that lie at the root of his wealth. The initial destruction of the native populations is simultaneous with European settlement and coincides—as Chamoiseau is careful to emphasize—with the building of plantations and cities: "Caribs and Arawaks are exterminated as slave sugar plantations and cities grow" (*T*, 3). The plantation and city are therefore not only spaces that symbolize European conquest but are also the material tools of colonial rule, which changes and controls the landscape as much as it controls social relations. In a potent reversal characteristic of *Texaco*, however, the freed slaves such as Esternome become squatters on the land of a colonizer—the initial squatter whose geographic illegitimacy has been conveniently forgotten. In creating this circular problem of location and ownership, Chamoiseau interrogates any form of intrusion and conquest, but does so in a nonbinary and nonlinear manner.

According to Chamoiseau's main premise, the centralized order requires its marginal chaos, while the peripheral chaos regenerates the sterile center. In order to condemn the slum (or the "war" for its survival), one would have to sacrifice the creative energy of illegitimate life and preserve instead the infertility of the established urban order. Texaco, however, struggles to assert the right of illegitimate growth, as the weed or the mangrove of the city: "In its old heart: a clear, regulated, normalized order. Around it: a boiling, indecipherable, impossible crown, buried under misery and History's obscured burdens. If the Creole city had at its disposal only the order of the center, it would have died. It needs the chaos of its fringes. Beauty replete with horror, order set in disorder. Beauty throbbing in horror and a secret order right in the heart of disorder. Texaco is Fort-de-France's mess; think about it: the poetry of its Order" (*T*, 184). The spatial configuration of the City and the slum, which the urban planner learns to perceive from Marie-Sophie's story, seems to reveal a potentially hostile relationship between "le coeur ancient" (the center) and "une couronne bouillonnante" (the effervescent crown of the city). The "disordered" and indecipherable periphery is instead the only thing that gives the normalized and regimented center of the city its possibility of remaining alive. The urban planner and, through him, the writer/ethnographer learn to recognize that the meaning of the city lies in its contrasts and battles, not in its homogeneity and artificial harmony. *Texaco*'s reflection on the right of the destitute squatters amounts to posing at least two crucial questions: What is the future of the relationship between the disdained periphery and the monumental center? And what hope is there for integration that is neither assimilative nor destructive?

To express the particularity of Texaco as an alternative urban space, Chamoiseau resorts to the metaphor of local vegetation, the mangrove, striving for multiple interpretations offered by such an image. First, he combines in one phrase, "la mangrove urbaine," the possibility of organic and inorganic life. This oxymoron, which also defines the urban phenomenon of terrain vague, fuses the built with the natural world. This move is reminiscent of Chamoiseau's literary predecessors who have thought of the Caribbean landscape as closely tied to the particularity of Caribbean culture. From the Doudouists to Glissant, the natural features of the land are constructed into metaphors of the social and artistic world. The urban mangrove is itself one such image, in which the two concepts are linked by a mysterious though suggestive notion of growth. Like weeds or fungi, the slum grows at the edges of the city, feeding on it and feeding it in turn. The persistent growth of the mangrove—"the haphazard whirls of the living" (*T*, 257)—becomes a model for Texaco and strives to express something essential about the slum and its people. As Christ explains in one of his notes to the Word Scratcher, Marie-Sophie's story teaches him to perceive the city as "an ecosystem" (257), which does not accept the model of Darwinian evolution and thus neither progresses nor recedes. Instead the mangrove is described as a growth in between: it is neither of the land nor of the sea, neither a root nor a stem, neither a plant nor a creature. In its in-betweenness it evokes powerful images of mythical monsters (it is described as an "aberration" [244]), which, as David Punter shows, become one of the most powerful literary tools of postcolonial imagination.[13] Chamoiseau's original contribution to this already existent postcolonial imagery is to attribute a kind of productive "monstrosity" to a specific urban space and examine it as a spatial relation.

The image of the urban mangrove—a city slum transformed into a force and ruse of nature—has its philosophical precedent in Deleuze and Guattari's "rhizome." They matter to Chamoiseau, at least in part, because of the work of Glissant, who draws on *A Thousand Plateaus* and in turn "infects" a great number of his postcolonial followers with its language. In *A Thousand Plateaus*, Deleuze and Guattari rely on the rhizome to evoke a cultural and theoretical alternative to the arboreal imagery that affirms and organizes European history and self-imagination. It is time, they claim, to do away with the tree: "To be rhizomorphous is to produce stems and filaments that seem to be roots, or better yet connect with them by penetrating the trunk, but put them to strange new uses. We're tired of trees. We should stop believing in trees, roots, and radicles. They've made us suffer too much. All of arborescent culture is founded on them, from biology to linguistics. Nothing is beautiful or loving or political aside from the underground stems and aerial roots, adventitious growths and rhizomes" (15). Deleuze and Guattari propose an image that can indirectly illuminate the structure of *Texaco* precisely in terms of the squatter's spatial intrusion that guides my analysis: the rhizome penetrates into and invades the centralized structure of a tree. It is, in this case, a parasitical growth that insinuates itself into the main structure, *radically* changing it in the process. The relationship between the root and the rhizome rests on reversibility of meanings and functions. The one always contains the possibility of the other; the root and the rhizome coexist and can generate one another endlessly.

This same structure of mutual reversibility characterizes the relationship between the slum and the City in *Texaco*. It will depend on the context and its very concrete set of coordinates what meaning we will give to each concept and how we will judge its outcome. What matters, however, with respect to *Texaco* is the rejection of any dichotomy in favor of the multiple, connective, and heterogeneous system of shoots that form the rhizome. It is fundamentally unpredictable, indestructible, and chaotic, just like Chamoiseau's slum. But most important the rhizome traverses and conquers space; it is capable of movement, adaptation, and spreading; its intention is territorial. In this moment we can fully appreciate the meaning that Deleuze and Guattari have for *Texaco* since the "bidonville" is itself a rhizomatic structure that seeks to reverse the relationship between City and slum. It spreads, according to Chamoiseau, like the mangrove with its in-between and resilient nature. Texaco is thus the chaotic and nonlinear reversal, a suburb-guest preying on the city-host, but also the contrapuntal heart of that city. It is ultimately the invasive and survivalist nature of the slum that should trigger a radical transformation of the city center.

The fascination with l'En-ville described by Marie-Sophie sends us back to the abolition of slavery in the French colonies in 1848, when the move to the city meant a final and definitive break with plantation slavery and its legacies. Yet although the city represents a multiplicity of chances, destinies, and stories and, at least in imagination, offers itself as a solution to the enclosed and oppressive space of the plantation, it also reveals itself to be a hostile place that partitions communal space into solitary nuclear housing, deprived of fellowship and marked instead by "civilized indifference" (*T*, 256). A house of one's own is, paradoxically, what Marie-Sophie and many former slaves dream of but recognize as the seed of dissolution of their traditionally communal existence. In order not to destroy "the heart and flesh" of communal life, Christ will realize that the cold City must receive and be changed by the "morne"-like organization of the slum. In this way the interwoven proximity of the country life will have moved into the city and made it more humane. As Christ concludes, if l'En-ville is to become anything other than "the *béké's kitchen*" (281, original emphasis), it must accept the transformation, which a periphery like Texaco will bring to it: "Texaco was what City kept of the countryside's humanity. And humanity is the most precious thing for a city. And the most fragile thing" (281). The cold City stands in sharp opposition to the "mornes," and the slums that mirror them, where the crisscrossed lanes and leaning huts allow an intimate encounter with each inhabitant's life: "All these huts formed a trapdoor spider's web in which we all lived in clusters. Before there was a community of people, there was one of huts carrying each other, tied through one another to the sliding land, each getting its bearings from the other. . . . Dreams touched each other. Sighs mingled. Miseries shouldered each other. Forces knocked each other out until you saw blood. It was a sort of rough draft of City, but warmer than City" (277). The laws of the "morne" are established on the bases of proximity by which the sheer multitude of interconnected huts shelters each individual hut. In such a context the notion of solitude is the opposite of survival. Most important, however, Marie-Sophie's story gives to the arrangement of houses precedence over community: the group affiliation and solidarity follow from the spatial organization of the "morne" and the quarter. Conversely the cold separation of the regulated city housing could just as easily destroy the community. From this perspective, the cold City is just another version of the master's house, which survived the time of slavery and has multiplied into an impenetrable city center: "Tall City. Massive City. City from whose memory they were excluded. For them City remained impenetrable. Smooth. Waxed. What to read in this wrought iron, these painted wood shutters, these enormous cut stones? These parks, these gardens, of which all these city people seemed to master the secret? Bonbon once said to him, and he was right, that City was a Big Hutch. The Big Hutch of all Big Hutches. Same mystery. Same power. This made Esternome my papa a tad bit sick" (80). Relying on her father's experience and stories, Marie-Sophie communicates here the problem of the City's fundamental illegibility. The fascination with the city points to its promise of diversity; its threat comes from what is unknown to the newcomers and what escapes their capacity to interpret, narrate, or remember. The City is thus an echo of the plantation's Big House, which, in Esternome's eyes, offers a carceral solidity: "The Big Hutch rose in the center of the outbuildings, sheds, and straw huts. From it poured the fields, gardens, the coffee-sown lands climbing the slope of trees (with precious wood). It dominated the whole, seemed to inhale all" (44). The hermetically closed space, which has the power to swallow its surroundings, is a token of a hermetically closed history, which, composed by and for the conqueror, will not accommodate the squatter, the guest, or the former slave. Marie-Sophie's key question, "What to read" (80), reminds us of her main quest: to change the text(ture) of the city by infiltrating it, to insert her story into an already written (prescribed) history, to make legible what her people cannot read, to conquer back, in space and language, the sites that have been denied. This technique of squatting structures the relationship of Creole to French, of slum to city, and even of Chamoiseau's literary endeavor to the French theory it references. When he gestures toward Deleuze and Guattari, for example, or Glissant and Césaire, Chamoiseau does not succumb to the "grand-grec" status of literary elitism but instead reaffirms the principle of infiltration that dominates his novel. The heterotopian space of Texaco returns to haunt and transform the so-called orderly and legitimate spaces that create heterotopia in the first place. Yet these theoretical and literary references are also illegal occupants—squatters—of his text and challenge any single interpretation we may feel tempted to produce.

Although he sees in the squatters' urban retaliation the inexorable logic of the pendulum and the beauty of phoenix-like survival, some implications of Chamoiseau's notions of territory and place ("lieu") remain contradictory in appearance. Is *Texaco*, in the end, interested in the reconquest of territories or the assertion of place? Chamoiseau's "lieu" owes its existence to the meaning that separates it from the unspecified and abstract domains of space and territory. Spatial meaning, he suggests, arises from the many stories of which a place is composed. The huts of Texaco, for example, grow on us because we come to know their inhabitants and their trajectories, dreams, and memories. The more familiar we become with the place, the more we accept and like it, mimicking in this respect the gradual transformation of Christ-the-Urban-Planner. Chamoiseau's strategy is to root and localize a grand historical narrative in an infinitely smaller and more modest space, which becomes the concrete battlefield of history.

Yet if a place—a small local unit, which exists in solidarity with all others—is so important for Chamoiseau, why is his novel also concerned with the conquest of territories? The uncertain origin of the word *territory* is often linked to the notion of fright or terror: a territory is a space from which people are warned off. In the case of Texaco, to conquer a territory is to reclaim a forbidden city-center and tear down the invisible walls that bar one population from mingling with another. The problem of spatial containment and defiant trespassing sends us back to the history of slavery as *Texaco* traces the former slaves' need to move freely and unrestrained through any space. It is not conquest that Chamoiseau attempts to claim and celebrate but rather a need to free up space for any people, culture, or story to live there. As in the final sentence of Bessie Head's *A Question of Power*, the solution is in the very relationship between a community and its location. Head's protagonist puts her hand on the ground, touching, we are told, her land: "As she fell asleep, she placed one soft hand over her land. It was a gesture of belonging" (206). This image of a person who, although herself always dispossessed, claims a place by touching it, echoes Mr. Biswas's need to claim his "portion of the earth" (*HMB*, 11) by building his own house. In *Texaco* Marie-Sophie asks herself the question Mr. Biswas would not have dared to ask but which shapes his entire life: "Why this obsessing about owning my own hutch? In City, to be is first and foremost to possess a roof" (275). To exist is, then, to exist in a place, but also to tell about that existence.

Chamoiseau's storyteller Marie-Sophie is, along with all her friends and neighbors who build and defend the quarter of Texaco, concerned with the preservation of place, "le lieu," and its fundamental relationship to language and narrative. In the end we are told that the squatters will, of course, not conquer l'En-ville and all it stands for—"lui qui en fait nous gobait" (it was City that gobbled us)—but they will live in it and, most important, name it. The movement of traditional revolt, such as the maroons were capable of in the times of slavery, is now perceived as obsolete: "No one sees the békés in City any more. So how can we get at them? No more Big Hutches, so where are we to maroon out of? No more factory, so what blind toil to give in to? What you call the Power turns into farce" (*T*, 294). City makes stark social oppositions invisible, and even though they are still there to animate the social organization from the inside, the cause and direction for battle is less and less visible on the surface. As a result there is something farcical, as the wise Mentoh points out, in the attempt to wage war against something that cannot be located. It turns out that the political (binary) opposition is made obsolete by the opacity of the contemporary city, whose seeming complexity successfully hides its basic inequalities. For this reason Chamoiseau chooses to redefine the concept of marooning into a particular kind of poetic resistance that can recognize the mobile mosaic of the contemporary world without relinquishing its will to intervene in it.

The survival of Texaco depends, in the end, on the gesture of naming: Marie-Sophie, led by the Mentoh's counsel, names the quarter of Texaco. The secret name is meant to protect and empower the slum, even when in reality it appears to be on the verge of destruction. Whenever her strength and faith seem to wane, Marie-Sophie invokes this name, summoning through it the reality and future of Texaco. Borrowing again from the biblical tradition of the world-creative naming, Chamoiseau finally renounces (and denounces) territorial conquest in favor of the story and the words that wield power. The novel ends with the word *authority,* unfortunately lost in translation: "I wanted it to be sung somewhere, in the ears of future generations, that we had fought with City, not to conquer it (it was City that gobbled us), but to conquer ourselves in the Creole unsaid which we had to name—in ourselves and for ourselves—until we came into our own [jusqu'à notre pleine autorité]" (390). The word *authority* seems to suggest an invitation not to fight against the normative immensity of the city center (and, by extension, the postcolonial metropole) but to discover and assert Texaco's communal agency and its ability to author itself and its place of existence. Such authority over self and language, or more precisely the ability to create and make them grow, is forged in the narrative battle for the ownership of names. This emphasis on the act of naming of an urban locale is echoed in Christopher Winks's definition of the city as a place for the autonomous (literally, "self-naming") and self-regulating community (xiii). Chamoiseau's "lieu" is contained in this name and in the stories that unfold around it. This name opens onto the language of a people; the language in turn contains its history, while history reveals the place of its unfolding. The battle for Texaco is, in the end, a battle for spatial and linguistic (self-)recognition. "Blurring the lines between narrative, history and ethnography, *Texaco* lays claim to the rewriting of the imagined/real community and the world through extended and ongoing processes of creolization" (Knepper, *Patrick Chamoiseau*, 129). If such a battle is also a utopia and a dream and does not succeed in changing the fate of real people and places, it at least commemorates their stories and gives authority to what would otherwise remain silent and buried in the official records. In an "illegitimate" struggle for a squatted place, in a marginal language, Texaco triumphs: it succeeds in asserting stories over History and places over Territory.

5 Heterotopia of Old Age in Beryl Gilroy's *Frangipani House*

Do not go gentle into that good night,
Old age should burn and rave at close of day;
Rage, rage against the dying of the light.
—Dylan Thomas, "Do Not Go Gentle into That Good Night"

In this chapter I explore the figure of the house as an exclusionary space where the allegedly burdensome and deviant aspects of social life are supposed to be safely contained. One such dimension of social reality is old age, which we—uncertain how to treat its gradual loss of productivity and social function—increasingly isolate. Homes for the elderly provide the space where visible traces of old age are conveniently kept out of sight. Through Beryl Gilroy's *Frangipani House* (1986), I explore this marginalization of old age by means of heterotopia, a concept that allows us a critical view of the relationship between the space and identity of the aging and "unproductive" body as it loses its social role. In contemporary society age increasingly appears as a relation of oppression since "most old people are stigmatized as sick and unattractive, receive little deference, and find themselves pushed from positions of responsibility even if they want to work" (King, 49).[1] The exclusion of old people from relevant sociocultural networks and from the labor market shows that the decline of the body constitutes one of the most significant problems in societies based on production and consumption. The human body and its spatiotemporal meaning thus require a critical examination of exclusionary social norms and their spatial configuration.

In the Caribbean context this problematic of the body and its productive function is especially important because the reliance on slavery in Caribbean colonialism transforms the human body into a tool of wealth accumulation. Although the body is a key component of production, it also ceases to have any autonomous meaning. Hortense Spillers famously argues that the "New-World, diasporic plight marked a theft of the body—a willful and violent (and unimaginable from this distance) severing of the captive body from its motive will, its active desire (67)."

By turning the body into "a territory of cultural and political maneuver" (67), this theft produces the denial of gender differences and marks the captive body as an expression of absolute physical otherness—an "object" whose powerlessness serves to confirm the captor's "subject" position. The actual treatment and symbolic interpretation of the captive thus annuls the very notion of the body. In Spillers's terminology, the body becomes "flesh": it is branded by unrestrained violence and so carries the physical and symbolic traces of objectification. The body is thus both essential to the practice of slavery and, paradoxically, through the impact of that practice, made irrelevant and replaceable. This dual effect of slavery—the reduction of a human being to his or her body and then the complete denial of that body's specificity—clarifies why the question of corporeality emerges as one of the most prominent topics in Caribbean discourse. In Dash's compelling account, "The body or corporeal images provide an insight into the psychic condition of the enslaved individual. The body—like the mind in the world of a slave—is numbed, impotent, inert, ultimately someone else's possession. Consequently, self-assertion is inevitably linked to a sensuous physical presence, to an active body, to standing 'upright and free,' in the words of Césaire's *Cahier.* Freedom for the enslaved is seen in terms of unrestricted physical movement" (introduction, xxvii). The recurring attempts at self-assertion through physical presence and unrestricted movement also organize the struggle for autonomy of Gilroy's protagonist Mama King, "old, ill, but splendidly her own woman," who is put away by her family in Frangipani House, "a Dickensian rest home on the outskirts of Georgetown" in Guyana (Salkey, 670).[2] Made destitute by the concrete physical impact and abstract social interpretations of old age, Mama King foregrounds the relationship between the spaces of freedom and captivity on the one hand, and the corporeal experience of autonomy and subjugation on the other. Mama King's story can thus be approached, as I intend to do here, as a salient example of corporeal objectification that provides a powerful link between two kinds of heterotopias: the heterotopia of old age and the heterotopia of spatial captivity. My ultimate purpose in this chapter is to investigate the alternative space and selfhood that emerge from Gilroy's critique of these two heterotopias of exclusion.

The winner of a prize in the Greater London Black Council Literature Competition in 1985, even before it was published, *Frangipani House* initially received mixed reviews. While some critics praised Gilroy's "insight of a psychologist, the eloquence of a poet, and the compassion of a kindred spirit" as well as her ability to exceed the confines of a protest novel (Knowles, 84–85), others considered that the novel was "badly served by a hyperbolical, self-conscious style" (Gilkes, 1372) and found "something forced" in Mama King's "matriarchal dauntlessness" where "beneath the rightful protest there is a curious undertow of emigrant's regret" (Deveson, 1187). However, her writing is probably best seen as resisting easy interpretation as it faithfully explores "Caribbean figures as culture bearers," depicted between anguish and comic irony (Anim-Addo, 131). Regardless of the position the reader takes in response to these diverse critical evaluations, Mama King's rebellion against the institutional structure of the nursing home allows me to explore the novel's central problematic of corporeal and spatial dispossession. Most important, I examine the kind of space that the body requires, occupies, is forcibly assigned, and seeks to challenge. Following Lefebvre's analysis, I explore the way social space and spatial identity emerge in relation to the body and its contestation of prohibitive spatial structures: "The whole of (social) space proceeds from the body, even though it so metamorphoses the body that it may forget it altogether—even though it may separate itself so radically from the body as to kill it" (*PS*, 405). Heterotopia of old age is certainly one such social space, which isolates and transforms the aging body in reductive and potentially destructive ways. Gilroy's novel invites us to contemplate and critique that space and its effect on identity.

The contrast between the place one wants to inhabit and the place one is assigned reveals our social perception of the body and its function in general, and also the particular conditions of "enslavement" that persist in the heterotopian segregation of the elderly: "Many nursing homes still fulfill Goffmann's [*sic*] (1961) criteria of total institutions. They have a tight daily schedule, enforce a strict set of rules, and leave little personal freedom for the residents. Residents tend to be deprived of their individuality because tight routines leave little space for their specific wishes and needs" (Pasupathi and Lökenhoff, 211). The reference is to Erving Goffman's study *Asylums: Essays on the Social Situation of Mental Patients and Other Inmates*. According to Goffman, "total" institutions exercise complete control over their residents' lives through ritualized processes of admission and subsequent degradation, such as the loss of privacy and submission to rules. As a result "residents' identities are stripped away and then reconstituted within the institutional system; a person becomes a resident, who is defined by his or her age along with specific medical diagnoses" (Pasupathi and Lökenhoff, 211). Insofar as it confines its inhabitants, depriving them of control over their place and movement, the nursing home evokes—to a limited degree we must not exaggerate—the conditions of slavery and incarceration. One difference lies, of course, in the question of productivity: while slavery presupposes the unbridled exploitation of the enslaved body, the nursing home "enslaves" in order not to deal with the waning of bodily power. In this respect the notions of slavery and ageism act as reverse images of one another, intersecting only in terms of denied agency and forced location. Nevertheless, as Lefebvre repeatedly shows, it is in the persistent excesses and implicit rebellion of the body, its ability to challenge any established order through its performance of unreason, that the body constitutes the last bastion of resistance to the abstract logic of prohibitive space represented by heterotopias, which in Foucault's account cover sites as diverse as prisons, asylums, nursing homes, and colonies. Despite their evident differences of structure and purpose, these institutional spaces share the goal of containing and policing human excess by means of corporeal control.[3]

I approach the dialectic of spatial inclusion and exclusion, which assign and deny corporeal meaning, through one of the most seminal texts of contemporary spatial analysis, Foucault's 1967 lecture "Different Spaces."[4] In it Foucault juxtaposes the realities of social space and their imaginary rearrangements, arguing that our age is increasingly an age of spatial "emplacement" (a constant calculation and classification of where human beings fit within available space) and the interpretations derived from the spatial positioning of cultural practices. Whether "Different Spaces" is discussed as the inaugural moment of critical spatial theory, a "silly" text, or a text characterized by "enchanted breathlessness," Foucault's reflection on the imaginary and real functions of space certainly constitutes a recurring reference in contemporary elaborations of spatiality.[5] In this brief but rich discussion of contemporary emplacements, Foucault reflects on those rather extraordinary spaces that serve to "suspend, neutralize or reverse the set of relations that are designated, reflected or represented [*réfléchis*] by them" ("DS," 178); they have a curious feature of being linked to all other spaces yet at variance with them by both reflecting and contesting them. These spaces are, Foucault suggests, utopias (emplacements that have no real spatial existence but maintain an inverse analogy with real social space) and heterotopias (real emplacements that are best described as actualized utopias; they represent, contest, and reverse the real space to which they remain external and inextricably linked). Both utopia and heterotopia constitute the radical "other" of the existing social space but differ in that one actually exists (heterotopia) and the other is entirely imaginary (utopia). From that point on, Foucault is interested in listing and exploring various heterotopian spaces, their historical transformations, and the way these spaces reveal our social practices and norms. The term *heterotopia* (literally "other places") points "to various institutions and places that interrupt the apparent continuity and normality of ordinary everyday space," thus injecting "alterity into the sameness" (Dehaene and De Cauter, "Heterotopia in a Postcivil Society," 3–4).[6] As a site of spatial alterity, heterotopia connects to Lefebvre's theorization of the spatial effect of the body, namely its ability to produce difference: "Differences endure or arise on the margins of the homogenized realm, either in the form of resistances or in the form of externalities (lateral, heterotopical, heterological). What is different is, to begin with, what is *excluded*" (*PS*, 373, original emphasis). When it emerges as disruptive, as in the case of old age, the body is certainly one such excluded social element, radically other and thus capable of mobilizing and reappropriating otherness as a form of spatial practice. The excluded body is thus reflected in the spatial function of heterotopia, itself an excluded space, "open but isolated, of controlled access and egress" (Faubion, 31), which serves to organize the unaccommodated dimensions of social life.

With respect to my reading of *Frangipani House* and its spatial rendering of the social status of aging, one type of heterotopia is of particular importance: Foucault's heterotopia of crisis and deviation, which allows us to perceive and analyze the way a particular society deals with deviant behavior (through psychiatric hospitals, prisons, retirement homes, etc.) and what constitutes deviation in the first place and what, by extension, the required social norm may be. According to Foucault's fluid schema, old age is situated on the cusp between crisis and deviation. As an interstitial social phenomenon, old age thus reintroduces my concern with dual and ambiguous categories. Since such categories are also mobilized by the figure of the house itself, both the representation of aging and its segregated space require a sustained reflection on a "third" alternative solution against a reductive spatial dichotomy through which social inclusion and exclusion operate.

The heterotopia of crisis, whose origin Foucault locates in the so-called primitive societies, initially designates a privileged space reserved for those individuals, such as adolescents, menstruating or pregnant women, and the elderly, who are in some form of temporary crisis in relation to the rest of their community because they are undergoing a particular physical transformation. In contemporary societies, however, these spaces, notably with respect to old age, are becoming heterotopias of deviation, because "in our society, where leisure activity is the rule, idleness forms a kind of deviation" ("DS," 180). The same concern with the way industrial (as opposed to "traditional") societies deal with aging and its relation to productivity characterizes Susan Sontag's famous discussion of the gender-based double standard by which old age is experienced and evaluated (31). As the main currency of societies organized around production and consumption, youth ceases to be part of human temporality and becomes an isolated value with no connection to old age. Old women in particular become exiles from this "materialistic world that places higher value on physical appearance than it does on mental and spiritual attributes" (Wilson, 189).

In an attempt to avoid reducing old age to a time of physical decline, some researchers have recently engaged in the development of a "new gerontology," proposing the notion of "'successful aging'—that is, the many factors that permit individuals to continue to function effectively, both physically and mentally, in old age" (Rowe and Kahn, xii). Not looking or appearing old becomes central to this quest for the positive aspects of aging. Staying fit, for example, turns into "highly valued social capital": "The body becomes central to identity and to aging, and the maintenance of its youthful appearance has become a lifelong project that requires increasing levels of work" (Calasanti and Slevin, 3). Although feminist studies have tended to overlook old age as a pressing question of oppression and inequality,[7] many cultural practices of resisting age are persistently seen as the domain of women. As recent studies in population geography show, classical positivist and data-driven analyses often engage in a kind of homogeneous understanding of old age, largely interpreted as threatening to the social and economic development of nation-states. This means that old people are routinely depicted as "more financially dependent on the state, requiring higher levels of health care and social assistance, and as having a minor role in achieving the political, social and cultural aspirations of nations, when compared to the 'working age' population" (Davies and Amity, 2). Such interpretations of aging marginalize "the value of 'non-production' and 'non-consumer' activities" while also "grossly miscalculat[ing] the considerable contribution older people make to social, economic and cultural landscapes of nations" (3). Inspired by the alternative "cultural turn" in human geography, which incorporates "cultural meanings into explanations of demographic processes" (3), I am concerned here with the literary representation of aging as a social and spatial marker of exclusion within the abstract system of production and efficacy. The connection between perpetual youth, productivity, and the accumulation of wealth is an important element of the capitalist worldview that measures life cycles and their significance by their contribution to the systems of industrial production. The implementation and development of this capitalist model in the colonies leads to its continued dominance in postcolonial societies as well. Parts of the life cycle, such as aging, are perceived negatively because of the alleged shortcomings in the productivity of the body. Nevertheless the question that persists and is tackled in *Frangipani House* is how the traditional family- and community-based model of aging intersects with and challenges the capitalist model of productivity and profit.[8] Discussing the merits of *Frangipani House*, Lucy Wilson points out that it not only depicts the isolation, suffering, and indignities that accompany old age but also suggests "the untapped potential of older women as a source of wisdom, insight and self-esteem for younger generations" (189). Gilroy's concern with unquantifiable human value as opposed to material criteria of wealth and productivity mobilizes in turn the two types of spatiality that I explore in this chapter: the heterotopia of repressive institutions and the freely chosen and fully accepted heterotopia of social otherness.

In *Frangipani House*, which, according to Gilroy, represents "a praise song for grandmothers" (Bradshaw, 392), the contrast between the traditional African approach to old age and its Western counterpart serves as an important backdrop to the conflict among Mama King's children and grandchildren as they try to decide what to do with her. While Mama King's granddaughter Cindy laments the coldness of her family, her husband, Chuck, who has spent time in Africa, reminds them that they are dealing with old age as if it were a problem: "We are trying Caucasian solutions. We have to go back to the African village for answers. The old in Africa have a place and a function. They are never cast aside" (*FH*, 100). Although this contrast between "Caucasian solutions" and "the African village" appears idealized, Gilroy is attempting to emphasize the meaning of human life and its temporality outside the normative structures of productivity, progress, and upward mobility. She reflects on the alternative: the necessity of extricating the value of human life from its quantifiable social function. According to Roydon Salick, Gilroy's third solution between the socioethnic binaries of Caucasian and African family customs consists in placing Mama King among Indo-Guyanese beggars. They are significant because their socioeconomic position marks them as outcasts and their ethnic origin falls outside the African-European dichotomy posited by Mama King's family: "Gilroy is suggesting an alternative that exists in the Caribbean, an alternative that is viable and to be found among Indo-Caribbean people generally, and specifically among the Indo-Caribbean peasantry" (Salick, 104). This alternative is meant to counter the fact that "you lose your identity as you get older" (Bradshaw, 392) and foregrounds instead the aging woman's vital quest for self-reliance and relevance within a given community. Mama King is able to reclaim herself thanks to the respect offered her by those who, like the group of Indo-Guyanese beggars, still know how to live and relate outside the abstract spaces of money, social status, and self-interest. By contrast, "Frangipani House is but an extension of the system of care for the old predominant in Europe and North America. . . . Though she has remained in Guyana, Mama King has been effectively made to fit into a home built by the colonizers and run according to their ethos" (De Souza, 159). In a society that chooses Frangipani House as a solution, old age can no longer be properly appreciated as a source of experience, memory, or wisdom but is relegated instead to the marginal position of deviant bodily phenomena. This deviation of age brings us back to the idea that the body whose social productivity and effectiveness can no longer be quantified becomes an exception and thus threatens to disrupt the carefully codified system of normative social expectations.

In her novel *Boy-Sandwich* (1989), a sequel to *Frangipani House*, Gilroy continues to explore the problem of the nursing home, this time in London, and resolves it by allowing the elderly Caribbean emigrants eventually to return to the island of their origin.[9] In this familiar location, which they perceive as their alternative and genuine "home," they are seamlessly integrated into a community and the flow of its daily life: "The people around her accept old age and its handicaps. They measure persons against life rather than against youth. In Britain the young alone matter and elderly people are regarded as used-up and intractable simply because they are old" (104). Here Gilroy develops more sharply the contrast between England and the Caribbean, which in *Frangipani House* takes the triangular shape Guyana–United States–Africa, and uses it to emphasize a viable alternative to the instrumental spaces of the Western world. In the Caribbean, by contrast, the easy conversation, spontaneous get-togethers, and ultimate irrelevance of age revitalize old people and make them inextricably part of the social fabric of the island: "The Islanders never number their years. 'Something' is used to denote any number between one and nine" (106). As a result the grandparents of the main protagonist, Tyrone, will probably live to be "eighty or ninety-something" (106). They are liberated from the burden of counting their time, social role, and contributions to the world around them; instead their life is again unquantifiable and measured only by the free flow of their relations with others. Gilroy recognizes, however, that this "ideal" location, with its communal character, is oppressive to young Tyrone, who actually misses the anonymity London offers him. He experiences his family as "a tight knot" that threatens to strangle him with its closeness (117) and wishes only to flee them. In his view and in the view of many young islanders, "home is for when you young and when you old. In between you go and grow somewhere else" (114). *Boy-Sandwich* ends with Tyrone's departure; like Naipaul's narrator in *Miguel Street* and many other emigrant protagonists in Caribbean fiction, he boards the airplane to return to England, realizing with a tinge of cynicism that "coming home is not a panacea but a service for old folk seeking a familiar graveyard" (122).

In both of these novels, however, the heterotopian space of the nursing home excludes the elderly within the social fabric they inhabit. By closing them off into specialized institutions that homogenize old age, families seek to offer benevolent protection to the elderly while keeping them away from the ordinary flows of daily life. The heterotopia of the nursing home partakes of Lefebvre's *abstract space*, whose repressiveness is manifested through reduction, functional localization, the imposition of hierarchy, and segregation (*PS*, 318). In this manner the elderly are a deviation from the busy socioeconomic productivity that dominates our perception of daily life and are also excluded from the quotidian spaces, Lefebvre's *lived spaces*, which are crucial for resistance to the regulated spaces of institutional control: "Confined by the abstraction of a space broken down into specialized locations, the body itself is pulverized. . . . In abstract space, and wherever its influence is felt, the demise of the body has a dual character, for it is at once symbolic and concrete: concrete, as a result of the aggression to which the body is subject; symbolic, on account of the fragmentation of the body's living unity" (*PS*, 310). Deprived of *lived space*, the elderly in nursing homes are permanently relegated to prohibitive spaces of carefully scheduled and mapped behaviors, which we claim to have provided for their own good. What falls out of this picture and what Gilroy daringly interrogates in her novel is the dignity of living according to one's own choice and the dangers of losing that dignity if one's choices, with the pretext of age, are handed over to experts and specialists to the detriment of what Lefebvre calls "the body's living unity." The active agency of the elderly is transformed, through the kind of space they inhabit, into an imposed passivity deemed appropriate for the aging body. This aging body, however, serves to remind us of the "supreme difference" (*PS*, 396) of our corporeal existence: because of old age and its proximity to death,[10] bodies of the elderly are also the ultimate reminder of those aspects of human existence that cannot be brought in line with productivity, quantitative gain, accumulation, or any rational schedule. The "fleshly body [*le corps charnel*] of the living being" and "the spatial body of society" (*PS*, 396) produce differences that cannot be easily organized, rationalized, or accommodated; therein lies their ultimate revenge on the abstract and homogenizing spatial order of the state and its institutions.

Nevertheless, although heterotopias function by exclusion and serve to order and segment social space, they also hold the opposite potential: challenging the order they have helped establish, providing, as Foucault puts it, "a kind of contestation, both mythical and real, of the space in which we live" ("DS," 179). In other words, as soon as a space is created to uphold imaginary social barriers and keep the deviant at the margins of social life, that same space also offers a vantage point from which centrality and order can themselves be perceived and challenged. In analyzing Frangipani House as a heterotopia—a space meant to confine the inherent alterity of old age, but also a space that foregrounds the possibility of resistance embodied in Mama King's struggle for dignity and freedom—I read Gilroy's novel as an instantiation of Lefebvre's "right to difference," "the right to be free from externally imposed, pre-established classifications of identity" (McCann, 181): "The 'right to difference' is a formal designation for something that may be achieved through practical action, through effective struggle—namely, concrete differences. The right to difference implies no entitlements that do not have to be bitterly fought for. This is a right whose only justification lies in its content" (*PS*, 396). Mama King's fight against the imposed classifications of identity that accompany old age and her various attempts at establishing her "right to difference" despite her waning physical strength constitute Gilroy's central narrative concern. In the course of this battle, Mama King's rejection of the coercive order of the nursing home also signals her attempt at establishing personal autonomy through spatial claims.

Once again, as in *A House for Mr. Biswas* and *Texaco*, space and identity are treated as fundamentally interconnected and dependent on one another: the denial of spatial autonomy amounts to Mama King's destitution—the denial of her identity, her past, and her human dignity. Yet

Gilroy's novel clearly shows that one can be made destitute precisely by being housed, even comfortably, against one's wishes and sense of self. This kind of destitution consists in the obliteration of personal autonomy through the forcibly assigned social location. Paradoxically Mama King's liberation comes from being homeless among the beggars, but with a sense of freedom to be so on her own terms. In *Frangipani House* the nursing home is a place of destitution, while living among the destitute amounts to finding a substitute home. The nursing home and the roaming beggars' community thus constitute inverse heterotopian experiences: while the nursing home offers a compensatory space where old age is made emotionally destitute but socially safe, the beggars' material destitution unfolds a series of "contesting counter-sites" (Boyer, 56) that paradoxically provide Mama King with a sense of emotional belonging.

At the very beginning of *Frangipani House*, we learn that the forty-three women inhabiting the nursing home and "paying for the privilege of confinement" while waiting to die in it represent "relics of work-filled bygone days" (1). In contrast to their once active and independent lives, they are now expected to rest out of sight, peacefully sequestered in an attractive prison. Yet even before we realize how our rebellious protagonist, Mama King, really feels about this "privilege of confinement," we are already wary of the house itself. Gilroy describes it as a respectable, overdressed lady, circumscribed by her sumptuous clothes, set apart from the rest of the world, and locked in by heavy vegetation:

> Anyone who came upon the house sitting sleek and comfortable on the town's edge, stopped outside its finely wrought iron gate as if under a spell. It was that kind of house—eloquent, compelling and smug. Sleepy headed windows dressed in frilled bonnets of lace and fine, white cotton, hibiscus shrubs that danced their flower bells to the songs of the wind, and a mammee apple tree that kept the grounds clean by never bearing fruit, marked the house as a place of professional comfort, care and heart's ease.
>
> A circular skirt of closely-cropped grass, with ruched panels of bright low-growing flowers offered familiarity and friendship to passers-by. But it was the ring of frangipani trees, just inside the slender, white painted spears of railings that marked the limits of the grounds, which named the house and caused folk to whisper darkly "Over yonder—Frangipani House! People dies-out dere! They pays plenty to die-out inside dere! Death comes to lodgers in Frangipani House!" (1)

This "eloquent" house speaks of respectability and comfort but is also "sleek," "smug," and "compelling." The frills, lace, and layers of architectural "fabric," which bear down on the spectator as much as on the lodgers themselves, give the word *compelling* an ominous tone: we are compelled by the heaviness of ornament and signs of comfort that ultimately conceal what the house might really hold in store. In keeping with Anthony Vidler's discussion of the inherently ambiguous and "uncanny" nature of the house, the respectable and neat outer trappings of Frangipani House suggest entrapment of the lodgers within. The description of the house immediately signals, as Salick points out, "the ambivalence of the institution" (100). For Isabel Hoving, who reads *Frangipani House* as part of the feminist literary tradition of intertwining gender and space, the house we usually imagine as a site of protection and intimacy actually "strangles and eradicates with brutal finality" (77). This ambivalence constitutes Gilroy's "cynical comment on what a house might mean as a home, a sign for one's own identity" (77).

As we explore the impact of repressive space on identity, Gilroy's description of the nursing home as barren and isolated serves to signal the alienation of its elderly lodgers. The unsettling ambiguity of the house/home is further emphasized by the fact that the lush garden offers "familiarity and friendship to passers-by," orienting the entire space outward: the house seeks to impress the passing visitor more than it cares for those who inhabit it. Paradoxically the nursing home is a public space whose ostentation targets the middle-class need for visible affluence and comfort while simultaneously canceling out the private life and autonomy of its residents. This dichotomy between public and private is also reflected in the temporality of the nursing home: the present is related to the public dimension of the home, while the past is Mama King's private world of memories and feelings.[11]

Gilroy offers a perfect summary of the nursing home's purpose: it gives "professional comfort." The phrase suggests an almost oxymoronic imbalance between rational purpose and fellow feeling. The house cannot bring them together but presents instead a series of tensions and contrasts: lush big trees bear no fruit, thick vegetation makes it hard to access the house, the circle of frangipani trees actually fences in the house and its lodgers, while sleepy windows offer a limited view. The entire house is meant to seduce the passer-by by giving the illusion of a perfect shelter for the elderly, although, in reality, they are brought there merely to die in style. And despite the "eloquence" of its ease and luxury, the house does not convince. The passers-by recognize it as a manicured tomb for "aged old folk—black women" (1).[12]

As a typical heterotopian space, Frangipani House is located "on the town's edge," physically excluded from the daily flows of communal life. As such, it is a place of "incarceration" (1), where the elderly appear insane, tossed between frenzied laughter and random song, talking to themselves and the ghosts from their past or remaining locked in silence. Gilroy further underscores the dual nature of this heterotopian house by suggesting its ability to simultaneously expose and disappear its lodgers: "Those who still felt the pulse of life, however weakly, found soon enough that not only did the walls of the house recede to leave them exposed and vulnerable, but suddenly it compressed them enough to cause consternation before they adjusted to their new surroundings. The hopes and emotions the women shared grew hazy with the passing of time. Finally they disintegrated leaving only faint smudges when they were finally blown away" (2). The space of the nursing home only seems static, for it hides a capacity for nightmarish mutability. The walls retract to expose or close in to crush the inhabitants. In both images the house itself possesses an uncanny power to determine the shape of the women's identity and daily life; even if they grow accustomed to their environment, they will slowly transform into "faint smudges," presumably crushed by the house itself and then blown away like dried husks. The outcome of living in the nursing home is, Gilroy suggests, a slow disintegration of the elderly because "confinement and do-nothing destroy people" (52).

The frills of the house and its dainty appearance also signal a traditional cast of gender roles. Elderly women are housed in this feminine-looking edifice characterized by the utmost passivity and complacence of its residents. Quite in keeping with Sontag's description of age and gender, here too "'femininity' is identified with incompetence, helplessness, passivity, noncompetitiveness, being nice. Age does not improve these qualities" (31). There is, in other words, a reassuring timelessness and static endurance of the "proper" feminine features. Yet in the case of Frangipani House lodgers, and particularly Mama King, the architectural femininity of the anthropomorphized house is misleading. Mama King, along with many other "inmates" of the nursing home, is a hard-working woman who has spent her life struggling and surviving by her own wit and strength while generously taking care of others, whether they be family, friends, or neighbors. Her past is filled with hard menial work: "I use to do plenty work—bake, wash, sell, scrub, domestic work" (12). She even remembers taking the job of breaking bricks and carrying heavy loads on her head. For this reason, her strongest rejection of the nursing home life has to do with its constitutive idleness: "More than anything else she wanted work. She always had a special relationship with work. Her body needed it as it needed food and clothes" (20). Attached to work as a vital dimension of her personality, Mama King is therefore the diametrical opposite of Sontag's middle-class Western woman, with her infantile craving for perpetual youth, comfort, and protection. She is a heroine "unique in West Indian fiction, embodying that indomitable urge—so often stifled by male conditioning and female self-effacement—the Caribbean woman has for self-realization and freedom of expression" (Salick, 98). Toward the end of the novel, Mama King's quest is expressed with powerful simplicity: she wants to be treated like she is "somebody" (99). This "somebody" is not defined by age, gender, or class, but is instead a simple formulation of a need for full and autonomous personhood at all levels of life and in all of its constitutive moments. Sontag describes this alternative kind of womanhood at the end of her essay on gendered aging: "Women have another option. They can aspire to be wise, not merely nice; to be competent, not merely helpful; to be strong, not merely graceful; to be ambitious for themselves, not merely in relation to men and children" (38). Of course, unlike the women Sontag has in mind, Mama King is already wise, competent, strong, and self-reliant rather than nice, subservient, or graceful. Ironically her problem consists in the way old age places her within the category of stereotypical femininity she never wanted to occupy and to which she never belonged. Her struggle to flee Frangipani House is thus also an attempt to flee the gradual falsification and standardization of her identity and recover, in the process, the person that she used to be: someone willful, persistent, and brave enough to live in accordance with her own design regardless of age.

The imagined comfort of the nursing home is purchased for the aging parents by children who have prospered abroad and are now attempting to remedy the problem of physical distance that prevents them from showing their care. The nursing home is therefore an institutional substitute for their love and a symbolic balm for their filial anguish. Mama King's confinement to Frangipani House can therefore be read as reflecting "the changing value system of a class of Americanized West Indians who leave elderly family members to fend for themselves or who believe that leaving the elderly in expensive homes is a substitute for love. These depersonalized homes are West Indian Bantustans where the soul is left without spiritual vegetation" (Tarver, 127). The solution to the difficult question—what to do with the aging parent—comes in the figure of

Olga Trask, the matron who runs Frangipani House and reigns supreme over its fragile inhabitants. She is a "predator of a woman" (*FH*, 2), whom we meet from the outset as the negotiator of costs. The opening scene reveals the hard material facts behind the seductive frills of the Frangipani façade: the nursing home is expensive, and the matron is experienced in driving a hard bargain. Mama King's daughters agree to pay the price that initially leaves them speechless: five hundred dollars a month in order to get "superior" care (2). One of the daughters, Token, specifies, "We will pay. But we want white people to care for her" (3). This requirement signals Token's interest in status: if they can afford for their mother to be nursed by white people, then they will have successfully purchased a higher social position. In their view the black woman cared for by white nurses is a sign of comfort and luxury. And since the family is not nearby but scattered across the United States, pursuing the dream of upward mobility, it becomes important to show to the local community and to anyone who might ask that Mama King's daughters spared no expense. This exchange precedes the reader's encounter with the main protagonist and introduces the question of money, in both its material and symbolic roles, as the backdrop to the narrative of shelter, nursing, and care. Frangipani House is thus also a space where money intersects and inevitably clashes with expressions of concern and love, bringing us back to the ultimate inadequacy of the notion of "professional comfort."

By contrast, Mama King's relation to money has always been so transitory and functional that she feels as though she has never really held money in her hands. When another resident, Miss Mason, gives her two five-dollar bills she has stolen from the matron, Mama King studies them with curious detachment: "Mama King examined the bills carefully. She had never found time to look at one closely before. She had never kept one for more than a few minutes, or savoured it or made friends with it. What little came her way had always been a servant of her altruism, her unselfishness and her concern for the needs of others" (39–40). The difference between Matron Trask and Mama King is obvious: while one implicitly "savors" money, the other has no taste for it. In Mama King's case, money has no autonomous value or emotional content; it is merely a means to different altruistic ends, allowing her to support others. By itself, money has no appeal for Mama King, and she does not care to "befriend" it. While in the case of Olga Trask and even Mama King's daughters, money possesses irresistible power and, acquiring a life of its own, becomes the master of all of their interactions, for Mama King money remains a "servant" to her generosity. Their respective relationship to money marks the fundamental difference between various characters in the novel. Most of the younger, "working-age" protagonists are attached to money and ruled by it. Olga Trask is even described as someone with "eager, seeking hands that would confiscate the copper pennies on the eyes of a corpse" (2). Meanwhile the elderly, like Miss Mason and Mama King, do not particularly care about money. Miss Mason steals the money and then gives it away like a meaningless object, while Mama King remembers it only as a functional necessity that allows her to manifest her care for others.

When, during her brief escapade with the Indo-Guyanese beggars, Mama King earns some money telling fortunes in the fish market, "the feel of money lift[s] her into the air" (69) not because she values it for its own sake but because it reminds her of the times she used to earn money "to get more and more for her grandchildren" (69). It is because of this money that she is later mugged and severely injured by a group of market thieves (another set of money-starved youngsters) who mistakenly assume that she has much more than is visible in her hand. This erroneous impression comes from the thieves' misreading of Mama King's jubilant attitude as she enters the cake shop: they assume that her smile, "broader than that of a contented bride" (71), signals wealth. Instead Mama King merely rejoices at the prospect of using her shiny coins "to buy a large bottle of mauby to share with all her friends" (70–71).[13] In this episode we rediscover Mama King's generous orientation toward others and her desire to provide for them before she even considers herself. More important, her well-being depends on her ability to contribute to the happiness of others. This is one of the reasons why her confinement in Frangipani House, where she is deprived of communal responsibility, leads to her mental collapse. Neither her family nor the matron can understand the fact that Mama King is incapable of being a consumer of care and attention. She demands instead her right to give and to be defined by that giving, with its inherent call to reciprocity.

In her initial encounter with Mama King (Mrs. Mabel Alexandrina King), Miss Trask—so accurate when it comes to money—mispronounces her name, calling her "Marma King." The elderly woman vehemently protests this misidentification that already promises her gradual disintegration in Frangipani House. The immediate loss of the proper name compounded with the reduction of the person to an object of monetary exchange can be read, as Pascale De Souza suggests, as evocative of "the erasure of the African name during the times of slavery": Mama King's contemporary version of this experience of dispossession begins with the moment when she is "denied a name, made to obey a daily routine, subjected to degrading conditions of life and even to physical abuse" (148). By her own admission Gilroy is explicitly interested in reflecting on "what identity is and how we experience it, both emotionally and within a social group" (Bradshaw, 382), inviting her readers and fellow Caribbean writers "to ask ourselves what has replaced colonialism and how we are reflecting this in our writing" (Gilroy, "The Woman Writer and Commitment," 15). In this sense her concern with questions of identity is also a direct examination of the colonial legacy in the Caribbean and its continued impact on Caribbean people's, and particularly black women's, self-perception.

Although the orderly rhythms of Frangipani House initially help Mama King recover from pleurisy, she quickly starts to feel "the urge for freedom" (*FH*, 4) as the days of reassuring routine morph into days of monotony and boredom. This urge for freedom permeates the novel as a whole: no matter what is offered in recompense or what reason is given to justify her confinement, Mama King remains obsessed with freedom as the only real value. Despite the lavish comfort of the nursing home, she is always painfully aware of the loss of self she is invited to suffer for her own good. Yet, as we find out, "nothing could ease that cutting sense of loss she felt for all the things she had once called her own" (7). Gilroy's language suggests that Frangipani House is always only a place of dispossession and imprisonment, and its lodgers are its more or less conscious inmates. Worse still, they are kept compliant through the constant use of sedatives that deprive them of their free will and their ability to assess their position and the ways they are being manipulated. As time passes we witness Mama King's increasing mental confusion and wonder if it is old age itself or the way old age is treated that precipitates the gradual disintegration of the mind. As a refrain to her story, the same question is repeated by several characters who witness her apparent insanity: "What could have brought her to this? Why did they do this to her?" (37); "What had they done to her?" (51). Mama King's visitors all realize that old age is not enough to explain her despair and degradation: "As long as she lives, she has to be active. Sitting around made her mad" (37).

The first stage of this mental breakdown is marked by the filtering of Mama King's contact with the outside world: "Since her entry into the home, she had begun to see the world through the glass window of her room as was the destiny of many old people" (5–6). Used to being an active participant, she is suddenly relegated to the role of a passive spectator. Her seat by the window suggests a transition to a life of distant observation that removes her far from real-life events and shifts her into the world of contemplation and memory. According to Lefebvre, it is precisely this emphasis on the visual experience of the world that characterizes the impact of *abstract space* as it transforms the body "by transporting it outside itself and into the ideal-visual realm" (*PS*, 309). In this kind of space, where the body is reduced to visual agency and has to relinquish all other aspects of its sensuous existence, the subject herself becomes an abstraction and is able to relate to the space around her as if that space were merely a sign, an image, or a flat surface: "So what escape can there be from a space thus shattered into images, into signs, into connected-yet-disconnected data directed at a 'subject' itself doomed to abstraction? For space offers itself like a mirror to the thinking [*réfléchissant*] 'subject,' but, after the manner of Lewis Carroll, the 'subject' passes through the looking-glass and becomes a lived abstraction" (313–14). Condemned to sitting quietly by the window, Mama King herself becomes this kind of lived abstraction whose life is no more than a projection of her past onto the empty screen of the glass-filtered garden in front of her. Her station by the window allows her neither a real view to the outside nor a reflection of her interiority, and so she effectively passes, like Carroll's Alice, to the other side.[14] In her case, however, the other side of the mirror is a form of temporary insanity, a mental dissolution produced by imposed passivity, loneliness, and the absence of interlocutors.

The alienation experienced by the nursing home lodgers consists in their loss of relevant material and symbolic location. The effect of *abstract space* on its users consists in replacing "residence" (*l'habitat*) with "housing" (*l'habiter*), thus signaling the loss of intimacy and meaning Lefebvre attributes to the notion of truly residing somewhere (*PS*, 314). Instead the elderly are merely *housed* in the nursing home: they are put away as irrelevant bodies awaiting death, slowly stripped of their self-awareness and social meaning. It is no wonder that in such circumstances they can only regress to frivolous girlhood; Miss Mason, for example, dresses up in garish girly clothes, dancing and giggling around the house like an aged child. The nurses like her for the entertainment she offers; her mental degradation and infantile antics make their workday go by quickly. Like Miss Mason, the other lodgers are similarly objectified, reduced to their most visible and least representative features, understood as bodies without function or interiority. At the lowest point of her mental dissolution, Mama King lies on the bed in her room "curled up like a foetus" (*FH*, 38), completing her cycle of regression. The women's descent into a kind of decrepit childhood is generated, to a large extent, by the general atmosphere of carefree aimlessness that Frangipani House offers as its main luxury.

In response to her spatial isolation, Mama King begins to rely on the continuous evocation of her past in order to remind herself that she still exists and was once an active participant in her own life and in the lives of others.[15] As she "prowl[s] round and round and round the room like a caged animal" (*FH*, 21), she talks to herself in an attempt to imbricate her personal narrative into the impersonal spaces of the nursing home. Her behavior is, of course, perceived as demented and is contained by the nursing staff through generous dispensation of sedatives. Yet despite the efforts to subdue Mama King's excesses, she succeeds in transforming her daily reality into a constant encounter between her present circumstances and her memories of the past. Her stories, although addressed to no one in particular and spoken into the void of her room, begin to animate the otherwise quiet and regulated spaces of the nursing home. Her narratives appear in italics, disrupting the central storyline of Gilroy's novel and signaling the old woman's stubborn intervention into the orderly linear flow of her nursing home experience. Whenever she sits by the window and engages in her interminable monologues, she is striving to reappropriate the dominated spaces of the rest home by filling them with the content of her past. Her gaze always locates her past nearby, projected onto the otherwise neutral and indifferent surroundings. The space around her is thus endowed with new meaning: it becomes a screen that receives and sends back the images of herself, affirming the threatened materiality of her existence. Although Frangipani House effectively annuls any outside (except as a limited view through the window), "the lodgers are granted another space in which to seek refuge: they can turn themselves in upon themselves and escape 'inside'" (Hoving, 84). In this way Mama King struggles against the alienating effect of heterotopian space by mobilizing the Lefebvrian notion of *lived space*, where our efforts to reclaim our right to the immediate environment proceed by means of symbolic and imaginary acts.

People she once loved, like her husband, Danny, and her various family members—notably her daughters and grandchildren—come to visit her as the ghostly figures of her reminiscences precisely because they do not visit her in reality.[16] In this way her storytelling, without audience or interlocutors, serves as an inadequate but necessary substitute for her daily emotional destitution in the nursing home. By considering Mama King destitute precisely when she is housed in the rest home, I mean to emphasize her being out of place and forsaken within a power structure that deprives her of her autonomy and agency. In the Caribbean context, this spatial deprivation also evokes the enduring legacy of colonialism. Mama King's isolation in the nursing home results from the large-scale Caribbean migration into the former colonial metropoles and more affluent Western countries in general, leading the younger generations into an economic exile and leaving the elderly without the sheltering structure of the family. In its absence Mama King, "a haunted ghost with a haunting past" (*FH*, 51), remembers her family and its history and almost loses herself in the fantasy of filial relations. Nevertheless when reflecting on her family in the present, she is painfully aware of their estrangement: "Nobody know if I sad, or hungry, or alone. I slave for all of you. You all go away leave a wound that fester more and more. Is easy to love from a distance—with the wide ocean between us" (51). As an abandoned old woman, Mama King becomes, in her own eyes and in the eyes of others, a festering wound and therefore something that her family can only wish to see gone.

Gilroy resorts to various metaphors of rejection and irrelevance in order to emphasize this heterotopian dimension of the nursing home, where the elderly amount to social jetsam produced by the practice of spatial exclusion. She describes the old women as "relics" (1) or "just trash to throw out" (8). Talking at one point to her grandson Markey, who briefly comes to visit, Mama King explains, "Them throw me out like rubbish" (51). And when she is assaulted by robbers in the market, she "looked like debris often seen along the shore when the tide was out" (72). Her sense that the elderly are treated as something superfluous, to be discarded no matter how much they may have given to their families in the past, confirms the role of Frangipani House as the space of containment and, more cynically, as temporary storage for the aging parents. Mama King is convinced that, no matter how much money they spend on the illusion of her comfort, her daughters and grandchildren are ultimately waiting for her to be gone so that they can be free of her needs. Her daughter Token vehemently declares, "I want *me* back! Your demands, her demands, everybody's demands at some time for some thing, have me bound up like the lianas in the jungle. I am using my cutlass and cutting, and cutting so I can find a way out to me, my life, myself" (103, original emphasis). In Token's protest against the demands of her family, "me" dominates, possibly because she has, as

Gilroy puts it, "learned the callousness of the acquisitive society" ("I Write Because . . . ," 200). She is concerned above all with the protection of a self she is fearful of losing. Nevertheless her claim to independence is radically different from her mother's: Token's self-assertion is predicated upon an idea of selfhood that excludes others or perceives them as threatening. Instead of seeing her family as a web that keeps her afloat, she describes it as a rampant jungle that needs cutting. Ironically her vision of her own liberation presupposes the imprisonment of her mother. This kind of freedom, whose price is someone else's confinement, has nothing in common with the kind Mama King strives for. Mama King's version of freedom does not deprive others of their identity or position but is instead established with a sense of communal sharing and group identity in mind. In other words, Mama King claims her autonomy without resorting to the vocabulary or ethics of isolated individualism but succeeds in finding it through her active participation in a community and even through self-renunciation. Paradoxically her liberation and self-awareness come from her ability to leave herself behind and exist among others simply as "somebody," without the need to claim the enclosed "me" that Token values so much.

Mama King's model of identity is alien and slightly distasteful to her children and grandchildren, who, immersed in a world of self-interest and possessions, consider "selfishness" to be a desirable trait: "She wanted little, too little, I say. She was also so giving, so content, so eager to help. She was too unselfish. A good parent is a little bit selfish, I say" (*FH*, 104). In this new and lopsided view of family and parenthood, a "good parent" should be selfish, thus authorizing her children and grandchildren to reciprocate, when the time comes, with the same kind of selfishness. But the excess of their mother's lifelong generosity is precisely the burden that Mama King's children cannot bear. Gilroy's version of freedom and autonomy challenges this notion of selfish and isolated identity associated with the Western bourgeois world and celebrates instead what can be considered a Caribbean version of relational identity, evocative of the composite and communal identities of yard novels.

Mama King's deliberate acceptance of her marginalization and her ability to embrace old age as a state of spatial and social exile leads her to flee Frangipani House and join a group of Indo-Guyanese beggars. Their social status of overt destitution marks their symbolic and material kinship with her. While her prospering family is no longer really interested in its familial ties to her, the beggars turn out to be her symbolic relatives. The traditional family is here substituted with the circumstantial family rooted in class solidarity. As an outsider, Mama King belongs to and is wholeheartedly accepted by those who can understand and share her plight. Although this narrative move can be read as "an attack of wishful symbolism" (Deveson, 1187), its value lies in its unwavering preference for a world without money or material comfort. Out of her luxurious confinement in Frangipani House, Mama King flees into the open spaces of destitute errantry and finds a sense of belonging precisely among those who are marginal to normative social structures. Yet Gilroy is far from idealizing the solution of poverty: the very fact that her episode among the beggars ends in life-threatening violence makes it clear that Mama King cannot stay with them, no matter how much she praises their generosity. The precariousness and real dangers of their outsider status are ultimately shown as an inadequate answer to the destitution of the old woman precisely because of her increasingly vulnerable body and its need for proper protection. Mama King must, in the end, find a place in her own family, even if she seems reluctant to do so.

Resolved to escape her comfortable prison, Mama King waits for the Indo-Guyanese beggars to approach Frangipani House. At first she does not see but hears them: "She could hear the scrape, trudge and clatter of their feet, the dull structural chanting of the men, and the plaintive shrieking of the women. Children indifferently echoed whichever melody they chose" (*FH*, 61). We detect in this group of beggars the community Mama King may be looking for, that is, a harmonious mix of different generations joined in a common cause, but we also perceive a shift from the abstract visual order of the nursing home to the revival of other forms of perception, in this case hearing. Frangipani House offers a quiet place for looking out onto the distant world outside, and the chants and noises of the beggars now enter to disrupt its order. After the matron ceremoniously gives them charity, Mama King follows the beggars as they leave, hoping to blend in and escape, shielded by their multitude. The bodies of the beggars are now meant to protect her from view. Trying not to draw attention to her flight, Mama King can only gesture to them not to give her away. The escape sequence thus relies on the triumphant return of the body: bodies that will shield the desperate old women and the supplicating gestures with which she will communicate her plan, which the beggars then "instinctively" understand, encircling her and leading her away (62).

From the world of disjointed ramblings to no addressee dominated by wistful contemplation and visual surveillance, we are now entering the world of sound, gesture, touch, and movement. The space is no longer a ready-made container for the body but is instead created by the body and its activity. The space of the beggars is, in other words, the space of a particular social practice and not an abstract space of static containment. When she later remembers the appeal of this experience, she emphasizes the beggars' genuine ability to care for her and the adventurous character of their daily life (*FH*, 101). Life with beggars does not rely on the abstract and tired notions of love or family. In addition, Mama King's rebellion against old age and its social insignificance is contested by her claim to adventure. Even at the very beginning of her journey, the possibility of living in the midst of risk and struggle instead of being artificially protected from them makes all the difference to her; although she is quickly overwhelmed by the heat and her feet hurt from the uneven road after her months of passivity in the nursing home, the simple fact that she is active again gives her courage to press on. She tells Pandit Prem, the leader of the beggars, that she belongs to no one and might as well stay with them: "I ent belong to nobody. I jus' ole. Nobody care 'bout ole" (63). We know that she was previously well cared for, if caring can be reduced to the purchasing of comfortable accommodation; Frangipani House is certainly an adequate rest home with pleasant-enough rooms and relatively competent staff. Yet what Mama King means by "care" is something quite different; although she never really spells it out, we can reconstruct an alternative model of caring by tracing her relationship to the beggars.

In a symbolic gesture marking her acceptance into the community, one of the women, Sumintra, takes Mama King's shoes and throws them away, saying, "You beggar now!" The beggars then form a "protective ring" around Mama King, sharing with her the stories of their suffering and particularly the scars on their bodies: the marks left by stones thrown at them, by dogs that had been set upon them, and the cigarette burns inflicted on them (*FH*, 64). Their bodies are a living record of their lives, their corporeal history. These scars mark their outsider status as well as the random physical violence to which they are subjected. Paradoxically, as an unprotected social group, the beggars are able to create a "protective ring" around Mama King. Their gesture is one of solidarity: they empathize with the woman who is herself isolated and whose body, through the markings of old age, carries a similar corporeal history on its skin. Mama King experiences this simple and immediate acceptance as happiness. Tired, barefoot, and penniless, without a clear destination or connection to anyone, she is suddenly a member of a community that shares her experience of exclusion. In the spirit of Glissant's idea of Relation, where the "experience of the abyss can now be said to be the best element of exchange" (*Poetics of Relation*, 8), Mama King shares with the beggars the intimate knowledge of suffering and can thus feel a profound sense of connection to this group.

After the incident of violent robbery in the marketplace, when Mama King—ironically mistaken for someone with money—is severely injured and taken to the hospital, her children and grandchildren finally arrive and are gathered around her bed, engaged in an endless discussion of their needs, plans, preferences, and regrets. In their reflections on Mama King, one thing that puzzles and infuriates them is her decision to leave the dearly purchased comfort of Frangipani House in favor of a miserable errant life with the beggars. For her proudly middle-class children, her decision is so shocking as to be unintelligible. The neighbors and acquaintances share this view: "They envied her the care that had been bought for her, but she had ungratefully run off to go with the poor, to be happy with the starving poor" (*FH*, 89). Because these people share the conviction that comfort and care can be bought, and are potentially even more valuable if they are bought, the great puzzle of Mama King's choice resides in its implicit claim that one can be "happy with the starving poor." For my purpose, this question is important because it emphasizes destitution as something that can be actively chosen rather than passively suffered. In Mama King's case, one passively suffers the spatial isolation of wealth and individual care, while communal poverty, with its outdoor and errant spaces, appears infinitely more welcoming. Although this narrative choice may indeed be viewed as wishful symbolism, it is worth examining why it seems to be the only option left to an aging woman.

The answer can be found in Mama King's attempt to break out of the repressive institutional space of the nursing home. Instead of quietly suffering the regulation of this heterotopia of containment, she enters a contestatory heterotopia of her own choosing. The beggars belong to the margin, the space of difference, whose very existence challenges normative social spaces. Their spontaneous appropriations of space cannot be regulated or contained. The heterotopia of the nursing home is of a different kind: it is a place established to contain what can no longer be seamlessly accommodated within those social spaces where productivity is the norm. Mama King's ungratefulness is therefore attributed to the fact that she embraces the heterotopian space of the beggars and in so doing exposes the fact—skillfully concealed by the external affluence of the nursing home—that she has already been discarded from the daily life of her children and community. Her destitute life with the beggars not only elevates destitution to a utopian pedestal of freedom, but it also, and more important, reveals the segregation of the elderly to be a far worse form of destitution than material poverty itself. Between genuinely shared material poverty and the alienating isolationism of comfort, Mama King—to everyone's consternation—chooses to be poor. This poverty is marked by outdoor spaces, reminiscent of the Caribbean yard novel, where communal ties are forged in the street, among those people who must define their identity outside of the abstract spaces of ownership. Because the world of houses, landed property, and other material possessions is historically the world of the colonial master, Mama King's choice of poverty as a form of liberation is also a move against the house as a symbol of colonial domination. Like the runaway Caribbean slaves of colonial times, Mama King engages, at least temporarily, in a kind of marronage from Frangipani House in an effort to achieve self-emancipation against the cold and rationalized domination of the matron, her symbolic overseer. When the matron, on her conciliatory hospital visit to Mama King, protests the presence of the beggars as "these dirty people," Mama King counters, "You go away! You is the sickening one" (97). In this vehement reversal, we realize that Mama King's revulsion arises from the repressive falsehood of the matron's professional concern, and she openly rejects it in favor of "dirty" people who are, at the very least, exactly what they appear to be.

In answering her daughters' impatient and puzzled queries, Mama King explains, "The only real kindness I ever get was from beggars. They was kind. They was good—sharing, protecting—giving me respect and friendship. They have little but they give a lot. They give me back my senses because they treat me like I was somebody" (99). Her loss of "all the things she had once called her own" (7) alerts us to the fact that ownership, in this as in all other cases I discuss in this book, means something very different from material possession. Things that Mama King once called her own and wishes to recover are elements of her personality, not elements of wealth; it is her self that she wishes to call her own, to be that somebody her family seems so keen to abolish. From her description of the beggars and their attitude toward her, we also realize that in order to have any form of selfhood at all, Mama King must claim it as her own achievement and receive it as a gift from others who recognize her as an autonomous individual. Her sense of self is thus inextricably bound to a community in which a person acquires his or her role in collaboration with others. Echoing Lefebvre's discussion of the spatial function of the body, Gilroy's novel embraces the body as a central component of identity and as "the generator (or producer) of space" (*PS*, 407). The particularity of Mama King's rebellion lies in this spatial claim to selfhood: by contesting the heterotopia of exclusion represented by the nursing home, she rediscovers herself in a freely chosen heterotopia of destitution. This reversal shows that excluded difference can be challenged by an alternative spatiality produced by each person's and each community's realization and appropriation of their "right to difference." And it is, in part, through storytelling and narratives of resistance like Mama King's that Caribbean postcolonial writers—particularly women writers—assert, in Gilroy's own words, that they "have always been there, cutting the barbed wire, rocking the pickets, weakening the structures, clambering over the stones" ("Women of Color at the Barricades," 152) in claiming this right to difference.

6 Upper and Lower Stories

Raphaël Confiant's *L'Hôtel du Bon Plaisir*

A house that has been experienced is not an inert box. Inhabited space transcends geometrical space.

—Gaston Bachelard, *The Poetics of Space*

In Raphaël Confiant's *L'Hôtel du Bon Plaisir* (2009), the spatial approach to multiple (post)colonial histories, both personal and cultural, shapes the way we interpret the intersecting destinies of his protagonists. As a matter of fact the titular hotel turns out to be the most important protagonist of all, showing that shared space creates community and shelters its evolving history. Although Confiant's novel shares with Chamoiseau's *Texaco* a profound thematic and methodological kinship centered on exploring through the category of space the nonhierarchical multiplicity of Créolité, the intertwined narratives in *L'Hôtel du Bon Plaisir* emerge as part of a vertical structure, which both represents and parodies the notion of racial and class hierarchy inherited from the colonial system in Martinique. While Chamoiseau's squatters stubbornly defend the horizontal and rhizomatic nature of their illegal settlement, Confiant's haphazard assembly of destitute tenants in the almshouse-cum-hotel inhabits an architectural project perpetually under construction. Despite the building's growth, however, Confiant deliberately shatters the implicit hierarchy of its verticality by weaving multiple voices and stories into the fractured totality of a single space. Similarly to the huts in *Texaco*, the new storeys of Confiant's hotel are built with different building materials, from concrete to crate wood.[1] Ironically the progressive degradation in building materials goes hand in hand with narrative enrichment. Each new storey announces further material deterioration of the edifice and, at the same time, the addition of another story to its history. The hotel Bon Plaisir thus seeks to represent a Martinican microcosm, with its various communities assembled in a single architectural space—an improvised and dilapidated house—where alternative living and forgotten people find a home. Drawing on

Bakhtin's theories of the carnival and the grotesque and on Lefebvre's admiration for this Rabelaisian principle with respect to *lived space*, I discuss how Confiant's protagonists' stories resist the order and grammar of imposed hierarchies and in so doing maintain the hotel as a space of creoleness. Confiant structures his novel as a "Creole comedy" in six acts (chapters), using the hotel and the novel itself as the stage for an exuberant and often grotesque Creole theater. The poverty and marginality of the protagonists are constantly veiled, if not completely suppressed, by the sense of festive and joyous plurality for which the building serves as setting and monument. When the hotel burns down in the end, the exuberant human diversity, deprived of its space, must also scatter. Confiant's novel is thus a celebration of and a lament for the kind of spatiality that allows creoleness to exist and grow.

In an interview about Martinique and its ecological situation today, Confiant points out that, since Martinique became a French overseas department (DOM) in 1946, there has been a steady draining of Martinican cultural resources in favor of French culture and language. This voluntary assimilation and gradual loss of Creole identity leads Confiant to assert that "Creole culture does not have a lot of future" because it has no means of expression through the media and is therefore forced to recede (Gosson, "Cultural and Environmental Assimilation in Martinique," 150). The transition from the status of colony to that of overseas department should have given the former French colonies in the Caribbean—Guiana, Martinique, and Guadeloupe—the same privileges as any other metropolitan department, allowing them an autonomous cultural development within the French political and economic system. But, as Randolph Hezekiah points out, "In practice, a new system of exploitation was put in place whereby the DOM became increasingly dependent on France for basic commodities (food and clothing, for example) at prices far in excess of French prices" (379), thus discouraging local entrepreneurship and leaving Caribbean intellectuals and writers to deal with the true nature of the unequal relationship between France and its overseas territories. In his interview with Renée K. Gosson, Confiant emphasizes the devastating impact of Martinique's economic dependence on France, with its increasing "de-industrialization" of the island and the emergence of an "Economie-Prétexte" (pretense economy): "A pretense to give appearance of an economy, that there are people who go to work, etc., but in reality, our country has been, and is, economically ruined" (Gosson, "Cultural and Environmental Assimilation in Martinique," 144). Despite the fact that keeping its overseas territories is costly to France, Confiant insists "it absolutely wants to keep its territories in the Americas, even if it is expensive, but at least it can say 'I have territories in the Americas.' And the only European country that still has territory in the Americas is France" (148). In this context of continued economic and cultural tutelage, Hezekiah suggests, "The terrible effects of the slave trade linger and reverberate through the pages of French West Indian literature, and the drama of the master-slave relationship has left a scar on the West Indian psyche that only the artist seems qualified to heal" (379). Confiant shares this view of the writer's role in the Caribbean: "Our reality demands responses, it demands that we be engaged writers, that we reflect upon our reality" (Hardwick, "Du français-banane au créole-dragon," 270, my translation). Such engaged writing resists French cultural dominance rooted in the economic dependence of Martinique, which may turn Martinicans into "a people for whom identity is not cultural but racial because there isn't any cultural difference any more" (Gosson, "Cultural and Environmental Assimilation in Martinique," 150–51). Aware of this danger and devoted to the idea of promoting the specificity of Creole culture through an emphasis on Creole language and its oral tradition, Confiant attempts to show in *L'Hôtel du Bon Plaisir* how spatial coexistence generates dialogue between disparate cultural traditions, potentially incompatible people, and seemingly contradictory ideas. The hotel is thus an architectural expression of cultural polyphony (although "cacophony" may be Confiant's preferred term) and unharmonized yet mutually enriching differences.[2] In this way Confiant shows his continued attachment to the principles of Créolité, which he already formulated along with Chamoiseau and Bernabé in "L'Eloge de la Créolité" ("In Praise of Creoleness").

In this famous literary and cultural manifesto, the three writers lament the gradual erasure of Creole language and interpret this process as no less than a "cultural amputation" (Bernabé, Chamoiseau, and Confiant, 899). In the Caribbean the Creole language itself represents "the purest example of the kind of cultural hybridization that occurs when different peoples are thrown together" (Caldwell, "Créolité and Postcoloniality," 302). Although often reserved, according to Sabine Hofmann, for linguistic phenomena, the notion of creolization is here extended to "all kinds of practices of cultural crossing . . . , of which the creole language represents an exemplary instance" (278). Creole language provides in this case "a model for a cultural mixture whose structures and procedures can be imitated even when writing in French" (281). The creative infiltration and appropriation of the French language is thus part of the process of creolization. The sense of identity that emerges from this complex diglossia and its cultural history is, as Glissant argues, not a root identity but a relational identity with no single origin, essence, or end point (*Poetics of Relation*, 11–15). Relational identity that characterizes creolization is instead dynamic and collective, "a limitless *métissage*, its elements diffracted and its consequences unforeseeable" (34). And although Glissant "depart[s] from the concept of creoleness" as soon as the "processes" of creolization become understood as its "contents" (*Poetics of Relation*, 89), the idea of creolization as he defines it certainly plays a large role in the Creolists' formulation and literary pursuit of this concept and practice.[3]

Although they focus on the reform of individual consciousness rather than of the public sphere, Bernabé, Chamoiseau, and Confiant seek to expand their intervention through creolization, "the process of cultural hybridization which will be the future dynamic of global cultural politics" (Caldwell, "Créolité and Postcoloniality," 302). In the face of an initially imposed and subsequently accepted cultural self-alienation (or "exteriority," as they put it), begun with colonialism and continued through the departmentalization of Martinique, the purpose of Créolité is to counter the false universality, monolingualism, and purity that the Creolists attribute to the European worldview. Créolité is instead an expression of a "kaleidoscopic totality, that is to say: *the nontotalitarian consciousness of a preserved diversity*" ("IPC," 892). Influenced by Glissant's aesthetics of "chaos-monde," understood as a nonharmonized plurality with a deliberate opening toward the "archipelago of languages" (*Poetics of Relation*, 84), Bernabé, Chamoiseau, and Confiant insist on promoting the kind of diversity whose totality remains fractured and dynamic. This approach is most vehemently opposed to any form of homogenization or totalitarian dominance of a single principle in aesthetics, linguistics, or daily life and resists both the African matrix of Césaire's Négritude and the regionalist orientation of Glissant's Antillanité. The ambition of Créolité is the world.

Eloge thus defines creoleness as a particular feature of the Caribbean but extends it beyond the boundaries of the archipelago to include the world at large. From this perspective, the very process of globalization is, in effect, a process of creolization of all world cultures, whose inevitable mutual dependence and ever-growing awareness of one another leads to a new form of consciousness about cultural identity and its location. The Caribbean is yet again, as I argued in chapter 1, projected beyond itself to become a model for a world culture by pointing a metaphorical way for global cultural unity that does not assimilate or annihilate differences. Because "the world is evolving into a state of Creoleness" ("IPC," 902) from this process of cultural complexification and multilingualism, a "new humanity" emerges as well: "A new humanity will gradually emerge which will have the same characteristics as our Creole humanity: all the complexity of Creoleness. The son or daughter of a German and a Haitian, born and living in Peking, will be torn between several languages, several histories, caught in the torrential ambiguity of a mosaic identity" (902–3). More than a literary or aesthetic concept, creoleness is also a way of inhabiting and understanding the world. Exceeding a mere idea, the principle of creoleness becomes a theoretical and literary affirmation of an existing cultural practice for which the Caribbean is an emblematic location but which is far from being enclosed in that region. The Caribbean is here a cultural space whose historical experience of ethnic, racial, and linguistic plurality encapsulates a similar and growing complexity of the broader world and provides a blueprint for a different global future.

As Ernest Pépin points out, however, French Caribbean literature faces the contradiction of trying to forge its identity through writing that actually "dissolves that very identity into the vast world-wide ocean of textuality" (2). As a result it is often perceived as meandering between "the ideological, aesthetic, and political claims staked out by various literary movements or strata, from exoticism to *créolité* via *négritude* and *antillanité*" (2). Despite this implicit tension between defining and dissolving its identity, the spatial extension of creoleness traces the world as a series of synchronous and diachronic sites, that is, as geographic locations seen in a single contemporary moment and telescoped through history, and connected through shared narratives, intersecting destinies, and chance encounters. A child of a German and a Haitian living in Peking is as much in the state of creoleness as a person whose mother tongue is Creole and who lives somewhere in the Caribbean. Such a person is "caught in the torrential ambiguity of a mosaic identity" ("IPC," 902–3). This image of geocultural ambiguity relies on spatial linking of diverse and distant sites and histories into a complex narrative of the "mosaic" identity that the Creolists celebrate and Confiant explores in *L'Hôtel*. In choosing to think of identity as plural and cross-cultural, Confiant refuses a "dichotomous vision of our reality" and integrates into the contemporary notion of Caribbean identity not only colonization and slavery but also all the people who have been part of the Caribbean, from the Amerindian to the black, white, and Hindu ancestors:

"We refuse to choose among our ancestors. . . . We have a Creole identity, an identity which allows us to reconcile all our ancestors" (Gosson, "Cultural and Environmental Assimilation in Martinique," 152). Although the notion of multiple and open identity may appear to be a utopian and purely textual construct, Confiant invites us to remember that "intellectuals are there to produce utopia, right?" (153).

One such utopia is the hotel Bon Plaisir, its world a perfect instantiation of creoleness, which nevertheless remains marginal and destitute. Yet despite both its utopian spirit and its material precariousness, Confiant's spatial creoleness serves to remind us of the intimate link between space and cultural identity. So in what manner do multiple identities shape physical space? Conversely, to what extent are "mosaic" identities produced by and in a particular space? In my analysis of *L'Hôtel du Bon Plaisir* I am interested in showing that space and identity produce one another and determine the kind of everyday life we are able to envision. In the case of contemporary Caribbean writing, this vision is, moreover, not limited to the Caribbean geographical setting but aims, as I already mentioned, to include the world as a whole, seeing the Caribbean in its cultural and linguistic plurality as a model for global relations across and beyond national borders. The Caribbean is therefore a concrete cultural setting and a vision of cultural possibility, a material location of an actual people and a metaphorical projection for a new humanity. The intersection of the concrete and the imaginary, the literal and the metaphorical happens here, as in all other novels I analyze in this book, through a particular space, that is, as a consequence of a spatial practice.

These two functions of space—its ideal, mental reality and its concrete, practical reality—are, according to Lefebvre, not antagonistic but rather complementary dimensions of a spatial dialectic, in which the pure mental form of space and its concrete existence can never be separated (*PS*, 292). Hezekiah describes the historical scars of the West Indian psyche as something "only the artist seems qualified to heal" (379); for many Caribbean intellectuals and writers, a meaningful transformation of the concrete location requires an alternative imagining of its reality, a utopian vision that Confiant suggests is the primary task of the intellectual. The creative encounter between the imaginary and the real is, moreover, a typically Antillean reality: "We never know when we are in reality or when we are in the world of the imagination" (Hardwick, 273, my translation). The two worlds are always linked; as in the case of the Creole and French languages, they are part of "a double-world" (272).

This alternative imagining of the real puts into (literary) practice Lefebvre's notion that *lived space* has the potential to challenge and transform dominated social spaces through the impact of the symbolic content of ordinary users on the abstractly regulated spaces of institutions and their mechanisms of power. We thus discover a similar challenge in both Caribbean postcolonial literature and spatial analysis: against an imposed abstract order (the lingering colonial order for Caribbean authors and the capitalist order for spatial thinkers), alternative spatiality can be constituted only through a multiplicity of voices and experiences of ordinary people, on a smaller scale, from below, and even from the place of destitution. Only such spatial experience, with its capacity to incorporate the disorderly and unpredictable into a spontaneous reinvention of social life, will be able to accommodate the joyous, unrestricted, and carnivalesque nature of human diversity in the Caribbean and elsewhere. In this way Confiant's novel, like Chamoiseau's *Texaco*, presents itself as a literary proposal for an alternative version of cultural identity, its location, and its value. For both authors, the unaccommodated humanity and its destitute spaces contest any imposed order and invite us to reflect on the importance of the unregulated heterogeneity of ordinary people and their spatial practice.

The focus of Confiant's novel is on the popular and underprivileged districts, on marginal and "fallen" people, and on the effervescent plurality of their coexistence. The hotel allows us to engage with intersecting histories of various protagonists, becoming, in the process, a symbolic microcosm of creoleness understood as an identity or linguistic marker and, more important, as a way of being in the world. *L'Hôtel du Bon Plaisir* is, in a way, evocative of the yard novel and continues to develop and renew its tradition, namely the encounter of the carnivalesque protagonists and histories in a single delimited space, which serves as a kind of theater for the destitute. In this spatial context the central characteristic of the novel lies in its penchant for the grotesque and the extraordinary as a means of revealing the most valuable aspects of ordinary life. In leading us through the intertwined histories of the building and its unusual tenants, Confiant's novel allows me to cast another look at the role of space in exposing and asserting the centrality of everyday spatial experience of the ordinary user. Confiant's interest in the common people, popular storytelling traditions, Creole language, and marginal spaces represents a remarkable instantiation of Lefebvre's principle of spatial transformation attributed to the symbolic and storytelling capacities of the common users of space. At the same time, Confiant's challenge to spatial hierarchy through a depiction of destitute people and their destinies leads us to a kind of Bakhtinian model of carnivalesque "debasement" whose purpose is the ultimate exaltation of the ordinary human being and an unabashed celebration of his or her raw corporeality and rowdy linguistic inventiveness. As Roy Chandler Caldwell Jr. points out with respect to Confiant's *L'Allée des soupirs* (1994), "What emerges from the novel's cacophony is no official, unitary, authoritative discourse, but a collective voice—indeterminate and vibrant and derisive, essentially contestatory" (304). If the central impulse of Caribbean imagination is indeed, as Dash argues, the process of self-formation and self-appropriation ("Writing the Body," 609), then it is also important to remember, as Mary Gallagher points out, that "the 'self' in question can be, and often is, collective in tenor" ("Genre and the Self," 55). This fugal multiplicity of singular voices generates a collectivity gathered together in a given space. It is my aim to explore in this chapter precisely the spaces of this collective voice as a literary rendition of Lefebvre's *lived space*, reclaimed by the grotesque characters of an architectural carnival through which Confiant seeks to challenge the notion of social discrimination based on wealth, educational privilege, and racial supremacy in the former colonial setting.

In his essay "Forms of Time and of the Chronotope in the Novel: Notes toward a Historical Poetics," and more elaborately in his book on Rabelais, Bakhtin famously argues that the aim of the carnivalesque novel is to "materialize the world" (187). This kind of narrative strives to ground the literary in a world of common daily concerns, affirming the earthly and human against any form of lofty transcendence. All elements of such a novel, from its protagonists to its language and setting, are chosen to emphasize exaggerated and grotesque events and people whose role is to mock established conventions. They are larger, louder, and more disorderly than anything we associate with novelistic refinement, which often reflects class hypocrisy and conceals social injustice. In this case, the grotesque and its principal figures of social rebellion—the clown, the rogue, the fool—aim at "destroying the established hierarchy of values, at bringing down the high and raising up the low, at destroying every nook and cranny of the habitual picture of the world" (177). The embodiments of irony such as the rogue, fool, and clown serve, in other words, "to refract monologic authorial intentions through a process of the 'making strange' or defamiliarization of received wisdoms" (Gardiner, 57). The goal of such a novel and of the popular traditions from which it derives is "the struggle against conventions, and against the inadequacy of all available life-slots to fit an authentic human being" (Bakhtin, 163). It celebrates instead "the right *not* to understand, the right to confuse, to tease, to hyperbolize life; the right to parody others while talking, the right to not be taken literally, not 'to be oneself'; the right to live a life in the chronotope of the entr'acte, the chronotope of theatrical space, the right to act life as a comedy and to treat others as actors, the right to rip off masks, the right to rage at others with a primeval (almost cultic) rage—and finally, the right to betray to the public a personal life, down to its most private and prurient little secrets" (163). Bakhtin's brilliant description of the contestatory nature of the mask and the grotesque, with their ability to affirm by negating, centers on their historical continuation in the novelistic form and sums up the effects of Confiant's novel as well. The Creolist novel can therefore be understood as the rhizomatic offshoot of the Rabelaisian tradition of resistance and contestation; although the novelistic examples in Bakhtin refer to an entirely different sociohistorical context, they share with the Creolist novel a humorous and hyperbolic attack on conventions, which establish and normalize the high-and-low social structure. Confiant's destitute tenants of the hotel Bon Plaisir are, for various reasons, people fallen from social grace or who have always been incorrigible outsiders. Their obstinate marginality is in itself a challenge to an orderly picture of the world. In the hotel most of what goes on seems to be upside down, hilariously reversed and presented to the reader as a form of revolutionary irreverence for any kind of norm. Moreover we recognize in Confiant's writing the principles of creoleness: through the use of Creole and the playful modifications of standard French, he explores the multilingual resistance to the rigid conventions of monolingualism. The "appetite" of creoleness, its Gargantuan linguistic gluttony, is to incorporate and celebrate all languages of the world: "Creoleness is not monolingual. Nor is its multilingualism divided into isolated compartments. Its field is language. Its appetite: all the languages of the world" ("IPC," 901).

Following this logic of appropriation that characterizes Creole language, creoleness is itself a Bakhtinian mask, an aesthetic and linguistic "rogue" striving to disrupt conventions. According to Glissant, in the context of plantation slavery, oral expression in Creole served as the slaves' secret code. A form of linguistic mask, Creole represented, in fact, a means of resistance and an act of survival against the brutal plantation system and its "chosification" (thingification) of people (Glissant, *Poetics of Relation*, 66–68). Creole language is thus a form of "diversion" through a systematic process of derision: "The slave takes possession of the language imposed by his master, a simplified language, adopted to the demands of his labor (a black pidgin) and makes this simplification even more extreme. You wish to reduce me to a childish babble, I will make this babble systematic, we shall see if you can make sense of it. Creole would then become a language that, in its structures and its dynamics, would have fundamentally incorporated the derisive nature of its formation" (Glissant, *Caribbean Discourse*, 20). For Glissant, as Sabine Hofmann explains, "the variability of creole is due to its history, to its origin in the plantations. Utterances in creole are often polysemic; very frequently one utterance contains two messages or even more. One of these is destined for the ears of the overseer or master; the other is aimed at other slaves and is incomprehensible to masters and foremen" (282–83). Creole language is thus a form of "camouflage," a language "constituted around this strategy of trickery" (Glissant, *Caribbean Discourse*, 21). As a result of plantation slavery and the kind of expression that emerges from such space, "the climax of Creole speech does not release an appreciative smile, but the laughter of participation" (21). I would add that it also constitutes implicit opposition, where the comedic, exaggerated, and trickster nature of language seeks to subvert, while feigning innocence, the power relations of the colonial system, aiming, as A. James Arnold suggests, "to colonize in reverse" (22).

Confiant's grotesque characters, always engaged in this kind of trickery and capable of eliciting Glissant's "laughter of participation," fulfill Bakhtin's promise of radical materialization of the world in order to unveil genuine material discrimination while laughing at the social structure that generates and maintains it. This is why destitution remains, albeit humorously, the central feature of Confiant's hotel: although we marvel and laugh at our boisterous protagonists as we follow, for instance, their frenzied hunt for a resident zombie or their casual passions unleashed on staircases and landings, we remain painfully aware of the enclosed marginality of this population and wonder what historical and social forces produce a heterotopian site like Bon Plaisir. By focusing on the common person and his or her ordinary struggles, which only become extraordinary through the particular use of language and manner of narration, Confiant seeks to accomplish the same goal Bakhtin attributes to Rabelais: to accommodate concrete human corporeality in the real spatiotemporal world. "Here the human body becomes a concrete measuring rod for the world, the measurer of the world's weight and of its value for the individual" (Bakhtin, 171). Bakhtin's individual, however, is not the private and isolated self of the traditional novel but a particularized representation of a larger community and a tangible sign of its fluctuating plurality, exactly as in the yard novels of the Caribbean. Even the body in Bakhtin's approach is an "impersonal body, the body of a human race as a whole" (173). In each instance of this novelistic procedure, what is single and material strives, at the same time, to become emblematic and transcendent but keeps itself in check somewhere on the edge of such dichotomies. Similar ambiguity constitutes the core of Créolité and of many postcolonial approaches to literature. We must recognize in them, as in Lefebvre's notion of *lived space*, a kind of Rabelaisian principle of down-to-earth humanity, essential for its deliberate failure to rise up and transcend itself.

Interestingly enough, as Andy Merrifield reminds us in his critical introduction, Lefebvre himself "adores Rabelais's laughter" (16). He is excessive not only in his private life, ignoring abstinence and austerity, but also in his writing. Merrifield describes Lefebvre's oeuvre as "effervescent and vital yet repetitive and overblown" (17). In a recent pioneering attempt to link Bakhtin and Lefebvre, Michael E. Gardiner argues that there are significant complementary features in their respective projects, notably an emphasis on embodiment and the everyday life, the irreducibly open-ended nature of human agency, an idea of dialogical humanism, and, most important for my present argument, "a considerable stress on the subversive, utopian potentialities of art and the festival" (52). For both thinkers, the ironic register serves "as a potential vehicle for socio-cultural criticism" (51). Excess is here a political force: in Bakhtin's interpretation of Rabelais's literary vision and in Lefebvre's own experience and orientation, the festival (like Bakhtin's carnival of masks and fools) has the most tremendous liberating power: "[Lefebvre] envisages festival as a special, potentially modern form of Marxist praxis that could erupt on an urban street or in an alienated factory. The festival was a pure spontaneous moment, a popular 'safety [valve],' a catharsis for everyday passions and dreams, something both liberating and antithetical" (Merrifield, 17–18). Confiant's hotel follows the same model of opposition: the grotesque and unruly community calls into question all conventional social expectations, from scholarly excellence to marriage, professional success, and economic interest. Bon Plaisir is therefore an architectural parody, a site of unplanned opposition and, ultimately, the enclosed location for an interior carnival, which seems to have fled from the street into the rooms and hallways of the dilapidated hotel. If Caribbeanness is indeed, as Benítez-Rojo asserts, "a system full of noise and opacity, a non-linear system, an unpredictable system, in short a chaotic system beyond the total reach of any specific kind of knowledge or interpretation of the world" ("Caribbean Culture," 203), and if such a system expresses itself best through the carnival, then Confiant's novel is certainly an attempt to capture, through a carnivalesque and chaotic narrative, this crucial dimension of Caribbeanness. In so doing *L'Hôtel du Bon Plaisir* incorporates into written form the paradoxical aspects of the carnival: "Ultimately carnival is paradoxical practice, a paradoxical foundation; that is, a machine for inverting, for a short period of time, hierarchies of race, culture, class, and gender" (212). In the case of Confiant's novel, these inversions of hierarchy are held together and given shape by the space where they unfold so that the architectural setting itself becomes carnivalesque and fulfills its goal of inversion and contestation.

Bakhtin argues that the Rabelaisian chronotope structures the novel still unconcerned with the enclosed spaces of rooms, where private family life unfolds in relative secrecy. Instead the Rabelaisian chronotope "unfolds under the open sky, in movement around the earth, in military campaigns and journeys, taking in various countries" (167). From this perspective, it would seem that the hotel in Confiant's novel represents precisely the opposite of the Rabelaisian unrestricted spatiality: it is an enclosed space where individual rooms hide the privacy of their inhabitants. Yet despite its apparent spatial enclosure, *L'Hôtel du Bon Plaisir* focuses on the explosive exteriority of stories and relations that also characterize the theater of the destitute in the yard novel. Like the yard, the hotel is by definition a space of encounter, with its multiplicity of rooms and inhabitants. At the same time it is a disorderly architectural setting where the stories of its protagonists unfold in intermediate and ambiguous spaces like stairs and hallways, reminiscent of Bakhtin's "chronotope of the entr'acte." Confiant is never really interested in what goes on in individual rooms. He focuses instead on the hotel as a totality internally fractured by the whimsical movement of the central narrative as it skips from tenant to tenant. These individual strands of the story continually intertwine to construct the overall history of the building. The hotel is therefore Confiant's central protagonist, "infused with smells, desires, dreams, hatreds and sorrows of its inhabitants" (*HBP*, 299).[4]

Already in *L'Allée des soupirs*, Confiant affirms the profound connection between Creole culture, its physical spaces, and the kind of literature it should produce in order to capture and preserve its physical and conceptual specificity. Through the striving novelist Jacquou Chartier,

Confiant explores this connection: "One must, as a matter of fact, invent a new form, a different architecture capable of, how to say . . . capable of espousing every meander of reality without for all that pretending to exhaust it. One should construct a Creole novel with unfinished panels. Make legible a heterogeneous world, modeled on your Creole shacks. Look at those of Terres-Sainville or Morne Pichevin: two sheets of corrugated iron here, three planks there, some hastily piled bricks covered with a slab of asbestos cement, the whole sealed with dry coconut leaves or laths of 'ti-baume' wood" (298–99, my translation). The dynamics of creoleness permeate Chartier's interpretation of local architecture and his vision of an ideal literary form, turning architecture and literature into two profoundly connected and mutually constitutive modes of cultural expression. According to this view, the Creole novel should reflect the architectural tradition of the poorer and popular neighborhoods, where Creole language and culture resist the assault of French domination and shape their inhabitants' everyday life. The inherently improvised nature of these neighborhoods, where found and randomly assembled materials contribute to the distinctive style of the built environment, could lead—if properly transposed—to a new type of literature as well. Such literature, Chartier implies, would make use of what is already there; like the scattered planks of wood and slabs of asbestos collected and repurposed for the building of a shack, the writer would collect and reassemble the elements of popular speech and oral tradition. This attention to the repurposed elements of an existing multiplicity characterizes, in Wendy Knepper's analysis, the art of bricolage in the Caribbean as "the process of taking the materials at hand and using them in an improvisational fashion" ("Colonization, Creolization, and Globalization," 71).[5] Bricolage, with its focus on building something new out of what is already there, is thus another way of theorizing Caribbean identity and aesthetics as marked by the process of creolization.

From the very beginning of the novel, the hotel Bon Plaisir is characterized as "strange" (*insolite*); each of its floors (four floors and a garret) was built at a different time, with different and gradually cheaper building materials, from the respectable cement for the ground and first floors to the exposed bricks for the second floor, asbestos for the third, and recuperated wood for the fourth floor. Finally, the fifth floor is not even really a floor: it is a grotesque-looking garret assembled from cardboard and wooden crates. Its only tenant, Etienne Beauvallon, builds it haphazardly from found and recuperated materials, like a true monument to improvisation and architectural bricolage: "Etienne ended up building a real camp from sundry materials: used tarpaulin from trucks, cases of dried cod, broken barrels of salted pork meat, ship ropes stolen from the harbor, cardboard of all colors. With its lively front and its machicolation, the whole resembled, at the same time, a pirate ship and a ruined medieval castle" (*HBP*, 218). The passage of time is thus clearly marked in the hotel's building materials, but so is the slow degradation of its economic value and the progressive blurring of its function. Over its thirty-seven years of existence, the hotel has served as a poorhouse, a brothel, and, finally, a hotel whose residents are permanently settled in their rented rooms and apartments. But while the purpose of the hotel changes, its main residents remain, suggesting that the community of inhabitants is what gives the hotel its true function and character. Conversely, the building connects and structures the intertwined stories of its tenants, endowing them with temporary stability.

The history of the hotel is conveyed through what seems to be authorial intervention into the narrative: parts of the text appear in smaller font and present us with a linear history of the building. This orderly presentation of the setting stands in sharp contrast to the meandering and random telling of the stories of the hotel's inhabitants. These stories are conveyed in bits and pieces, like debris slowly gathered in the telling. In the epilogue, Confiant writes that it is not only people who have character: spaces are themselves infused with character, filled with all the longing, dreams, and sorrows of their tenants: "Human beings are not the only ones who live long. Men and women are not alone in forging a character, confronting difficulties, enjoying moments of tenderness, suffering the strokes of fate. Their residences—whether they be shacks, houses, villas, palaces or castles—accompany them, in silence, on that improbable journey. If we commonly affirm that walls have ears, it is also important to recognize that each tile, each wall, each beam, in short, every inch of our residences is infused with our smells, desires, hatreds and sorrows" (299). The hotel is therefore the collective character of all the inhabitants, fused together into an architectural totality that both preserves and overcomes all the differences and contradictions between its individual members. The edifice allows us to contemplate the incongruous nature of its making and invites us to understand it as a cacophonous unity of disparate yet mutually intertwined parts.

The hotel covers a portion of Martinican history from 1922 to 1959 and allows us to follow the inception and subsequent changes in the hotel's function. Initially the hotel is built as a charitable institution by three white Creole sisters named Vigier de Lamotte: the leader of the project, Louise-Julie, affectionately nicknamed "Dame Béké," and her two younger sisters, nicknamed Tête d'Or and P'tite Papotte. After an unsuccessful attempt at leading a monastic life, the three sisters decide to expand their Christian generosity outside organized religion and for the benefit of the underprivileged people of Fort-de-France. The result is the chaotic and painstaking building of L'Hôtel de la Charité Saint François de Sales. The name of the almshouse commemorates the man who renounced his noble origins to devote his life to the Christian faith and was declared a saint in 1665. The sisters implicitly see themselves as making the same magnanimous gesture as they leave behind the privileges of their class and devote their lives to charity. The building of the poorhouse is financed by their successful and wealthy brother-in-law, Pierre-Marie de La Ramée, who agrees to help in order to placate his odd sisters-in-law. But initially whatever is built during the day is mysteriously demolished overnight, until it seems that an evil spirit opposes the erection of the building. To pacify this angry ghost and finish the project, the sisters agree to abandon cement for bricks and, later on, bricks for asbestos. The degradation of the chosen materials seems to calm the spirit, or rather Pierre-Marie de La Ramée, who is secretly suspected of interfering with the construction by commissioning adversarial witchcraft so as to reduce the building costs.

Louise-Julie conceives of the hotel as a gathering place for all the needy and destitute of Fort-de-France. Her "hotel" is an almshouse in which, even before the building is finished, the three sisters "would happen to give provisional shelter to battered wives or concubines, abandoned kids or old women who no longer had family. For seventeen years, that is, until the break-out of the second Great War, the Charity Hotel of Saint François de Sales relieved the extreme misery of the people of Terres-Sainville and its surroundings" (*HBP*, 90). This particular attention to the needy and destitute distinguishes the three sisters from most other privileged citizens whose white or lighter skin color marks their corresponding social prestige. When he wonders about the motivation behind their incongruous charity, Pierre-Marie de La Ramée receives the following answer from one of his colleagues visiting from France: "Maybe, dear friend, your sisters-in-law are trying with all their devotion to . . . how to put it . . . to atone, there, that's it! To atone for the crimes committed by their ancestors during slavery" (139). Although Pierre-Marie vehemently rejects this view, irritated by any mention of "crimes during slavery" and the Frenchmen's hypocritical self-righteousness, this reminder of the origins of destitution and wealth in Martinique and their unequal distribution along color lines serves as a mockery of the magnanimous deed. Similarly the three pious sisters are mocked for their desire to eradicate, along with poverty, local rituals and pagan creeds (89). The act of charity strives to relieve the suffering of the poor, but it is also a reminder of the unresolved persistence of profound inequality. Moreover their interest in poverty gives the sisters something to do once it becomes clear that they will never marry: the destitute are their pastime and their cause. This cynical view of charity is part of Confiant's carnivalesque irony, which reverses all expectations and presents us with an irreverent view of good intentions of dubious motive.

The upper classes' pervasive and always implicit contempt for the underprivileged is expressed by the tongue-in-cheek voice of the randomly focalized omniscient narrator, who refers to the poor as "populace" (rabble) and "plèbe" (plebs or riffraff). These lower-class citizens (no longer slaves but still held in very low social esteem) are also mockingly referred to as "the proletariat of the northern neighborhoods of the City" (89) and are often described as "indigent." For the lawyer Dorimont, the ultimate owner and secret chronicler of the hotel, those who seek shelter in it are the "vulgum pecus"—a contemptuous expression in corrupt Latin he uses to refer to the "ignorant masses" that surround him.[6] Despite his distaste for this "vulgum pecus," however, it is these Creole-speaking, uneducated, marginal, and failed people whose stories fascinate him and whose lives he wishes to uncover in the novel he secretly composes. Through Dorimont and his attitude toward the lower-class tenants that both repel and attract him, Confiant calls into question the role of the writer, possibly a Creolist writer like himself, who seeks to collect and transpose into the lofty and marketable literary works in French the daily lives of Creole-speaking people.

One reason for Dorimont's sense of superiority is the fact that he is a "mulâtre," a lighter-skinned Martinican, born of one white and one black parent or of parents who are themselves "mulâtres." He lives on the first floor of the hotel, just one floor above the white sisters, and is thus only one step below them in the implicit spatial hierarchy of race. Above him, on upper floors, live darker-skinned people mostly of African origin, an East Indian family, and a Syrian. All are of lesser social significance because their color, as much as their inadequate financial means, designate them as inferior in Dorimont's eyes. Although, having lost his fortune and job, he no longer belongs to the middle class, Dorimont is nevertheless a former member of "the little colonial world of the colored Martinican bourgeoisie, with its ridiculous etiquette, its outdated speech, its old school French mannerisms and its often false respectability" (156). He is therefore particularly irritated to be sharing the first floor with Man Florine, a strong and independent black woman who never succumbed to any man. Thinking about her and people like her, Dorimont mumbles, "Ah, the blacks! My God, what a breed!" (15). Still, their resilience in the face of destitution and the vibrancy of their stories attract his curiosity. From this perspective, he also personifies a mocking version of a potential reader's view of the destitute protagonists—that of a voyeur examining a world that seems marginal yet fascinating.

The carnivalesque reversal of meaning and structure is evident in the reversed order of spatial hierarchy in the novel: the top is bottom and the bottom, top. The white Creole sisters, who create and, through their brother-in-law, own the poorhouse, reside on the ground floor. The higher we climb in the building, the lower the social status of its inhabitants: "The conditions of life deteriorated to the extent that one changed floors" (*HBP*, 21). Similar hierarchy continues when, during World War II, the almshouse is temporarily turned into a brothel: although the outraged pious sisters continue to occupy the ground floor, the first floor is now inhabited by lighter-skinned prostitutes and their ranking clients, while the upper floors shelter the rank and file and soldiers without epaulettes: "*Mulâtresses*, *chabines*, and all light-skinned women took up residence on the first floor, in the renovated rooms with walls covered in dark red paint. The place was reserved for commanders, colonels, generals, and above all for lieutenants of ships, the marines having surpassed the land forces in prestige ever since the cream of the French naval fleet, fleeing Hitler's advance, was stationed in the harbor of Fort-de-France" (121). As an important military outpost of the Vichy government during the war, Martinique is also marked at this time by another kind of hierarchy, that of the French military in relation to the local population. While the rest of the island suffers from severe shortage of food and other goods usually imported from Europe (even salt and oil are rationed), the first floor of the hotel-cum-brothel continues to maintain relative prosperity. Luxury goods like gin, whiskey, and cigarettes are available to white Creoles only: "The white Creoles, landowners, continued for their part to be supplied normally and benefited first and foremost from the rationing established by the new strongman of the island appointed by Marshal Pétain, a man with a goatee and a flowery cap named Robert, Admiral by trade" (116–17).

After the war, when she can no longer financially sustain their project of sheltering the poor, Louise-Julie transforms the almshouse into a residential building with rooms and apartments for rent. From charitable figures, the three sisters become landladies of cheap apartments and rooms to let. Again the spatial hierarchy follows with grotesque persistence the reverse order of high and low. The price of the apartments changes depending on the floor: lower floors are more expensive than the upper floors of gradually lesser quality. Although the prices posted on the wall serve to dissuade the "vulgum pecus" from attempting to gain access to a place that once served to shelter them, the hotel remains known as "Charity." Its paying tenants range from having some money to having none, since, faithful to their initial dream of dispensing charity, the three sisters also accept some tenants who never pay. The hotel's residents are thus presented as destitute not merely because they are poor but also because they belong nowhere and have stepped into a spatial context of exteriority, that is, of being outside the social structures that used to shelter them.

For this reason the most destitute of all tenants, Etienne Beauvallon (Bougre Fou), who resides in the garret and will in the end burn down the building, describes the hotel as "a stranded ocean liner" where disparate tragic destinies come together to remind us of the historical tragedies of the island itself: "In fact, if we consider the Hotel of Bon Plaisir as a boat, or rather a stranded ocean liner, well then, my shipwreck is not as absurd as it seems. In that shaky building there gathered together, as if on purpose, the shattered destinies, secretly kept existences, exploded dreams or simply the most mundane, the most insignificant of troubles: that of living on a land where nothing will ever be possible. What could one do, in fact, with an island where the savage extermination of Amerindians was followed by the barbarism of slavery? Two founding tragedies, pontificates a local philosopher who just got a literary award in Paris! Foundations, what nonsense! Common graves, yes. Or rather the killing fields" (130). The specific reflection about the hotel and its character inevitably leads to a broader reflection on Martinique as a place. It is seen, with mocking distance, as an island where nothing can really change the already inscribed tragedies of colonial history that seem to reverberate through all subsequent moments, directing the destinies of the inhabitants toward resignation and irony. These historical tragedies are, according to the narrator, not "foundations" of Martinican culture but rather its "mass graves." Yet no matter what name we give to historical facts, they determine the scope of the real daily lives of ordinary people, with their "shattered destinies," "exploded dreams," and connection to Martinique as a particular location where, even if stranded, they are also inevitably anchored. For this narrator, the shipwreck of postcolonial destitution is therefore not absurd; it belongs to a discernible logic of initial violence and subsequent marginalization that all postcolonial societies face and struggle to overcome. Within these larger questions of history and cultural (dis)inheritance, the individual story is always only a miniature instantiation of an entire structure of relations, events, and possibilities. In the case of Bougre Fou, his destitution is a consequence of his sudden incensed rejection of a prestigious scholarship to Paris and, by that token, of French cultural dominance over Martinique more generally. No one ever understands why Bougre Fou deliberately changes, like someone possessed, from a successful and talented young student to a raving destitute. We know only that, in the end, before burning down the hotel, he yells at the anti-France protesters of December 1959, "I don't just want my life to be better, I want to change the order of the world!" (295).[7]

This reversal of order, shown physically in the structure of the hotel Bon Plaisir, symbolizes the demand for social change on a broader scale. Such a reversal would bring Creole culture and Martinican specificity to the fore, abolishing the obsequious and alienating orientation toward French culture and its tradition of socioeconomic hierarchy. Yet this order can be understood even more broadly as the inequitable order of capitalist socioeconomic exploitation at large. Such order, of which the history of slavery is only one salient example, oppresses and alienates ordinary human beings in any geographical context, bringing those who refuse to play their assigned roles, like Bougre Fou, to the garret (i.e., outside) of the legitimate social structure. This upside-down world, as the educated madman Bougre Fou believes, must be burned down. The fire ends the life of the hotel and scatters the stories that it once held together, suggesting that the change of order, if accomplished by a destructive act, destroys the good along with the bad. And the good in the hotel is precisely its rich chaos of stories and relations, its already reversed and sometimes entirely abolished order of things. The final episode of Bougre Fou's burning of the hotel shows that an already reversed and derisive structure cannot be willfully changed. Any direct and programmatic intervention leads to its undoing. The essential value of the hotel lies in its spontaneous and fluctuating character, in the paradoxically unsettled identity of this residential building. Because, in practice, the hotel respects no existing order, Bougre Fou's cry for fundamental transformation brings the life of that building to an end and, with it, its spatially constructed creoleness.

The narrative of derisive reversals in *L'Hôtel du Bon Plaisir* is predicated upon the central role of the destitute community whose main figure is paradoxically not a desperate indigent but a "nègre hilare," a hilarious black. The mocking and provocative reference to a black minstrel mask as the clownish stock character of a racist society and its theater reminds us, without false pathos, of the unequal status of the Martinican people in relation to the French and then of the further pernicious hierarchy of color within the island society itself. The hotel is, as Confiant puts it, a "refuge for the disinherited" (*HBP*, 101), whose dispossession must be understood as a historical phenomenon begun with slavery and passed on to the present day. Yet however much the narrator wishes to depict the hotel's residents as overcoming poverty through the resilience of their stories and their vernacular, it is difficult to believe in their "hilarity." The reader knows that the image of the "nègre hilare" has to be false: it is a mask that conceals and, in so doing, draws attention to what is masked: "*One would swear that certain words were invented to characterize certain races. Take for example the word 'hilarious'! Does it not suit the blacks to perfection? A hilarious black—it sounds good, it rings true. In short, it goes without saying, does it not? And don't come telling me that it is an all-purpose expression or a racist stereotype! In the hotel 'Bon Plaisir,' there is nothing but hilarious blacks even when they are being difficult. . . . Even when the black is scowling or takes himself seriously, he is no less hilarious. Comical and ugly, wrote Césaire*" (*HBP*, 176, original emphasis). Although the narrator insists on there being no other adequate description of black people except for the word *hilarious*, no matter what their circumstances or disposition, it is precisely this blanket insistence on the "happy" stereotype that drives home, quite uncomfortably, the horror of such hypocritical inventions, which seek to trivialize the suffering of the underprivileged by representing them as merrily enjoying their destitute condition. The narrator's reflection concludes by evoking the verb *lugubrer* (177), a neologism of Haitian Creole attributed to Boisrond-Tonnerre, secretary to Jean-Jacques Dessalines, the founder of the Haitian Republic. In contrast to *hilarious*, *lugubrer* ("to lugubriate," i.e., to darken, to grieve) evokes the pain of a specific collective memory: that of a slave chained in the belly of the slave ship. The only language that can capture this memory while resisting it is Creole language, "le langage bricolé" (the language cobbled together). So what happens to the "hilarity" of the black who carries in him the ancestral memory of the Middle Passage and slavery, dreaming at night, like the narrator, of the rocking of the slave ship in the storm, or of running? His hilarity is a mask hastily put over the face of historical sorrow. This black speaks Creole to express and hide (from those who do not share his language) the magnitude of his dispossession, which leads him to realize that in French the word *creole* is an anagram for "anger," *colère* (131). This means that under the deceptive surface of the hotel, where absurd, comical, and lopsided stories unfold from floor to floor and all human suffering seems to amuse us with its oddity (as it does the aspiring writer Dorimont), there lies hidden the silent rage of the wretched. For this reason it is appropriate that the novel should end with a fire that consumes the seeming "hilarity" of the hotel: to the extent that the effervescent unfolding of stories and unexpected events distracts us from the fact that the inhabitants are marginal and, to a large extent, socially irrelevant, the fire reveals, by destroying the hotel, the falsehood of its "happy" creoleness. The novel thus ends by reminding us of the other face Confiant gives to creoleness, its hidden meaning that spells "anger" and designates a culture at risk of losing its space and specificity.

Dorimont, whose legal practice comes to an end as a result of his gambling, womanizing, and general inability to keep things straight, strives to become a writer and put on paper everything that fascinates him in the hotel. He personifies all that is problematic with writing and written records of a culture based primarily on oral expression. His investigations into the lives of various tenants allow us to follow their stories, but we also realize that the tenants never fully disclose who they are and how they came to live in Bon Plaisir. Nor is Dorimont, limited by his deep affiliation to the Martinican bourgeoisie, able to understand the Bon Plaisir people, whose choices and modes of living depart radically from his own. As readers, however, we find out through our omniscient narrator more than is ever available to Dorimont and can assess all the ways his project must ultimately fail. We realize, at the same time, that there is a profound need, a necessity even, to translate the oral into the written in order to preserve and keep it alive. The epigraph to the sixth and final act of this Creole comedy spells out this task: "One must narrate the untellable. One must laugh at deep sadness. One must mock disgrace" (229). Yet because the traditional storyteller—"le maître de la parole" (the master of the word)—has lost his significance and today no one listens to him anymore, the unknown narrator of the novel takes up the task of "propagating the spoken and the written" (229).[8] Confiant uses the word *bouturer*, "to propagate from cuttings." The reference to the vegetal world and the metaphor of growth concealed in it suggests that the encounter between the spoken and the written in the contemporary Caribbean novel must, according to Confiant, yield a new form of life in which both of the initial components continue to exist and grow. The outcome is a genuine narrative hybrid, an expanding life form that preserves and at the same time overcomes the individual characteristics of its constitutive parts. This ideal narrative form, a Creole novel, is closely connected to the idea of space; the same way life unfolds, spontaneous and unpredictable, in the impoverished neighborhoods of Fort-de-France, so must the novel engage in reproducing and preserving the chaotic, lively nature of oral storytelling, with its complex rhythm of symbolic invocations, digressions, and repetitions. Such a novel must also preserve the dialogical and polyphonic character of spoken words; it must seek to include the reader into the circle of telling by creating a space where the reader can "hear" the multiplicity of stories spun in front of him or her. It is in this way that the novel must "narrate the untellable," as Confiant puts it. Its task is to create a utopian narrative space where the characteristics of a living culture can be captured without damage to its vitality.

In his encounters and discussion with Bougre Fou, who, despite his apparent madness, is one of the most educated and thoughtful residents of the hotel, Dorimont develops his theory of the novel and its purpose in Martinique. Bougre Fou is a passionate reader of poetry, particularly that of Aimé Césaire, while Dorimont prefers the novel. Bougre Fou explains that the time of the novel has not yet arrived in Martinique, a country still in need of voicing its cry of protest, which only poetry can do well (*HBP*, 254). His example of this successful poetic revolt is, of course, Césaire's *Notebook of a Return to My Native Land*. Dorimont prefers prose and believes that Martinicans must surpass the cry and engage in another kind of writing: "It is high time for us not to address the Other, he declared to Bougre Fou, surprised by his own peremptory tone, but to address ourselves. For ourselves. And that, my young friend, only the novel can do" (255). The former lawyer–turned-owner of Bon Plaisir engages in producing this new novel, the one capable of taking the literary expression of the region to another level: that of self-sufficiency and self-awareness without constantly evoking and including the Other. This Other is, of course, the European colonial world, and France in particular. The project with which he wishes to accomplish this goal is a "big and vast novel" (255) that chronicles the lives of the hotel's tenants. Like the hotel itself, the novel is also "un roman en chantier," a novel under construction (255), perpetually in the process of being made, undone, and made again. In addition, the project of writing, with an emphasis on its unfolding rather than on the finished product, is equated with the kind of social space available to the ordinary inhabitants. The novel should, in this case, strive to substitute for the material shortages that the people experience in their daily lives; moreover it should strive to incorporate the concrete material reality of the island into its structure. The task of the writer is to capture the reality of creoleness in the written form and to realize that its spatial unfolding and its architectural idiosyncrasies must guide the theoretical understanding of literature. Dorimont is nonplussed by the fact that none of the tenants talk to him openly or ever fully reveal their secrets. He decides to supplement what is missing by imagining the stories he cannot otherwise obtain and ultimately defines the novel as "the art of lying truthfully" (246).

Nevertheless the act of writing, although necessary in upholding the idea of a certain kind of education (in the metropolitan French style), is connected throughout the novel with the implicit violence of prescriptive grammar. Three tenants of Bon Plaisir have the dubious privilege of having had a "proper" education: reading and writing and admiring the illustrious names of French culture. This kind of education only puts them at a greater remove from their native Creole language and culture, marking their implicit alienation from their immediate environment. As a retired teacher, Victorin Helvéticus is one of those highly educated islanders who, in the context of the novel, represents a successful, fully adapted version of what Bougre Fou should have been: an award-winning student, a perfect ventriloquist for the French educational system, and a linguistic and literary snob. He is fully aware, nevertheless, of the futile distraction that such education seems to be. "In this little country, so far removed from its mother country," he declares, "there are two types of masters. Those who own land and have white skin and those who possess education and have black skin" (276). Seen from this perspective, education is partially a cover-up for a fundamental material inequality between the landowning white elite and the striving but materially dispossessed black elite. Still, both groups are "masters," towering over those who have neither land nor education, that is, ordinary Creole people such as those we find in the hotel. The precious education that allows Helvéticus or Dorimont to feel superior to their neighbors is fragmentary and chaotic, "in slices" ("en tranches"), as Dorimont realizes (253). The literary texts are excerpts from Verlaine or Lamartine, taken out of their actual context and always presented as part of a literary handbook. Colonial education is therefore as alienating and fragmentary for a Martinican francophile like Helvéticus as it is for Naipaul's Indo-Trinidadian Mr. Biswas. In contrast to the old storytellers, like Florine's former neighbor in Trénelle or Nini Jolicoeur's father, both of whom make a brief and nostalgia-ridden appearance in the novel, we mostly encounter formally uneducated Creole speakers or educated lovers of French who "are madly in love with the good old academic French" (25). It is partly because of this combined alienation through language and material dispossession that Florine declares that the black people have passed "from slavery to slavitude and from slavitude to servitude" ("de l'esclavage à l'esclavitude et de l'esclavitude à la servitude" [37]). Yet for someone like Helvéticus, the proper handling of proper French represents the summit of all instruction worthy of its name (106). This linguistic servitude is implicitly equated, in one of the epigraphs, to the cityscape burdened with public squares dominated by imposing statues of worthy French figures: "*We live under the scrutiny of these creatures frozen in marble and bronze and therefore in their power. That's why we live bowing down*" (107). Postcolonial Martinique, with its departmental status, which separated a people from itself (Chamoiseau, *Ecrire en pays dominée*, 250), is therefore a dominated land where every architectural and linguistic marker serves to distinguish the inhabitants along the vertical axes of class prestige inherited from the colonial times. This is why, in *Ecrire en pays dominée* (*Writing in a Dominated Country*), Chamoiseau emphasizes the impact of insidious "silent" domination, without armies, barbed wire, walls, or censorship; instead the departmental status of Martinique leads to a "deformation of spirit," turning the individual into his or her own jailor who controls the imagination itself (17–18). This means that any form of liberation must take into account the realities of political and economic independence and the liberation of the imaginary.

The hotel, haunted by a zombie (as everyone seems to believe), is therefore a grotesque miniature representation of Martinique: an island possessed by a destructive "spirit" of transatlantic domination where the tenants resist, with sometimes clownish humor and vivacity of spirit, the rigid structure of racial and class hierarchy. When the inspector Montagris finds a mutilated murder victim in one of the rooms, he is surprised to discover that, in addition to removing various parts of the victim's body, the murderer had also removed a portion of his tongue. In its place the inspector finds a neatly folded piece of paper: it is a page torn from a French grammar book containing the rules of usage for the subjunctive mood. Since the subjunctive mood in French expresses a reality that is not concrete (i.e., desires and hopes), a necessity or a need, a doubt, a subjective judgment, or a hypothetical situation,[9] it becomes clear that the removal of the tongue equals the abolishment of the spoken in favor of the written word in grammatically regulated "proper" French. French is thus an artificial tongue—a substitute for the real physical organ, the fleshy tongue that is Creole. This replacement of the real tongue by a page torn from a grammar book is indeed "subjunctive," a hypothetical situation that expresses desire, necessity, a subjective judgment: that French language, if it mutilates Creole, must be resisted.

Implicitly, French cultural domination over its former colonies and its alienating effect on the island's autonomous identity represented through the mechanism of grammar evoke a similar problem regarding the distribution and organization of space. As I have shown in previous chapters, Lefebvre's notion of dominated and abstract space revolves around the imposition of rules and limits on the ordinary user of the city and on the space itself. Although dominated space is always naturalized, it is nevertheless the result of a "cult of rectitude, in the sense of right angles and straight lines. The order of power, the order of the male—in short, the moral order" (*PS*, 305). The force of the state, its institutions, and various embodiments of economic power translate spatially into abstract spaces where the rigid morality of straight lines dictates the kind of social life that can happen. This kind of space is diametrically opposed to the Rabelaisian space of carnivalesque excess. Similarly the oral tradition stands in carnivalesque and improvisatory opposition to the rigid grammar of the written language and its abstract domination. In this sense, space and language, environment and expression echo one another, showing us, as Confiant's novel attempts to do, the intimate connection between location and cultural identity, spaces and people who inhabit them.

Dorimont organizes the stories he has collected into separate notebooks, one for each tenant, and each of a different color: red for Man Florine, blue for the Lamotte sisters, orange for Justina Beausoleil, brown for the clarinetist Jean-André Laverrière, white for Victorin Helvéticus, yellow for the Andrassamy family, and purple for himself. Each color corresponds to the person whose story it serves to distinguish. Thus the diversity of stories is reflected in Dorimont's notebooks and their various colors; like a kaleidoscope, the collection of notebooks reminds us of the multifarious narratives that intertwine and come apart throughout the book. Yet despite Dorimont's efforts, we also know that his writing is an inadequate substitution for what the building itself does: it gathers and keeps together in one place the stories of all inhabitants and all past events. Thus the hotel itself is the best keeper of history and memories, a genuine Creole "monument," unlike those frozen statues to the famous French. When the hotel burns down, all that it contained vanishes along with it, particularly the kind of life that its structure made possible. Since the hotel leads the tenants' stories to intersect, clash, and intertwine, without the building the stories themselves become homeless and destitute. Dorimont's notebooks and, on an extradiegetic level, Confiant's novel itself, serve as narrative substitutes for the house that makes the multiplicity of stories possible in the first place. They are, on two different narrative levels, attempts at creating a Creole novel. This novel, however, requires its space, so without the hotel—that is, without the house for the story—the Creole world of Confiant's novel remains destitute.

Even houses, Confiant concludes, can end up forgetting us. Where the hotel Bon Plaisir used to be, there is now an improvised parking lot. Other stories may develop there, but the thirty-seven years of history that the hotel witnessed and shaped are gone with the disappearance of the architectural and spatial dimensions of that history. More important still, the hotel houses a specifically Creole culture, its fluctuating and joyous orality and its carnivalesque irreverence. Without the building and its strange façade, the face of this culture also fades. In this manner, yet again, we are invited to contemplate the vitally close but fragile connection between space and cultural identity. They may depend on one another to such an extent that without a specific house or a spatial setting of some kind, there is no room for the tangible daily life of a people and their stories. In other words, with the vanishing of the hotel, the stories vanish as well. The ability of the written record, whether metadiegetic, as in Dorimont's notebooks, or extradiegetic, as in Confiant's own novel, to render these stories remains dubious and tortured; they belong to the concrete location and the daily lives of its inhabitants. The written record captures and preserves them, but it must also deaden them in the process (or murder them, as the subjunctive mood symbolically does one of the tenants). Despite the fact that the Creolists' writing strives today to maintain creoleness and its constitutive orality in the written form (through the use of "interlect," for example), it is the *lived space* that matters more: where people actually live, telling and sharing their stories, is where their cultural identity resides as well. The novel is, as Confiant recognizes, a necessary yet self-consciously poor substitute. But "intellectuals are there to produce utopia, right?" (Gosson, "Cultural and Environmental Assimilation in Martinique," 153).

Conclusion

Reflections on space, whether explicit or implied, permeate any study of colonialism and its postcolonial contestations. All major figures of postcolonial theory have in one way or another raised the question of postcolonial spatiality in terms of colonial domination, postcolonial independence, and nation building, or the place of the "Third World" in contemporary global politics. In a recent attempt to reinvigorate the term *postcolonial*, burdened, in my view, by the unproductive repetition of its binary problematics as well as its "interstitial" solutions, Ato Quayson proposes, for example, that "closer scrutiny of the *postcolonial* suggests that it contains mutually reinforcing periodizing and spatial functions" (342, original emphasis). Quayson reminds us, very much in the spirit of Clive Barnett's or Maeve McCusker's focus on the prevalence of spatial concepts in postcolonial studies (see my introduction), that the concept of space structures postcolonial discourses in a dynamic way and is as important to the internal organization of the field as the more common idea of postcolonial periodicity. The obvious contemporary penchant for rediscovering space wherever it can be found attests to its perpetually nascent popularity and to the genuine discursive and experiential importance of space. Nevertheless there is not enough explicit discussion of the mutually constitutive relations between space and identity in those places where the right to spatial and communal autonomy has historically been denied and has thus become the locus of a struggle for reappropriation. Even less has been thought, as Neil Smith and Cindi Katz write, about space as a metaphor—an imaginative and transformative category of fragile literary and artistic interventions within the realm of solid material concerns.[1] While I, along with many other postcolonial scholars, recognize that spatial thinking is generally relevant for postcolonial analysis, I seek to show that Caribbean postcolonial literature in particular relies on representations of space as its central strategy in formulating the specificity of the region. My aim in this book has been to address two related questions: What exactly constitutes spatial identity in Caribbean postcolonial literature? What is the transformative potential of spatial thinking when it is mobilized as a metaphor in postcolonial literature? I connect these two questions in the following way. Colonial domination alienates the colonized and enslaved peoples from the spaces they inhabit but do not own. Yet more important, it also alienates them from a meaningful sense of identity, both individual and communal. The two categories, space and self, thus become interchangeable; the absence of autonomous location results in the absence of autonomous identity. Dispossessed of place, the colonial subjects find themselves searching for a viable form of selfhood divorced from the notion of material ownership yet still connected to the space they inhabit. The result is the production of an alternative spatiality that rests on something other than material ownership of space. This alternative spatiality is constructed as symbolic; through daily, mostly communal use of space, the dispossessed lay claim to what is otherwise taken from them in material terms. It is here that space-as-metaphor becomes a powerful statement of resistance: space is no longer the subject of material property but rather of symbolic appropriation.

The perpetually fluctuating binary of destitution and substitution thus organizes my reading of space in Caribbean postcolonial discourse and unfolds a series of other binary oppositions and paradoxes that emanate from it. I argue that the reliance on the metaphor of space, rather than the reflection on space as such, produces an act of substitution. Time and again this substitution of an image for the thing emphasizes the reality of destitution, which underlies and motivates the imaginative act. In other words, the metaphor of space in the Caribbean context highlights the contested nature of postcolonial space, its historical unavailability, and the fact that claiming space remains a luxury most people do not have. It is precisely this denial of space—drawn into sharper focus by the proliferation of spatial images—that I examine by looking at the spatial concerns of Caribbean literature. Conversely, the absence of a legitimate location, so central to postcolonial reflections on space, triggers the proliferation of spatial images as imaginary substitutes for that absence of material location denied by the history of colonial destitution. In other words, the metaphor of space points not to space as such, but, as Lefebvre rightly observes, to the very absence of space. Because I am interested in the particular manner in which Caribbean authors interrogate this historical condition of spatial destitution and generate a necessarily failing literary substitute, I examine *space* as the structural narrative device of a literary text and as an analytical category crucial for the productive critique and future rearticulations of the spatial postcolonial paradigm. In my reading, the failure of the literary text to resolve the material problem does not underscore the traditional view that literary analysis ultimately has nothing to say about the world of material needs, nor does it emphasize the constitutive limitation of the utopian gesture. Rather the failure of the literary to resolve the question of material destitution, in its very obviousness serves to draw attention to the paradoxical centrality of both the material-real and the imaginative-representational components of any reflection on space.

Of course, in the Caribbean postcolonial context, this might sound like an easy and excessively hopeful solution. While the industry of tourism, for example, continues today along the exploitative path set by the colonial machine of the past, it would be irresponsible to claim that symbolic reappropriation successfully challenges the unequal distribution of wealth in the local manifestations of global capitalism. I attempt instead to recognize the profound limitation of literature when it seeks to construct a world-transformative representation even as I acknowledge, and even celebrate, its revolutionary impulse. Nevertheless it is important to recognize that, as Lefebvre shows, the symbolic dimension of our quotidian engagements with space constitutes one of the most important dimensions of social space and its production. This symbolic intervention into an otherwise prescribed spatial practice lies at the heart of our passive but persistent attempts to contest our lack of political agency and power. In Lefebvre's *dominated space*, the ordinary user reappropriates space by living and transforming it imaginatively. It is in this constant daily reappropriation, which remains quiet but stubborn, that imagination serves as a contestatory category. Even when it does not change the actual conditions of dispossession and marginalization we witness or experience, it draws attention to the unequal distribution of wealth and power that makes imaginative interventions so necessary. What interests me throughout this book is this powerful intervention of fiction into material spatiality in order to assert the right of the dispossessed to produce both space and self according to their own needs.

The etymological meaning of *destitution*, "to be placed outside," organizes my readings of the novels and creates a conceptual link between them. I argue that my selected texts share a concern with a fundamental paradox of colonialism: its practice of exclusion through forced inclusions. The systematic expulsion of the colonized from the geopolitical hierarchy of the global world rests, paradoxically, on the violently enforced participation of the enslaved peoples in the building of that hierarchy. Throughout colonial history and independently of specific locations we might focus on, the colonized are brought into the colonial system not only as the necessary contrapuntal other to the colonizing powers but above all as cheap labor or a kind of raw material of colonialism. By the same token, the colonized are brought inside in order to play the outsider. *Destitution* allows me to emphasize the double meaning of this socioeconomic exclusion: "to be placed outside" suggests that the outsider is forced out after having been brought in. Generally speaking, this is what colonization produces: an enforced and violent bringing of the colonized into the system only to expel them as that system's undesirable remainders. On this very general level, the novels I analyze in this book share a common concern with the lasting cultural and socioeconomic consequences of colonial hierarchy in which dominant cultures and languages derive their centrality from the creation of their cultural destitute. To be destitute in the colonial and postcolonial contexts means to suffer from an irresolvable split between material ownership and existential authenticity. The colonial subject is deprived of both by a single gesture that turns the colonized into property and substitutes human freedom for material possession. This colonial deprivation imposes on the colonial subject a desire for material spatial possession and ownership of self, which are falsely presented as interchangeable. But as these novels clearly show, a material pursuit does not gratify an existential need, nor does existential wealth resolve the problems of material poverty. Destitution is the concept that designates both the political and the textual aspects of this problem of ownership and authorship.

Although destitution allows me to bring different Caribbean novels together by focusing on the fact that they all construct identity through a spatial narrative, the answers we find in these novels differ profoundly. In the case of Mr. Biswas, for example, the answer to poverty and the sociocultural abyss of his existence resides in the continuously deferred dream of combining the physical shelter of a house with the idea of being socially recognized. Because Mr. Biswas's notion of self depends on his notion of ownership (of a house and, by extension, his own identity), his homelessness must ultimately result in the crumbling of self. Not only is his isolated marginality deprived of meaningful human connections, but he also fails to become an autonomous person because his dignity depends on precisely the material ownership from which he is precluded.

Mr. Biswas is the victim of the logic of ownership that structures colonialism in the first place, excluding him even as it presents itself as the sole means of self-possession. Ultimately, however, in failing to stand on his own, Mr. Biswas serves as the most moving reminder of what it means to try.

By contrast, in Chamoiseau's *Texaco*, Gilroy's *Frangipani House*, and Confiant's *L'Hôtel du Bon Plaisir*, all of which in their different ways build on the rich tradition of the Caribbean yard novel, the notions of autonomous self and location rely not on the concept of ownership but on the creative notion of communal sharing. Despite their poverty and personal tragedies, the protagonists of these novels succeed in weaving their narratives into a larger collective history, and, because their sense of identity is communal, they triumph in their resistance. The positive and enriching facets of spatial dispossession are derived from the daily life of its community, no matter how marginal it may appear on the surface. Although these three novels offer a powerful response to Naipaul's sense of irreparable loss, they cannot, despite their exuberant narrative utopias, neutralize or annul the profoundly relevant question that Mr. Biswas poses: What about those who do not succeed in standing on their own and have no one to stand with? All of the novels I discuss are connected by their deep concern with destitution born of colonialism, yet where some recognize the terrible limits of destitution, the others continue to imagine and expand, at least narratively, beyond such limits.

As Sartre points out in his preface to Fanon's *The Wretched of the Earth*, the material and symbolic violence of the colonial project consists in dehumanizing the victim while maintaining the ideology of universal humanism of the mother country: "Violence in the colonies does not only have for its aim the keeping of these enslaved men at arm's length: it seeks to dehumanize them. Everything will be done to wipe out their traditions, to substitute our language for theirs and to destroy their culture without giving them ours" (15). What interests me in this narrative of human hierarchy, which ultimately plagues the Western world as much as its historical victims, is the taxonomic gesture of finding, classifying, and naming the other in order to place him or her within a bound system of claims and rights only to deny them. Designating a subject of any kind is already an indexical gesture by which finger-pointing, so cogently exposed in Althusser's discussion of ideology, accomplishes the compulsory socialization of the unnamed stranger, a pulling into my world, and the violence of his or her potential expulsion from that same world. Such expulsion is what I have in mind when I read destitution as a category of spatial and ideological exteriority in Caribbean postcolonial fiction.

Spatially oriented Caribbean writers contribute to this important discussion of sociopolitical emplacement by drawing attention to the ambiguous and problematic status of the marginal location: the protagonists in the novels I discuss desire, reject, or create social and personal places that contradict our ideas of revolutionary postcoloniality as much as they dismantle the conservative status quo. No one in these novels wants to own a large suburban house and become a respectable white man (this would be ironic, as these authors are either *not* white or *not* men!), but they all want to own. This desire for housed property and reappropriation of identity—itself understood as a right to a proper name and place—centers these novels around the spatial configurations of identity, its realities and fictions. Such spatial configurations—houses, neighborhoods, and other domains of located identity—produce a complex view of the mutually constitutive notions of inside and outside, psychological and political, private and public. However, this notion of spatial property is, at the same time, a matter of linguistic and narrative reappropriation. In Chamoiseau's *Texaco*, for example, the battle for the slum of Texaco culminates in a battle for naming one's own location and identity. Paradoxically, then, Texaco and its inhabitants struggle for the right to "self-interpellation," if one may call it that, and attempt to assign themselves a subject position of their own choosing.

The spatial category depends, as Lefebvre poignantly argues, on a significant though entirely implicit tension: between authorized, legitimate, and surveyed spaces and marginal, illegitimate, and clandestine ones. In order to show this dimension of my selected novels, I focus on the destitute and their relationship to their living spaces. The defining characteristic of the destitute is their relation to the spaces they do not own and from which they can easily be expelled. Borrowed or threatened space, and the anxiety created by it, constitute the destitute's relationship to the owner and, by extension, to all other institutional forces that appear to be legitimate and, through ownership, fully grounded in their social and political territories. From this perspective, Caribbean spatial novels ultimately address the legitimacy of the subject and the way sociopolitical forces at large sanction or cancel subject positions. The notion of ownership matters here precisely because it raises the fundamental question of human freedom, of owning oneself or being owned by another. This matter of ownership is even more important in the postcolonial context, where the historical memory of slavery and indentured labor continually brings the question of ownership—over places and identity—back into focus.

Yet location and spatial identity cannot be thought without addressing their internal paradox: the reversible nature of placement oscillates between home and prison. A postcolonial subject like Mr. Biswas, for example, remains caught in an endless cycle of residential anxiety, fighting the arbitrary violence of colonial placement with wishful fictions about ideal place. These two types of physical locations translate into two corresponding versions of identity: one violently assigned, the other resisting.

The fundamental connection between space and the identities it either helps produce or prevents from coming into being is powerfully illustrated in Fanon's opening discussion of the wretched. He evokes, above all, their confined and squalid places of residence, physical and symbolic, architectural and ideological:

> The town belonging to the colonized people, or at least the native town, the Negro village, the medina, the reservation, is a place of ill fame, peopled by men of evil repute. They are born there, it matters little where or how; they die there, it matters not where or how. It is a world without spaciousness; men live there on top of each other, and their huts are built one on top of the other. The native town is a hungry town, starved of bread, of meat, of shoes, of coal, of light. The native town is a crouching village, a town on its knees, a town wallowing in the mire. It is a town of niggers and dirty Arabs. The look that the native turns on the settler's town is a look of lust, a look of envy; it expresses his dreams of possession—all manner of possession: to sit at the settler's table, to sleep in the settler's bed, with his wife if possible. The colonized man is an envious man. And this the settler knows very well; when their glances meet he ascertains bitterly, always on the defensive, "They want to take our place." It is true, for there is no native who does not dream at least once a day of setting himself up in the settler's place. (39)

Fanon insists here on the abject humiliation of the colonized, which stems, among other things, from the hierarchy of colonial locations: the native town is a "crouching village, a town on its knees." The inability of the native town to stand on its own shows that the fundamental problem of the postcolonial novel lies, as I argue, in its concern with destitution. Those who are pushed down to crouch, as Fanon puts it, and to "wallow in the mire" will continue to dream of and fight for their standing, upright position. Symbolically, but also literally, this should be the position of an upright human being, denied by the colonial system. Fanon makes a clear connection here between a place of residence, an urban and geographical location, and its direct link to one's sense of humanity. The way we live, where and how, allows for or deprives us of our human characteristics. In Fanon's text, the phrase "it matters not where, or how" recurs. The conditions of existence of the "lesser" human being are irrelevant. The mass of hungry, indistinguishable people replaces any notion of a particular human being, for and to whom we would feel responsible. Such a mass is stripped of its history and, possibly, its future. Instead it is a featureless agglomerate, deprived, as Fanon points out, of any "spaciousness." And having no "spaciousness," it has no meaningful identity.

One way of opposing such nothingness of location and self is already implied in Althusser's famous theory of the subject. If interpellation (and in this case it is the interpellation of and into the colonial system and its aftereffects) converts a "concrete individual" into an ideological subject, this conversion, since *it is* ideological, can itself be converted in order to transform one type of subjecthood into another. If Althusser's ideology is "imaginary," it follows that any subject who becomes conscious of the ideological underpinnings of his or her subject position can plot ways to be free of it by replacing it with a different kind of imaginary location. Since Althusser defines ideology as representing "the imaginary relationship of individuals to their real conditions of existence" (162), one form of opposition to the violence of (post)colonial interpellation would consist precisely in positing a different set of imaginary relations. Opposition would consist, in other words, in reimagining an alternative kind of subject. The utopian gesture of the postcolonial text would consist, then, in imagining a transformation of these real conditions of existence through alternative literary narratives, which offer a substitute subject location against the oppression of the available ones.

When viewing Caribbean postcolonial writing from the perspective of space, we must therefore question the relationship of actual to imaginary locations. More generally still, the focus on space requires a closer examination of the reasons why and the ways in which postcolonial writing often engages in transcendence of actual locations through metaphors of space. In my terminology, the spatial perspective in postcolonial literature reveals a rich tradition and an ongoing practice of dealing with actual destitution through the substitutive potential of literature. The metaphors of space in postcolonial writing must therefore fulfill a double role: they must always refer, quite accurately and poignantly, to the actual conditions they seek to critique, while at the same time offering the imaginative overcoming of those same conditions. In *Absolutely Postcolonial*, Peter Hallward offers a valuable critique—and ultimate recognition—of this postcolonial gesture of imaginative transcendence. Concerned with postcolonial theory's persistent refusal to name and work with its conceptual location, Hallward argues that "the signature postcolonial concepts—the hybrid, the interstitial, the intercultural, the in-between, the indeterminate, the counter-hegemonic, the contingent and so on—are so many attempts to evoke that which no concept can 'capture'" (xi). Favoring Fanon and other anticolonial thinkers over postcolonial ones, Hallward emphasizes that colonial relations are fundamentally divisive and exploitative, born of military conquest and dispossession, and are therefore not a matter of interstitial agency. He favors the revolutionary potential of the divisive anticolonial binary because, at the very least, it contains the possibility of reversal. Yet, shying away from dichotomies in favor of a single and unified world, postcolonial theory, according to this view, forsakes its promise of genuine political engagement and opts for an illusory harmonization of radically opposed polarities that *should not* be reconciled. Hallward's objection to postcolonial theory focuses on the way it seems to promise and then forsake the project of radical political critique. He understands this political and conceptual move to originate in postcolonial theory's preference for singular and singularizing terms, opposed, he argues, to the specific. These two terms, *singular* and *specific*, designate two abstract poles of distinction and structure his critique of the postcolonial project. The specific is relational, the singular nonrelational (xii). Postcolonial discourse, in its singularity, "will operate without criteria external to its operation" and will ultimately "act even in the absence of others as such" (xii). Instead of an interpretation of reality, postcoloniality will then offer a creation of reality of which it wishes to speak. Consequently everything about postcolonial theory is internal to its production and refuses a clear or relational reference to an outside of its conceptual premises. More than an issue of critical terminology, the problem lies in a general understanding of agency and context, and affects, more particularly, the very conception of politics and political action.

My choice to conclude this book by referencing Hallward's critique of postcolonial theory has to do with what I consider his very useful insistence on conceptual location: "Rather than debate the question of centre and periphery, then, I will identify the postcolonial orientation with a refusal of any identifiable or precisely located centre, in favor of its own self-regulating transcendence of location" (xv). Hallward's discussion of the postcolonial thus allows for a different question: *Why* is there in postcolonial theory and literature, as Hallward claims, this gesture of transcending place, of claiming to be outside, and, finally, of moving beyond the subject itself? As I show in this book, the "self-regulating transcendence of location" (as Hallward puts it), understood in spatial terms, happens precisely because the postcolonial must take into account and return, with some creative power, to the problems of being forcibly placed outside (destitute, in my discussion), defined as subjectless and deprived of relational reciprocity. Take as an example any narrative of enslavement: it addresses a systematic transformation of human beings into objects of exchange, denies these objectified subjects a possibility of autonomous or self-selected location, whether material or symbolic, and abolishes reciprocity of relations reserved for free human subjects only. In an attempt to remember these facts and do something about their continued geopolitical and cultural reverberations, postcolonial theory and literature tend to celebrate the denied subject, the impossible location, and the transcendence of relation itself. In this gesture there may well be, as Hallward suggests, a failure actively to redress the wrong of inequality by reversing the terms of engagement, but there is also much bold defiance. If we cannot all be equally free, choosing subjects, in possession of our selves and our location, if we cannot cross borders or speak back to the sources of our oppression, at least we can most certainly imagine a world beyond subjecthood, place, borders, and imposed relations. We can question the very premise of the binary world and refuse to choose between the two positions we did not create in the first place.

Hallward concludes his discussion by reminding us of the centrality of literature for those theories that, in their very core, have arisen as and should remain theories of reading. In acknowledging the fact that "any literary work, however mimetic its intent, involves some degree of despecification, some degree of imaginative transcendence" (333), Hallward emphasizes in the end that "the realm of the aesthetic invariably solicits the exercise of a *thought-ful* freedom" and that "what goes by the name of artistic or creative writing will continue to open a fragile space of relational detachment and imaginative engagement" (334). In his critique of the postcolonial position, Hallward objects to its persistent "suspicion of the 'soft' or 'creative' dimensions of literature" (334), to the point of abandoning its fundamental project of reading literature. The problem lies in seeing imaginative literary representation and the material dimensions of political history as mutually exclusive. Hallward is more than justified in rejecting this either/or reduction that too often postures as radical engagement: "If literature did not offer *some* degree of creative disengagement from material circumstances and still more from bureaucratic discourse it would have been buried long before its materialist critics began arranging its funeral. The more forceful Marxist critics sometimes seem to forget that the postcolonial criticism they attack is primarily literary criticism, i.e. a practice of reading designed first and foremost to account for certain particular literary phenomena" (334, original emphasis). I would suggest that postcolonial writers' insistence on the creative transcendence of place and subject has little to do with a refusal of radical politics of place and owes infinitely more to the nature of postcolonial location itself. To be postcolonial is to be stranded in a world of hierarchies where your position has, from the outset of the colonial conquest, been defined as minor. In such a context, "transcendence of location" appears to be almost inevitable. For people whose cultural and geographical location was denied, abolished, repossessed, and then undervalued, there seems to be very little left to do. This transcendence of location may be one productive and revolutionary move to be made. When, in the world of borders, one refuses to acknowledge the border and seeks to cross it by refusing its very existence, this move must be recognized as a radical one even when its wishful magic remains to operate in words only.

In his conclusion to *Absolutely Postcolonial*, Hallward suggests that "it would be absurd, of course, to retreat to the indefensible position that art has nothing to do with society or culture" (335), but he also wishes to preserve it from answering only to the demands of socioeconomic materialism. The problem of the postcolonial, as I attempt to read it in this book, lies in its constant and absolutely inevitable wavering between the material reality of destitution and the imaginative acceptance of this outsider's position in the name of some world in which there would presumably exist an option beyond the either/or of privilege and poverty, fiction and reality. Hallward himself suggests that "what goes by the name of artistic or creative writing will continue to open a *fragile space* of relational detachment and imaginative engagement" (334, my emphasis). This "fragile space" appears to exist in some realm beyond the binary opposition of radical social change, whether it be "left" or "right." It is obviously fragile, as it offers no quick answer, no sound-bite solution, no five-year plan. Instead it is a third solution between binaries that Aimé Césaire, with respect to Négritude, describes as "not a choice between alternatives, but an effort at reconciliation. Not a cold reconciliation, but reconciliation in the heat of the fire, an alchemical reconciliation if you like" ("The Liberating Power of Words").

I focus on this fragile third space "in the heat of the fire" between irreconcilable opposites in order to question the violence of forced locations and the impossible choices produced by such violence. The choice is, in other words, foreclosed from the outset because it merely reflects the existence of imposed "options," which draw into sharper focus the unfreedom of the predetermined conditions of choosing. In Chamoiseau's *Texaco*, for example, the slum community can do one of two things: remain where it is and face police brutality before it is forced to relocate, or relocate of its own "free will," that is, under threat and in order to avoid actual physical violence. The very purpose of the novel is to interrogate and ultimately refuse the reduction of a living community to an object of imposed urban design. Are these extremes worth calling "options"?

Ultimately postcolonial literary and theoretical work seems to claim both universal validity and particular application. The way a statement, whether it be theoretical or artistic, transcends its location in no way undermines the existence and meaning of that location. On the contrary, as Adorno shows, the very universality of art springs from its consistent particularization. Conversely, the particular opacity of an artwork (to borrow Adorno's language) in no way deters from its ability to communicate in some partial way, which can never exhaust its speaking potential (205). Tying this point back to my concern with specific literary texts of Caribbean postcolonial literature, my authors' insight into the problems of location in no way decides the matter of placement even when the texts offer imaginative alternatives to an imposed absence of meaningful choice. The questions posed by the yard novels of the Caribbean, and by Naipaul, Chamoiseau, Gilroy, and Confiant, are both universally meaningful and absolutely particular to the contexts they address. There may yet be something for binary politics of placement to learn from this stubborn paradox of art. In the context of postcolonial writing, this paradox is best revealed through spatial analysis; in viewing Caribbean literature from the perspective of spatial theory, we discover what is most crucial to its structure and its intention. It reveals a specific geographic location and its community as produced by the history of colonialism but also as productive of social and historical transformation through the imaginative reappropriation of space and self.

Notes

Introduction

1. For a discussion of conceptual mapping and its relationship to the shifting notion of space under the influence of globalization, see Cuddy-Keane.

2. See Gallagher, *Ici-Là*.

3. I return to the question of the miniature and its Bachelardian roots in chapter 2, where I discuss the house as a spatial representation of individual and communal claims to ownership and autonomy. Another treatment of this question can be found in chapter 3, where I analyze Naipaul's *A House for Mr. Biswas* and its use of miniature spaces and spatial images to foreground the quotidian tragedy of spatial dispossession.

4. In slightly varied forms, *sta* is found in a whole set of Indo-European languages, such as Sanskrit, Greek, Latin, the Teutonic group (Anglo-Saxon, Icelandic, Old High German), and Slavonic. It means "to stand."

5. For a discussion of the representations of poverty and potential as two coinciding modern literary and philosophical concerns, see Greaney.

6. On art as a form of everyday poetic practice, see Nadal-Melsió.

7. Lefebvre's critique of structuralist dogma is reminiscent of Marx's passionate attack on the Old and Young Hegelians in *The German Ideology*.

8. In *Thirdspace*, Soja renames this constellation "the trialectics of spatiality" (10).

9. For a detailed discussion of Lefebvre's relation to and critique of the Hegelian dialectic, see Schmid.

Chapter 1. Caribbean Spatial Metaphors

1. In the French Caribbean this Edenic and exotic view of the archipelago is expressed in the *doudouiste* ("folksy") literary tradition. See Pépin, 2.

2. This is the term Benítez-Rojo uses to describe Columbus's discovery of the New World (*The Repeating Island*, 220).

3. For a compelling discussion of European rivalry over the Caribbean islands, see also Williams, "The Cockpit of Europe."

4. For a cogent critique of the way hybridity as an umbrella critical concept, particularly in the Caribbean, "enacts a dehistoricizing conflation," see Puri (3). Puri argues that, although it is a term meant to resist racist purisms, *hybridity* also suppresses the many types of cultural and political diversity in the Caribbean that are better expressed and recognized through an existing multiplicity of terms such as *creolization*, *mestizaje*, *douglarization*, and *jibarismo*. According to Puri, hybridity is itself, and quite ironically, in the process of being subsumed under a still broader term, *globalization*.

5. A discussion of Benítez-Rojo's use of chaos theory and the rhizome to account for the Caribbean as a "complex system" can be found in Sprouse. Here chaos theory is understood as both a metaphor and a method for analyzing Caribbean cultural practices (80).

6. Introducing Glissant's famous collection of essays, *Caribbean Discourse*, Dash points out that "it is the composite reality of the bastard that obsesses Glissant, not the longing for a remote paternity" (introduction, xli).

7. Glissant's *Caribbean Discourse* and *Poetics of Relation* both feature a memorable depiction of the slave ship and place it at the center of Caribbean cultural consciousness. The slave ship is also a potent conceptual and metaphorical device in Paul Gilroy's *The Black Atlantic*. Merchant, pirate, and slave ships serve to structure the discussion of the Atlantic "hydrarchy" in Linebaugh and Rediker. A focused historical examination of the slave ship can be found in Rediker. The slave ship also appears—repeatedly and with great force—as a key image in various poetic and literary representations of the Caribbean, notably those regarding the *Zong* massacre that occurred in 1781 when some 150 slaves were thrown overboard and drowned in the interest of collecting insurance monies. The *Zong* incident is addressed in D'Aguiar; Dabydeen; Cliff; and, most recently, Philip.

8. For a discussion of the slave ship as simultaneously a primordial void and a generative matrix, which serve as spatial metaphors for the beginning of the Caribbean culture, see Radović. Using Casey's discussion of ancient cosmogonies, where the primordial chaos (the void) gives rise to the creation of cosmos (an ordered world), I reflect on Glissant's evocation of the slave ship as such a generative matrix in his own cosmological reimagining of the Atlantic slave trade.

9. The famous Haitian author René Depestre often refers to himself as "homme-banian" (banyan-man) or "géo-libertin" (geo-libertine) to designate the free, rhizomatic, and unrestrained nature of his geographical understanding of identity.

10. Salman Rushdie uses this same linguistic parallel when, in *Shame*, he writes, "I, too, am a translated man. I have been *borne across*" (23). (Post)colonial migrancy is thus seen as sharing in the processes of cultural translation in which something

is lost and gained. This translation is also an act of figuration: the circulation of images across perceived cultural borders. In their discussion of spatial metaphors and their proliferation, Smith and Katz also point to the centrality of translation as a process that connects material and metaphorical spaces (67).

11. With respect to spatial metaphors and their mode of operation, Smith and Katz write that "metaphors assist in reducing the unfamiliar to the familiar; they reinscribe the unfamiliar event, experience or social relation as utterly known. It is precisely this apparent familiarity of space, the givenness of space, its fixity and inertness, that make a spatial grammar so fertile for metaphoric appropriation" (68). The suggested metaphorical reduction of space is, of course, far from one-sided; it also implies the reverse movement, from the familiar to the unfamiliar.

12. For an ecocritical approach to place and landscape in Martinican fiction, see Gosson, "For What the Land Tells." This essay begins with the excerpt from Glissant that I give here and argues for the centrality of "the land as a repository for an otherwise unrecorded, misrepresented, and under-appreciated Martinican past" (233).

13. For a discussion of "the idiosyncratic types of realism" in Caribbean literature that seek to redefine the European genres of realism and socialist realism, see Ormerod (435).

14. Parry returns to this underexamined connection between materialist spatial and postcolonial critique in her collection of essays *Postcolonial Studies*.

15. Reflecting on Lefebvre's contribution to this analysis of spatial inequality, Harvey writes, "While Lefebvre perhaps exaggerates a touch, I think it is worth recalling his remark that capitalism has survived in the twentieth century by one and only one means: 'by occupying space, by producing space'" (376).

Chapter 2. A House of One's Own

1. A version of the idea that space is not merely an abstract set of shared features or an empty receptacle where objects are arranged, but is instead the very condition of their physical possibility and their interconnectedness can be found in Merleau-Ponty's *Phenomenology of Perception*: "Space is not the setting (real or logical) in which things are arranged but the means whereby the position of things becomes possible. This means that instead of imagining it as a sort of ether in which all things float, or conceiving it abstractly as a characteristic that they have in common, we must think of it as the universal power enabling them to be connected" (284).

2. For a widely influential and, to this day, invaluable analysis of allochronic discourse as a fundamental vehicle of Western domination and a means of legitimizing global inequalities (Bunzl, xiii), see Fabian, *Time and the Other*.

3. The French title is *La rue Cases-Nègres*, first published in 1950 by J. Froissart (Paris). In 1983 this novel was made into a film by Euzhan Palcy, with a script-writing credit by Patrick Chamoiseau.

4. A brilliant literary example of approaching the enclosed space (a room) as an occasion for imaginary travel can be found in Xavier de Maistre's *Voyage autour de ma chambre* (1794; Voyage around My Room). A similar quality of expanding enclosed interior spaces through imaginative practice characterizes Marcel Proust's *A la recherche du temps perdu* (1913–27; In Search of Lost Time).

5. A similar spontaneous gathering of an otherwise fragmented community during a picnic occurs in Sam Selvon's *The Housing Lark* (1965).

6. In making this distinction, Naipaul offers a literary elaboration of an idea we find in Bachelard's *The Poetics of Space*, that miniature and the seemingly insignificant detail may contain immensity: "Thus the minuscule, a narrow gate, opens up an entire world. The details of a thing can be a sign of a new world which, like all worlds, contains the attributes of greatness. Miniature is one of the refuges of greatness" (155).

7. In a recent documentary on Bob Marley directed by Kevin Macdonald (*Marley*, 2012), when Marley is asked, "Are you a rich man? Do you have a lot of possessions?," he responds, "Possessions make you rich? I don't have that type of richness. My richness is life, forever." This is another example of a Caribbean artist marking a clear distinction between living and being in the world as opposed to owning things with which to mark and furnish it.

Chapter 3. "No Admittance"

1. *A House for Mr. Biswas*, which focuses on the connection between independence and ownership, was published just one year before Trinidad gained its independence from the United Kingdom in 1962. In view of this fact, Mr. Biswas can be reinterpreted as an extensive reflection on the problem of cultural identity and its dependence on a claim to a national territory, that is, a politically autonomous "portion of the earth," a phrase Mr. Biswas repeatedly uses to depict his own quest.

2. For an extensive discussion of Naipaul's historically assigned and subsequently self-selected status of the literary outsider, see Célestin.

3. Here I take the binary pair "appropriation/expropriation" from Dovey's account of Lefebvre (52).

4. For a fascinating discussion of cosmos and chaos as two distinct and mutually exclusive types of places, see Casey.

5. Depictions of Hanuman House are based on the Lion House, belonging to Naipaul's maternal family in Chaguanas, Trinidad.

6. Mustafa suggests that the controversy that surrounds Naipaul's narrative choices of belonging to and distancing himself from various cultural and political contexts involves widely ranging evaluations of both the man and his work, from "objective" and "ahistorical" to "culturally ignorant" and "hysterical." Mustafa organizes Naipaul's career into a narrative frame that she sees as itself resembling a nineteenth-century bildungsroman in which "only certain events having to do with already codified achievements are privileged" (7).

7. Barnow draws attention to the relationship between the particular and universal in Naipaul's fiction: "Understanding is shaped by the when and where, the historicity of the observer. As long as the observer relates to the observed in the context of larger social and political concerns that direct his interest in them, understanding will not be value-neutral. Naipaul has always pointed his focus on the particular in the terms of its broader, 'universal' meanings, and he has been very open about finding some societies and some cultural conventions more conducive to a reasonably good life than others" (x).

8. For a brief survey of various assessments of Naipaul's personality and work, similar to the one I offer here, see Strachan's "Naipaul's 'Garden of Hell'" in his interdisciplinary study of Caribbean tourist discourse *Paradise and Plantation.*

9. Recognizing that critical positions on Naipaul's literary production can generate only "disagreement," Nixon emphasizes, as one of the central accomplishments of Naipaul's writing, precisely his "unimpeachable style" (3).

10. For a recent collection of essays concerned with reassessing Naipaul's literary achievements, limitations, and legacies, see Rahim and Lalla.

11. Rohlehr has recently pointed out that the "confessional" approach permeates Naipaul's fiction and nonfiction writing. The result is "the Trickster's triumph. . . : the privilege of becoming at one and the same time confessant and confessor; of achieving simultaneously the postures of self-exposure, self-diagnosis, self-healing and the flagellant's self-righteous joy in excoriating the hide of an already doomed old new world" ("The Confessional Element in Naipaul's Fiction," 97).

12. For an extensive discussion of literacy in *A House for Mr. Biswas*, see ten Kortenaar.

Chapter 4. Squatters in the Cathedral of the Written Word

For prompting me to think about the word *squatter* with respect to *Texaco*, I am indebted to Coursil's discussion of this novel.

1. In her recent critical introduction to Chamoiseau's work, Knepper argues that *Texaco* is "a kind of postcolonial utopia, produced as a critique of existing society, the depiction of a more perfect society, and a plan for reform" (*Patrick Chamoiseau*, 114). Yet this utopia is unique insofar as it relies on the processes of translation, dialogue, and rewriting of the ideal society with the aim of contesting the global and reasserting the local.

2. Using different theoretical means, Lincoln makes a similar point, that "the imaginative potency of literature might open a surprising path to a transformational future" (21). Although I adopt this point in much of my reflection on Caribbean spatial narratives, I also remain—along with Lefebvre and his followers—critical of the fact that, in Lefebvre's words, "the world of images and signs exercises a fascination, skirts or submerges problems, and diverts attention from the 'real'—i.e. from the possible. While occupying space, it also signifies

space, substituting a mental and therefore abstract space for spatial practice—without, however, doing anything really to unify those spaces that it seems to combine in the abstraction of signs and images" (*PS*, 389). In my view the conflict between these two positions must be preserved if we are to think of any alternatives to dominated space and dominant ideological narratives about real spatial practice. Literature and spatial images have a large role to play in this reconceptualization of spatiality, but only if they remain sources of critique and conceptual possibility rather than comforting gestures of substitution.

3. According to Bongie, Chamoiseau disrupts the linear historical narrative and the flow of storytelling with "metafictive passages that introduce an authorial double, an erudite town planner (*urbaniste*), who comments in pointedly theoretical and ethnographic terms" on the meaning of Texaco and its community. These intrusions serve "to distance the reader from the (predominantly oral) community that is being evoked in the main body of the text, transforming that community and its place into the object of (a necessary) memory, a (necessary) theoretical construct" (171).

4. For a compelling discussion of the overlaps and differences between heterotopia and terrain vague, see Dehaene and De Cauter, *Heterotopia and the City*.

5. This notion of a generative chaos is something that Chamoiseau takes from Glissant, whose definition of "le chaos-monde" posits the necessity of poetic deregulation, which contests all hierarchies but preserves the nonnormative logic of its own: "The *chaos-monde* is only disorder if one assumes there to be an order whose full force poetics is not prepared to reveal (poetics is not a science). . . . *Chaos-monde* is neither fusion nor confusion: it acknowledges neither the uniform blend—a ravenous integration—nor muddled nothingness. Chaos is not 'chaotic.' But its hidden order does not presuppose hierarchies or pre-cellences—neither of chosen languages nor of prince-nations. The *chaos-monde* is not a mechanism; it has no keys" (*Poetics of Relation*, 94).

6. Describing his interest in the productive encounter between the imagined and the actual, Chamoiseau says, "A mirroring between the imaginary and the real, the marvelous and the realist, the poetic and the prosaic, these are the scales of variation which are precious to me" (McCusker and Chamoiseau, 729, my translation).

7. See, for example, Leach. The first section of this collection bears the title "The Legible Metropolis." There Frisby suggests that the notion of the city as text persists in the understanding of architecture since at least the nineteenth century.

8. Geographically amplified, the same problems define the relationship between the colonial periphery and its metropolitan center. Between France and Martinique, for example, notwithstanding the fact that Martinique is today a French département d'outre-mer (DOM) and since 1946 technically no longer a colony, there remains a hierarchical relationship based on precisely the notions of centrality and marginality of cultures and geographical locations.

9. In *Poetics of Relation*, Glissant describes this pyramidal hierarchy in the following way: "A pyramid organization: everywhere after 1848 the origin of the mass of slaves, then workers was African—or Hindu in the Caribbean; the middle level, managers, administrators, and overseers, were hired men of European origin, a small number of whom were replaced early in the century by people of color—once again in the Caribbean; at the top of the pyramid were the planters, colonists, or *békés*, as they were called in the Antilles, who strove to constitute a white pseudoaristocracy" (64).

10. Bongie emphasizes precisely this irony of Texaco's structure. The town planner engages in preserving the shanty town as a "living monument" (171); "the irony of his situation, however, is that his disruptive presence in the text actually alerts the readers to the 'historical' . . . identity of this quarter of the 'ville créole.' The town planner's presence in this site of resistance to cultural oblivion is the sign of its contamination by history" (171).

11. This and the previous quote are from McCusker and Chamoiseau, 725. All translations of this interview are mine.

12. Already in this theoretical stance we recognize Chamoiseau's indebtedness to Deleuze and Guattari's *A Thousand Plateaus*, which I discuss later in this chapter. In the introduction to their book, we read a similar formulation: "The notion of unity (*unité*) appears only when there is a power takeover in the multiplicity by the signifier or a corresponding subjectification proceeding" (8). It is clear that for Deleuze and Guattari, unity is a moment of subordination of many meanings to a single one, which asserts its power over the multiplicity. Chamoiseau is invested in undoing any such domination and attempts to produce, in all of his writings, a return of the multiple against the dominant meaning.

13. Punter discusses the significance of the monstrous, hybrid, and creaturely in postcolonial literature in general, but his prime example is Rushdie's *Shame*.

Chapter 5. Heterotopia of Old Age

1. For a detailed discussion of old age and discrimination in the labor market, see Macnicol.

2. According to Roxann Bradshaw's interview with Gilroy, the inspiration for *Frangipani House* came when Gilroy was visiting a friend who owned a rest home in Barbados.

3. In her introduction to the recent special issue of *Occasion* on embodiment and aging, Goldman emphasizes the importance of exploring "alternative forms of bodily consciousness, phenomenological ways of living, and queer stylistics—alternative embodied forms that become increasingly significant when socially sanctioned forms of cognition, memory, and reproductive capacity are deemed compromised." This rich collection of essays on the embodied experience of aging, gender, and memory seeks to connect these phenomena to the aesthetic practice as it pertains to age.

4. An alternative translation and discussion of the reasons for and shortcomings of the translators' word choice (between *different* and *other*) can be found in Dehaene and De Cauter, *Heterotopia and the City.*

5. For a passing mention of Foucault's text as "silly," see Curry, 90. "Enchanted breathlessness" is in Faubion, 31. For more or less extensive references to Foucault's "Different Spaces"/"Of Other Spaces," see, for example, Soja's *Postmodern Geographies* and *Thirdspace*; Casey; Malpas; Minca; Kohn; and, most extensively, Dehaene and De Cauter, *Heterotopia and the City.*

6. The original application of this term can be traced to the medical context, where it designates displaced or dystopic tissue, that is, the condition of growth of normal tissue in unexpected places. For a discussion of this medical dimension of the term, see Sohn. See also Cenzatti.

7. For an overview of this marginal role of old age in feminist discourse, see, for example, Calasanti and Slevin. For a specific focus on the relationship between age and the body as determined by social meanings and practices, see Gilleard and Higgs, *Cultures of Ageing: Self, Citizen and the Body.*

8. For an explicit discussion of age and community, see Gilleard and Higgs, *Contexts of Aging: Class, Cohort and Community.*

9. In *Praisesong for the Widow*, Paule Marshall engages in a similar reevaluation of old age resulting from a journey to the Caribbean, where the protagonist, Avey Johnson, discovers the traditional function and value of old age during a transformative dancing ceremony in Carriacou.

10. As Maierhofer and Hartung note in the introduction to their special issue on aging, "While dealing with age and aging, we all realize that ultimately we are also talking about death and dying" (125).

11. This connection between the spatial coordinates of private and public and their temporal counterparts, the past and the present, is also made by Brodber.

12. In her discussion of *Frangipani House*, De Souza emphasizes the implicit and explicit parallels between old-age homes and "holes" reminiscent of burial plots (154). Mama King, for instance, sees Frangipani House as "a hole. A deep dark hole" (9).

13. Mauby is a refreshing drink made from the tree bark of a species of buckthorn and widely consumed in the Caribbean.

14. In her last interview Gilroy indicates her great love for Carroll's novel: "The first book that I ever read with colour in it was Alice's Adventures in Wonderland [*Alice in Wonderland*]. . . . it was my favourite book" (Bradshaw, 385).

15. On the relationship between old age and memory, see Katz.

16. In an interview with Anne Adams, Gilroy explains this ghostly dimension of Mama King's recurring memories of Danny as her writerly attempt to come to terms with her own husband's death: "My writing is a therapeutic process. When I wrote *Frangipani House* my husband had died, and I have never been able to come to terms with that loss; I could never work out that loss"

(Adams, 120). Later in the same interview she also suggests that this book constitutes her "coming to terms with [her] own old age" (125). These two observations about the deeply personal and psychological dimension of her writing can help us situate *Frangipani House* among those novels, like Naipaul's *A House for Mr. Biswas*, that blend—in complex and unexpected ways—the elements of autobiography and fiction in an attempt to elucidate the real through its imaginative elaboration.

Chapter 6. Upper and Lower Stories

1. In this chapter I deliberately use the spelling *storey* instead of *story* for a floor or level of a building in order to distinguish between *storey* as a physical architectural element of the novel and *story*, designating the narratives that unfold in the building. This spelling allows me to keep the pun while providing for the reader a clear distinction between the two concepts. Whenever possible, I will use the more common term *floor* instead of *storey* for the sake of convenience.

2. In Confiant's 1994 novel, *L'Allée des soupirs*, one of the protagonists, Jacquou Chartier, declares, "The Creole novel will be cacophonic or it will not be at all!" (436). He judges the word *polyphonic* to be suggestive of order and harmony proper to the Cartesian world.

3. For a critical assessment of the Creolists' use of the notion of creolization and particularly of Confiant's literary treatment of this process, see Arnold. Arnold emphasizes that the Creolists' novels tend to "reproduce the colonial relationship for the delectation of First World readers" (23). Moreover "the most serious problem with the fictional practice of the *Créolists* in Martinique is their exclusionary vision of the nation" (24). He notes that their East Indian or Middle Eastern fictional characters, for example, tend to play "stereotyped roles" (24).

4. Since *L'Hôtel du Bon Plaisir* has not yet been translated into English, all English translations from this novel are my own.

5. Knepper's point of departure is Françoise Vergès's idea that bricolage represents "a practice and ethics of borrowing and accepting to be transformed, affected by the other" (Vergès, 184).

6. The correct noun would be *vulgus* ("the masses"). The word *vulgum* does not exist in Latin. The whole expression "vulgum pecus" is derived, in corrupt manner, from Horace's "servum pecus" (servile flock). The irony here is that Dorimont feels above everyone else in the hotel, not the least for his superior education, but despises the "ignorant masses" in incorrect Latin.

7. In December 1959 a traffic accident involving a white French officer hitting a motorcyclist in Fort-de-France sparked violent anti-French nationalist riots. See Germain.

8. For a discussion of this retrospective, regressive and even nostalgic dimension of Creolists' writing, see Burton.

9. See "Subjunctive," Language Guide, http://www.languageguide.org/french/grammar/subj/.

Conclusion

1. Robert T. Tally's translation of Bertrand Westphal's *Geocriticism*, originally published in French in 2007, and his own exploration of the "spatial turn" in a recent volume entitled *Spatiality* signal a growing interest in the "interrelations of space, place, and literature" (Tally 140). Geocriticism, just like the currently more familiar ecocriticism, engages with the centrality of literary imagination in shaping actual places as opposed to merely representing them.

Bibliography

Adams, Anne V. "'Coming to Terms with My Own Old Age': An Interview with Beryl Gilroy." *Matatu* 3, no. 6 (1989): 115–25.

Adorno, Theodor W. *Aesthetic Theory*. Translated and edited by Robert Hullot-Kentor. Minneapolis: University of Minnesota Press, 1997.

Althusser, Louis. "Ideology and Ideological State Apparatuses." In *Lenin and Philosophy and Other Essays*, 85–126. New York: Monthly Review Press, 1971.

Anderson, Robert S. "Gardens and Forests on Caribbean Islands: Two Hundred Years of Environmental Institutions." In *Islands, Forests and Gardens in the Caribbean*, edited by Robert S. Anderson, Richard Grove, and Karis Hiebert, 1–18. Oxford: Macmillan Caribbean, 2006.

Anim-Addo, Joan. "Anguish and the Absurd: 'Key Moments,' Recreated Lives, and the Emergence of New Figures of Black Womanhood in the Narrative Works of Beryl Gilroy." In *Winds of Change: Transforming Voices of Caribbean Women Writers and Scholars*, edited by Adele S. Newson and Linda Strong-Leek, 131–43. New York: Peter Lang, 1998.

Arnold, A. James. "Créolité: Power, Mimicry, and Dependence." *Review: Literature and the Arts of Americas* 37, no. 1 (2004): 19–26.

Ashcroft, Bill, Gareth Griffiths, and Helen Tiffin. *The Empire Writes Back: Theory and Practice in Post-colonial Literatures*. Abingdon, UK: Routledge, 2002.

Ashcroft, Bill, Gareth Griffiths, and Helen Tiffin. *Post-colonial Studies: The Key Concepts*. London: Routledge, 2000.

Bachelard, Gaston. *The Poetics of Space*. Translated by Maria Jolas. Boston: Beacon Press, 1994.

———. *La poétique de L'espace*. Paris: Quadrigue/PUF, 2004.

Bakhtin, Mikhail M. *The Dialogic Imagination*. Translated by Caryl Emerson and Michael Holquist. Austin: University of Texas Press, 2001.

Barnett, Clive. "Postcolonialism: Space, Textuality and Power." In *Approaches to Human Geography*, edited by Stuart Aitken and Gill Valentine, 147–59. London: Sage, 2006.

Barnow, Dagmar. *Naipaul's Strangers*. Bloomington: Indiana University Press, 2003.

Baucom, Ian. "Specters of the Atlantic." *South Atlantic Quarterly* 100, no. 1 (2001): 61–82.

Benítez-Rojo, Antonio. "Caribbean Culture: A Carnivalesque Approach." In *A History of Literature in the Caribbean*, edited by A. James Arnold, 3: 203–13. Amsterdam: John Benjamins, 1997.

———. *The Repeating Island: The Caribbean and the Postmodern Perspective*. 2nd edition. Translated by James E. Maraniss. Durham, NC: Duke University Press, 1996.

Bernabé, Jean, Patrick Chamoiseau, and Raphaël Confiant. *Eloge de la Créolité*. 1989. Paris: Editions Gallimard, 1993.

Bernabé, Jean, Patrick Chamoiseau, and Raphaël Confiant. "In Praise of Creolness." *Callaloo* 13, no. 4 (1990): 886–909.

Bhabha, Homi K. "Freedom's Basis in the Indeterminate." *October* 61 (Summer 1992): 46–57.

———. *The Location of Culture*. London: Routledge, 1994.

———. "Naipaul's Vernacular Cosmopolitans." *Chronicle of Higher Education* 48 (26 Oct. 2001).Online.

———. "The World and the Home." *Social Text* 31/32 (1992): 141–53.

Bongie, Chris. *Islands and Exiles: The Creole Identities of Post/Colonial Literature*. Stanford: Stanford University Press, 1998.

Boyer, M. Christine. "The Many Mirrors of Foucault and Their Architectural Reflections." In *Heterotopia and the City: Public Space in a Postcivil Society*, edited by Michiel Dehaene and Lieven De Cauter, 53–73. Abingdon, UK: Routledge, 2008.

Bradshaw, Roxann. "Beryl Gilroy's 'Fact-Fiction'—Through the Lens of the 'Quiet Old Lady.'" *Callaloo* 25, no. 2 (2002): 381–400.

Brathwaite, Edward. "Houses in West Indian Novel." *Literary Half-Yearly* 17, no. 1 (1976): 111–21.

Brathwaite, Edward Kamau. "The Unborn Body of the Life of Fiction: Roger Mais' Aesthetics with Special Reference to *Black Lightning*." *Journal of West Indian Literature* 2, no. 1 (1987): 11–36.

Brathwaite, Kamau. "Roger Mais." In *Twentieth-Century Caribbean and Black African Writers: Second Series*, edited by Bernth Lindfors and Reinhard Sander, 78–81. Detroit: Gale Research, 1993.

Brodber, Erna. "Guyana's Historical Sociology and the Novels of Beryl Gilroy and Grace Nichols." In *Arms Akimbo: Africana Women in Contemporary Literature*, edited by Janice Liddell and Yakini Belinda Kemp, 205–18. Gainesville: University Press of Florida, 1999.

Brown, Stewart. Introduction to *The Oxford Book of Caribbean Short Stories*, edited by Stewart Brown and John Wickham, xiii–xxxiii. Oxford: Oxford University Press, 1999.

Bunzl, Matti. Foreword to *Time and the Other*, by Johannes Fabian, ix–xxxiv. New York: Columbia University Press, 2002.

Burton, Richard D. E. "The Idea of Difference in Contemporary French West Indian Thought: Négritude, Antillanité, Créolité." In *French and West Indian: Martinique, Guadeloupe, and French Guiana Today*, edited by Richard D. E. Burton and Fred Reno, 137–66. Charlottesville: University of Virginia Press, 1995.

Calasanti, Toni M., and Kathleen F. Slevin, eds. *Age Matters: Realigning Feminist Thinking*. New York: Routledge, 2006.

Calasanti, Toni M., and Kathleen F. Slevin. "Introduction: Age Matters." In *Age Matters: Realigning Feminist Thinking*, edited by Toni M. Calasanti and Kathleen F. Slevin, 1–17. New York: Routledge, 2006.

Caldwell, Roy Chandler, Jr. "Créolité and Postcoloniality in Raphaël Confiant's *L'Allée des Soupirs*." *French Review* 73, no. 2 (1999): 301–11.

Casey, Edward S. *The Fate of Place: A Philosophical History*. Berkeley: University of California Press, 1998.

Célestin, Roger. "Naipaul: The 'Exotic' View." In *From Cannibals to Radicals: Figures and Limits of Exoticism*, 175–215. Minneapolis: University of Minnesota Press, 1996.

Cenzatti, Marco. "Heterotopias of Difference." In *Heterotopia and the City: Public Space in a Postcivil Society*, edited by Michiel Dehaene and Lieven De Cauter, 75–85. Abingdon, UK: Routledge, 2008.

Césaire, Aimé. *Cahier d'un retour au pays natal / Notebook of a Return to My Native Land*. Translated by Mireille Rosello with Annie Pritchard. French-English bilingual edition. Tarset, UK: Bloodaxe Books, 1995.

———. "The Liberating Power of Words." Interview by Annick Thebia Melsan. 1997. Reprinted in *Journal of Pan African Studies* 2 (15 June 2008). Last modified 18 July 2013, http://www.jpanafrican.com/docs/vol2no4/2.4_The_Liberating_Power_of_Words.pdf.

Chambers, Iain. "Maritime Criticism and Theoretical Shipwrecks." *PMLA* (2010): 678–84.

Chamoiseau, Patrick. *Ecrire en pays dominée*. Paris: Editions Gallimard, 1997.

———. *Texaco*. 1992. Translated by Rose-Myriam Réjouis and Val Vinokurov. New York: Vintage International, 1998.

Chamoiseau, Patrick, and Raphaël Confiant. *Lettres créoles: Tracées antillaises et continentales de la littérature*. Paris: Hatier, 1991.

Chivallon, Christine. "Texaco ou l'éloge de la 'spatialité.'" *Notre Librairie: Cinq ans de littératures 1991 1995, Caraïbe* 1, no. 127 (1996): 88–108.

Cliff, Michelle. *Abeng*. New York: Plume, 1995.

Cobham, Rhonda. Introduction to *Black Fauns*, by Alfred Hubert Mendes, i–xvi. London: New Beacon Books, 1984.

Cohen, Ted. "Metaphor and the Cultivation of Intimacy." In *On Metaphor*, edited by Sheldon Sacks, 1–10. Chicago: University of Chicago Press, 1979.

Confiant, Raphaël. *L'Allée des soupirs*. Montréal: Mémoire d'encrier, 2008.

———. *L'Hôtel du Bon Plaisir*. Paris: Mercure de France, 2009.

———. "Traduire la literature en situation de diglossie." *Palimpsestes* 12 (2000): 49–59.

Coursil, Jacques. "L'éloge de la muette." *Césure, revue de la convention psychanalitique* 11 (1996). Last modified 17 June 2013, http://www.potomitan.info/travaux/muette.htm.

Crichlow, Michaeline A. *Globalisation and the Post-Creole Imagination: Notes on Fleeing the Plantation*. Durham, NC: Duke University Press, 2009.

Cuddy-Keane, Melba. "Imaging/Imagining Globalization: Maps and Models." Paper presented at Globalization and the Image I: Imagining the Global, 2002 MLA Convention, New York City, 28 Dec. 2002. Last modified 26 Dec. 2013, http://homes.chass.utoronto.ca/~mcuddy/mapping.htm.

Curry, Michael R. "Wittgenstein and the Fabric of Everyday Life." In *Thinking Space*, edited by Mike Crang and Nigel Thrift, 89–113. Abingdon, UK: Routledge, 2000.

Dabydeen, David. *Turner: New and Selected Poems*. Leeds, UK: Peepal Tree, 1995.

D'Aguiar, Fred. *Feeding the Ghosts*. London: Chatto & Windus, 1997.

Dash, J. Michael. "Exile and Recent Literature." In *A History of Literature in the Caribbean, Volume 3: Cross Cultural Studies*, edited by A. James Arnold, 451–61. Amsterdam: John Benjamins, 1997.

———. Introduction to *Caribbean Discourse: Selected Essays*, by Edouard Glissant, xi–xlv. Charlottesville: University of Virginia Press, 1992.

———. *The Other America: Caribbean Literature in a New World Context*. Charlottesville: University of Virginia Press, 1998.

———. "Writing the Body: Glissant's Poetics of Re-membering." *World Literature Today* 63, no. 4 (1989): 609–12.

Davies, Amanda, and James Amity. *Geographies of Aging: Social Processes and the Spatial Unevenness of Population Aging*. Surrey, UK: Ashgate, 2011.

Dawson, Ashley. "Squatters, Space and Belonging in the Underdeveloped City." *Social Text* 81 (Winter 2004): 17–34.

Dehaene, Michiel, and Lieven De Cauter, eds. *Heterotopia and the City: Public Space in a Postcivil Society*. Abingdon, UK: Routledge, 2008.

Dehaene, Michiel, and Lieven De Cauter. "Heterotopia in a Postcivil Society." In *Heterotopia and the City: Public Space in a Postcivil Society*, edited by Michiel Dehaene and Lieven de Cauter, 3–9. London: Routledge, 2008.

de la Campa, Román. "Resistance and Globalization in Caribbean Discourse: Antonio Benítez-Rojo and Edouard Glissant." In *A History of Literature in the Caribbean, Volume 3: Cross Cultural Studies*, edited by A. James Arnold, 87–116. Amsterdam: John Benjamins, 1997.

Deleuze, Gilles, and Félix Guattari. *A Thousand Plateaus: Capitalism and Schizophrenia*. Translated by Brian Massumi. Minneapolis: University of Minnesota Press, 1987.

DeLoughrey, Elizabeth M., Renée K. Gosson, and George B. Handley, eds. *Caribbean Literature and the Environment: Between Nature and Culture*. Charlottesville: University of Virginia Press, 2005.

DeLoughrey, Elizabeth, and George B. Handley, eds. *Postcolonial Ecologies: Literatures of the Environment*. Oxford: Oxford University Press, 2011.

de Man, Paul. "The Epistemology of Metaphor." In *On Metaphor*, edited by Sheldon Sacks, 11–28. Chicago: University of Chicago Press, 1979.

Derrick, A. C. "Naipaul's Technique as a Novelist." In *Critical Perspectives on V. S. Naipaul*, edited by Robert D. Hamner, 194–207. Washington, DC: Three Continents Press, 1977.

De Souza, Pascale. "Flotsam in the Migratory Wake: Relating the Plight of the Old in *Frangipani House* and *Un plat de porc aux bananes vertes*." *Comparative Literature Studies* 39, no. 2 (2002): 146–61.

Deveson, Richard. "The Life of the Political Past." *Times Literary Supplement*, 24 October 1986, 1187.

Dirlik, Arif. "Place-Based Imagination: Globalism and the Politics of Place." *Review (Fernand Braudel Center)* 22, no. 2 (1999): 151–87.

Doron, Gil. "Terrains vagues: Transgression and Urban activism." In *Heterotopia and the City: Public Space in a Postcivil Society*, edited by Michiel Dehaene and Lieven de Cauter, 203–13. London: Routledge, 2008.

Dovey, Kim. *Framing Places: Mediating Power in Built Form*. London: Routledge, 2008.

Fabian, Johannes. *Time and the Other: How Anthropology Makes Its Object*. New York: Columbia University Press, 2002.

Fanon, Frantz. *The Wretched of the Earth*. New York: Grove Press, 1963.

Faubion, James D. "Heterotopia: An Ecology." In *Heterotopia and the City: Public Space in a Postcivil Society*, edited by Michiel Dehaene and Lieven De Cauter, 31–39. Abingdon, UK: Routledge, 2008.

Foucault, Michel. "Different Spaces." In *Aesthetics, Method and Epistemology*, edited by James D. Faubion, 175–85. New York: New Press, 1998.

———. "Des espaces autres." In *Dits et écrits 1954 1988, Volume 2: 1976–1988*, 1571–81. Paris: Editions Gallimard, 2001.

———. "Of Other Spaces." In *Heterotopia and the City: Public Space in a Postcivil Society*, edited by Michiel Dehaene and Lieven De Cauter, 13–29. Abingdon, UK: Routledge, 2008.

French, Patrick. *The World Is What It Is: The Authorized Biography of V. S. Naipaul*. New York: Vintage, 2009.

Frisby, David. "The Metropolis as Text: Otto Wagner and Vienna's 'Second Renaissance.'" In *The Hieroglyphics of Space: Reading and Experiencing the Modern Metropolis*, edited by Neil Leach, 15–30. London: Routledge, 2002.

Gallagher, Mary. "Genre and the Self: Some Reflections on the Poetics and Politics of the 'Fils de Césaire.'" *International Journal of Francophone Studies* 10, no. 1/2 (2007): 51–66.

———, ed. *Ici-Là: Place and Displacement in Caribbean Writing in French.* Amsterdam: Rodopi, 2003.

Gardiner, Michael E. "Post-Romantic Irony in Bakhtin and Lefebvre." *History of Human Sciences* 25, no. 3 (2012): 51–69.

Germain, Félix Fernand. "Dangerous Liaisons: The Lives and Labor of Working Class Antilleans and Sub-Saharan Africans in 1960s Paris." PhD dissertation, University of California, Berkeley, 2007. Last modified 17 June 2013, http://books.google.ca/books?id=Y1Esz5p8MbMC&pg=PP2&lpg=PP4&ots=WgOQvp8d1a&dq=felix+fernand+germain.

Gilkes, Michael. "Caribbean Contrasts." *Third World Quarterly* 9, no. 4 (1987): 1371–75.

Gilleard, Christopher, and Paul Higgs. *Contexts of Aging: Class, Cohort and Community.* Cambridge, UK: Polity Press, 2005.

Gilleard, Christopher, and Paul Higgs. *Cultures of Ageing: Self, Citizen and the Body.* Upper Saddle River, NJ: Pearson Education, 2000.

Gilroy, Beryl. *Boy-Sandwich.* Oxford: Heinemann International, 1989.

———. *Frangipani House.* Oxford: Heinemann, 1986.

———. "I Write Because . . . " In *Caribbean Women Writers: Essays from the First International Conference*, edited by Selwyn Reginald Cudjoe, 195–201. Wellesley, MA: Calaloux, 1990.

———. "The Woman Writer and Commitment: Links between Caribbean and African Literature." *Wasafiri* 5, no. 10 (1989): 15–16.

———. "Women of Color at the Barricades." In *Winds of Change: Transforming Voices of Caribbean Women Writers and Scholars*, edited by Adele S. Newson and Linda Strong-Leek, 145–53. New York: Peter Lang, 1998.

Gilroy, Paul. *The Black Atlantic: Modernity and Double Consciousness.* Cambridge, MA: Harvard University Press, 1993.

Glissant, Edouard. *Caribbean Discourse: Selected Essays.* Translated by J. Michael Dash. Charlottesville: University of Virginia Press, 1992.

———. *Le discours antillais.* Paris: Folio/Editions Gallimard, 1997.

———. *Poetics of Relation.* Translated by Betsy Wing. Ann Arbor: University of Michigan Press, 1997.

———. *Poétique de la relation.* Paris: Editions Gallimard, 1990.

Godzich, Wlad. Foreword to *Heterologies: Discourse on the Other*, by Michel de Certeau, vii–xxi. Minneapolis: University of Minnesota Press, 2010.

Goffman, Erving. *Asylums: Essays on the Social Situation of Mental Patients and Other Inmates.* New York: Anchor, 1961.

Goldman, Marlene. "Aging, Old Age, Memory, Aesthetics: Introduction to Special Issue." *Occasion: Interdisciplinary Studies in the Humanities* 4

(15 June 2012). Last modified 26 Dec. 2013, http://arcade.stanford.edu/occasion_issue/volume-4.

Goonewardena, Kanishka, Stefan Kipfer, Richard Milgrom, and Christian Schmid, eds. *Space, Difference, Everyday Life: Reading Henri Lefebvre.* New York: Routledge, 2008.

Gosson, Renée. "Cultural and Environmental Assimilation in Martinique: An Interview with Raphaël Confiant." In *Caribbean Literature and the Environment: Between Nature and Culture*, edited by Elizabeth M. DeLoughrey, Renée K. Gosson, and George B. Handley, 143–53. Charlottesville: University of Virginia Press, 2005.

———. "For What the Land Tells: An Ecocritical Approach to Patrick Chamoiseau's *Chronicle of the Seven Sorrows*." *Callaloo* 26, no. 1 (2003): 219–34.

Greaney, Patrick. *Untimely Beggar: Poverty and Power from Baudelaire to Benjamin.* Minneapolis: University of Minnesota Press, 2008.

Hall, Stuart. "Old and New Identities, Old and New Ethnicities." In *Culture, Globalization and the World-System: Contemporary Conditions for the Representation of Identity*, edited by Anthony D. King, 41–68. Minneapolis: University of Minnesota Press, 1997.

Hallward, Peter. *Absolutely Postcolonial: Writing between the Singular and Specific.* Manchester, UK: Manchester University Press, 2001.

Hamner, Robert. Introduction to *Critical Perspectives on V. S. Naipaul*, edited by Robert D. Hamner, xvi–xvii. Washington, DC: Three Continents Press, 1977.

———. "The Measure of the 'Yard Novel': From Mendes to Lovelace." *Commonwealth: Essays and Studies* 9, no. 1 (1986): 98–105.

Harbison, Robert. *The Built, the Unbuilt, and the Unbuildable: In Pursuit of Architectural Meaning.* London: Thames and Hudson, 1996.

Hardwick, Louise. "Du français-banane au créole-dragon: Entretien avec Raphaël Confiant." *International Journal of Francophone Studies* 9, no. 2 (2006): 257–76.

Harvey, David. *Spaces of Capital: Towards a Critical Geography.* New York: Routledge, 2001.

Head, Bessie. *A Question of Power.* London: Heinemann, 1974.

Hess, Rémi. Foreword to *La Production de l'espace*, by Henri Lefebvre, v–xvi. Paris: Anthropos, 2000.

———. *Henri Lefebvre et la pensée du possible: Théorie des moments et construction de la personne.* Paris: Economica/Anthropos, 2009.

Hezekiah, Randolph. "Martinique and Guadeloupe: Time and Space." In *A History of Literature in the Caribbean*, edited by A. James Arnold, 1: 379–87. Amsterdam: John Benjamins, 1994.

Hofmann, Sabine. "Against Monolingualism: Roots, Rhizomes and the Conceptualization of Creole Language." In *A Pepper-Pot of Cultures: Aspects of Creolization in the Caribbean*, edited by Gordon Collier and Ulrich Fleischmann, 277–85. Amsterdam: Rodopi, 2003.

Hoving, Isabel. *In Praise of New Travelers: Reading Caribbean Migrant Women Writers*. Stanford: Stanford University Press, 2001.

James, C. L. R. *Minty Alley*. 1936. London: New Beacon Books, 1981.

———. "Triumph." 1929. In *The Oxford Book of Caribbean Short Stories*, edited by Stewart Brown and John Wickham, 35–49. Oxford: Oxford University Press, 1999.

Katz, Stephen. "Embodied Memory: Ageing, Neuroculture, and the Genealogy of Mind." *Occasion: Interdisciplinary Studies in the Humanities* 4 (15 June 2012). Last modified 26 Dec. 2013, http://arcade.stanford.edu/occasion_issue/volume-4.

King, Neal. "The Lengthening List of Oppressions: Age Relations and the Feminist Study of Inequality." In *Age Matters: Realigning Feminist Thinking*, edited by Toni M. Calasanti and Kathleen F. Slevin, 47–74. New York: Routledge, 2006.

Knepper, Wendy. "Colonization, Creolization, and Globalization: The Art and Ruses of Bricolage." *Small Axe* 21 (2006): 70–86.

———. *Patrick Chamoiseau: A Critical Introduction*. Jackson: University Press of Mississippi, 2012.

Knowles, Roberta Q. "Review of *Frangipani House*." *Caribbean Writer* 2 (1988): 92–3.

Kohn, Margaret. *Radical Space: Building the House of the People*. Ithaca, NY: Cornell University Press, 2003.

Kracauer, Siegfried. "On Employment Agencies: The Construction of a Space. Translated by David Frisby. In *Rethinking Architecture: A Reader in Cultural Theory*, edited by Neil Leach, 59–64. London: Routledge, 1997.

Lamming, George. "Caribbean Literature: The Black Rock of Africa." *African Forum: A Quarterly Journal of Contemporary Affairs* 1, no. 4 (1966): 32–52.

———. "The Occasion for Speaking." In *The Pleasures of Exile*, 23–50. Ann Arbor: University of Michigan Press, 1992.

———. *The Pleasures of Exile*. Ann Arbor: University of Michigan Press, 1992.

Larrier, Renée. "'Crier/Ecrire/Cahier': Anagrammatic Configurations of Voice in Francophone Caribbean Narratives." *French Review*, 69, no. 2 (1995): 275–83.

Leach, Neil, ed. *The Hieroglyphics of Space: Reading and Experiencing the Modern Metropolis*. London: Routledge, 2002.

Lefebvre, Henri. *Critique of Everyday Life*. Vol. 1. London: Verso, 1991.

———. *Everyday Life in the Modern World*. London: Continuum, 2002.

———. *La production de l'espace*. 1974. 4th edition. Paris: Anthropos, 2000.

———. *The Production of Space*. Translated by Donald Nicholson-Smith. Oxford: Blackwell, 1991.

Lee R. H. "The Novels of V. S. Naipaul." In *Critical Perspectives on V. S. Naipaul*, edited by Robert D. Hamner, 68–83. Washington, DC: Three Continents Press, 1977.

Letchimy, Serge. *De L'habitat précaire à la ville: L'example Martiniquais*. Paris: Editions L'Harmattan, 1992.

Lincoln, Sarah L. "Conquering City: The Poetics of Possibility in *Texaco*." *Small Axe* 36 (November 2011): 1–21.

Linebaugh, Peter, and Marcus Rediker. *The Many-Headed Hydra: Sailors, Slaves, Commoners, and the Hidden History of the Revolutionary Atlantic*. Boston: Beacon Press, 2000.

Lovelace, Earl. *The Dragon Can't Dance*. 1979. Harlow, UK: Longman, 1981.

Macnicol, John. *Age Discrimination: An Historical and Contemporary Analysis*. Cambridge, UK: Cambridge University Press, 2006.

Maes-Jelinek, Hena. "The Novel from 1950 to 1970." In *A History of Literature in the Caribbean*, edited by A. James Arnold, 2: 127–48. Amsterdam: John Benjamins, 2001.

Maierhofer, Roberta, and Heike Hartung. "Narratives of Life: Aging and Identity—Introduction." *Journal of Aging, Humanities, and the Arts* 1 (2007): 125–31.

Mais, Roger. *The Hills Were Joyful Together*. 1953. London: Heinemann, 1987.

Malpas, J. E. *Place and Experience: A Philosophical Topography*. Cambridge, UK: Cambridge University Press, 2007.

Marx, Karl. *The German Ideology: Part I*. In *The Marx-Engels Reader*, edited by Robert C. Tucker, 146–200. New York: Norton, 1978.

Massey, Doreen. "Don't Let's Counterpose Place and Space." *Development* 45, no. 1 (2002): 24–25.

———. *For Space*. London: Sage, 2005.

McCann, Eugene J. "Race, Protest, and Public Space: Contextualizing Lefebvre in the U.S. City." *Antipode* 31, no. 2 (1999): 163–84.

McCusker, Maeve. "No Place Like Home? Constructing an Identity in Patrick Chamoiseau's *Texaco*." In *Ici-Là: Place and Displacement in Caribbean Writing in French*, edited by Mary Gallagher, 41–60. Amsterdam: Rodopi, 2003.

McCusker, Maeve, and Patrick Chamoiseau. "De la problématique du territoire à la problématique du lieu: Un entretien avec Patrick Chamoiseau." *French Review* 73, no. 4 (2000): 724–33.

Ménager, Serge Dominique. "Topographie, texte et palimpseste: *Texaco* de Patrick Chamoiseau." *French Review* 68, no. 1 (1994): 61–68.

Mendes, Alfred. *Black Fauns*. 1935. London: New Beacon Books, 1984.

Merleau-Ponty, Maurice. *Phénoménologie de la perception*. Paris: Editions Gallimard, 1945.

———. *Phenomenology of Perception*. London: Routledge, 2002.

Merrifield, Andy. *Henri Lefebvre: A Critical Introduction*. New York: Routledge, 2006.

Miller, Hillis J. "The Critic as Host." In *Deconstruction and Criticism*, 177–208. London: Continuum, 2004.

Minca, Claudio, ed. *Postmodern Geography: Theory and Praxis.* Oxford: Blackwell, 2001.

Morris, Daphne. Introduction to *The Hills Were Joyful Together*, by Roger Mais, iii–xix. London: Heinemann, 1987.

Mustafa, Fawzia. *V. S. Naipaul.* Cambridge, UK: Cambridge University Press, 1995.

Nadal-Melsió, Sara. "Lessons in Surrealism: Relationality, Event, Encounter." In *Space, Difference, Everyday Life: Reading Henri Lefebvre*, edited by Kanishka Goonewardena et al., 161–75. New York: Routledge, 2008.

Naipaul, V. S. "East Indian." In *Literary Occasions: Essays*, 35–44. New York: Knopf, 2003.

———. *The Enigma of Arrival.* 1987. New York: Vintage Books, 1988.

———. "Foreword to *A House for Mr Biswas.*" In *Literary Occasions: Essays*, 128–35. New York: Knopf, 2003.

———. *A House for Mr Biswas.* 1961. New York: Vintage International, 2001.

———. "Jasmine." In *Literary Occasions: Essays*, 45–52. New York: Knopf, 2003.

———. *The Middle Passage.* New York: Vintage Books, 2002.

———. *Miguel Street.* 1959. New York: Penguin Books, 1979.

———. "Prologue: Reading and Writing, a Personal Account." In *Literary Occasions: Essays*, 3–31. New York: Knopf, 2003.

Nasta, Susheila. *Home Truths: Fictions of the South Asian Diaspora in Britain.* London: Palgrave, 2002.

Nesbitt, Nick. *Voicing Memory: History and Subjectivity in French Caribbean Literature.* Charlottesville: University of Virginia Press, 2003.

Nixon, Rob. *London Calling: V. S. Naipaul, Postcolonial Mandarin.* Oxford: Oxford University Press, 1992.

Ormerod, Beverly. "Realism Redefined: The Subjective Vision." In *A History of Literature in the Caribbean, Volume 3: Cross-Cultural Studies*, edited by A. James Arnold, 435–49. Amsterdam: John Benjamins, 1997.

Panwar, Purabi, ed. *V. S. Naipaul: An Anthology of Recent Criticism.* Delhi: Pencraft International, 2003.

Parry, Benita. "The Postcolonial: Conceptual Category or Chimera?" *Yearbook of English Studies* 27 (1997): 3–21.

———. *Postcolonial Studies: A Materialist Critique.* London: Routledge, 2004.

Pasupathi, Monisha, and Corinna E. Lökenhoff. "Ageist Behavior." In *Ageism: Stereotyping and Prejudice against Older Persons*, edited by Todd D. Nelson, 201–46. Cambridge, MA: MIT Press, 2002.

Pépin, Ernest. "The Place of Space in the Novels of the *Créolité* Movement." Translated by Mary Gallagher. In *Ici-Là: Place and Displacement in Caribbean Writing in French*, edited by Mary Gallagher, 1–23. Amsterdam: Rodopi, 2003.

Philip, M. NourbeSe. *Zong!* Toronto: Mercury Press, 2008.

Phillips, Caryl. *A New World Order: Essays.* New York: Vintage International, 2002.

Punter, David. *Postcolonial Imaginings: Fictions of a New World Order.* Edinburgh: Edinburgh University Press, 2000.

Puri, Shalini. *The Caribbean Postcolonial: Social Equality, Post-Nationalism, and Cultural Hybridity.* New York: Palgrave Macmillan, 2004.

Quayson, Ato. "Periods versus Concepts: Space Making and the Question of Postcolonial Literary History." *PMLA* 127, no. 2 (2012): 342–48.

Radović, Stanka. "The Birthplace of Relation: Edouard Glissant's *Poétique de la relation.*" *Callaloo* 30, no. 2 (2007): 475–81.

Rahim, Jennifer, and Barbara Lalla, eds. *Created in the West Indies: Caribbean Perspectives on V. S. Naipaul.* Kingston, Jamaica: Ian Randle, 2011.

Ramchand, Kenneth. Introduction to *Minty Alley*, by C. L. R. James, 5–15. London: New Beacon Books, 1981.

Rediker, Marcus. *The Slave Ship: A Human History.* New York: Penguin Books, 2008.

Ricoeur, Paul. "The Metaphorical Process as Cognition, Imagination, and Feeling." In *On Metaphor*, edited by Sheldon Sacks, 141–57. Chicago: University of Chicago Press, 1979.

Rogozinski, Jan. *A Brief History of the Caribbean: From the Arawak and Carib to the Present.* New York: Plume, 2000.

Rohlehr, Gordon. "Character and Rebellion in *A House for Mr. Biswas.*" In *Critical Perspectives on V. S. Naipaul*, edited by Robert D. Hamner, 84–93. Washington, DC: Three Continents Press, 1977.

———. "The Confessional Element in Naipaul's Fiction." In *Created in the West Indies: Caribbean Perspectives on V. S. Naipaul*, edited by Jennifer Rahim and Barbara Lalla, 79–98. Kingston, Jamaica: Ian Randle, 2011.

———. "The Ironic Approach." In *Critical Perspectives on V. S. Naipaul*, edited by Robert D. Hamner, 178–93. Washington, DC: Three Continents Press, 1977.

Rowe, John Wallis, and Robert L. Kahn. *Successful Aging.* New York: Dell, 1999.

Rushdie, Salman. *Shame.* Toronto: Vintage Canada, 1997.

Said, Edward. "Bitter Dispatches from the Third World." In *Reflections on Exile, and Other Essays*, 98–104. Cambridge, MA: Harvard University Press, 2000.

Salick, Roydon. "'Rampant with Memory': Theme and Technique in *The Stone Angel* and *Frangipani House.*" *Commonwealth* 14, no. 2 (1992): 98–105.

Salkey, Andrew. Review of Beryl Gilroy's *Frangipani House. World Literature Today* 61, no. 4 (1987): 670.

Sartre, Jean-Paul. Preface to *The Wretched of the Earth*, by Frantz Fanon, 7–31. New York: Grove Press, 1963.

Schmid, Christian. "Henri Lefebvre's Theory of the Production of Space: Towards a Three-Dimensional Dialectic." In *Space, Difference, Everyday Life: Reading Henri Lefebvre*, edited by Kanishka Goonewardena et al., 27–45. New York: Routledge, 2008.

Serres, Michel. *Le parasite*. Paris: Bernard Grasset, 1980.

Smith, Neil, and Cindi Katz. "Grounding Metaphor: Towards a Spatialized Politics." In *Place and the Politics of Identity*, edited by Michael Keith and Steve Pile, 66–81. London: Routledge, 1993.

Sohn, Heidi. "Heterotopia: Anamnesis of a Medical Term." In *Heterotopia and the City: Public Space in a Postcivil Society*, edited by Michiel Dehaene and Lieven De Cauter, 41–50. Abingdon, UK: Routledge, 2008.

Soja, Edward W. *Postmodern Geographies: The Reassertion of Space in Critical Social Theory*. London: Verso, 1989.

———. *Thirdspace: Journeys to Los Angeles and Other Real-and-Imagined Places*. Malden, MA: Blackwell, 1996.

Solà-Morales, Ignasi de. "Terrain Vague." In *Anyplace*, edited by Cynthia C. Davidson, 118–23. Cambridge, MA: MIT Press, 1995.

Sontag, Susan. "The Double Standard of Aging." *Saturday Review*, 23 Sept. 1972, 29–38.

Spillers, Hortense J. "Mama's Baby, Papa's Maybe: An American Grammar Book." *Diacritics* 17, no. 2 (1987): 64–81.

Sprouse, Keith Alan. "Chaos and Rhizome: Introduction to a Caribbean Poetics." In *A History of Literature in the Caribbean, Volume 3: Cross-Cultural Studies*, edited by A. James Arnold, 79–86. Amsterdam: John Benjamins, 1997.

Stewart, Susan. *On Longing: Narratives of the Miniature, the Gigantic, the Souvenir, the Collection*. Durham, NC: Duke University Press, 1993.

Strachan, Ian Gregory. *Paradise and Plantation: Tourism and Culture in the Anglophone Caribbean*. Charlottesville: University of Virginia Press, 2002.

Tally, Robert T. *Spatiality*. Abingdon, UK: Routledge, 2013.

Tarver, Australia. "*Frangipani House*: Beryl Gilroy's Praise Song for Grandmothers." In *Winds of Change: Transforming Voices of Caribbean Women Writers and Scholars*, edited by Adele S. Newson and Linda Strong-Leek, 127–30. New York: Peter Lang, 1998.

ten Kortenaar, Neil. "Mr. Biswas Finds a Home in the World on Paper: V. S. Naipaul." In *Postcolonial Literature and the Impact of Literacy: Reading and Writing in African and Caribbean Fiction*, 107–34. Cambridge, UK: Cambridge University Press, 2011.

Theroux, Paul. "Paul Theroux Claims New Biography Reveals the True Monster in V. S. Naipaul." *Sunday Times* (London), 6 Apr. 2008. Last modified 18 July 2013, http://www.thesundaytimes.co.uk/sto/culture/books/article83961.ece.

Tiffin, Helen. "'Man Fitting the Landscape': Nature, Culture and Colonialism."

In *Caribbean Literature and the Environment: Between Nature and Culture*, edited by Elizabeth M. DeLoughrey, Renée K. Gosson, and George B. Handley, 199–212. Charlottesville: University of Virginia Press, 2005.

Tuan, Yi-Fu. *Space and Place: The Perspective of Experience.* Minneapolis: University of Minnesota Press, 2011.

Tucker, Robert C., ed. *The Marx-Engels Reader.* New York: Norton, 1978.

Upstone, Sara. *Spatial Politics in the Postcolonial Novel.* Surrey, UK: Ashgate, 2009.

Vergès, Françoise. "Kiltir Kreol: Processes and Practices of Créolité and Creolization." In *Créolité and Creolization: Documenta 11Platform3*, edited by Okwui Enwezor et al., 179–84. Ostfildern-Ruit, Germany: Hatje Cantz, 2003.

Vidler, Anthony. *The Architectural Uncanny: Essays in the Modern Unhomely.* Cambridge, MA: MIT Press, 1999.

Walcott, Derek. "The Garden Path." *New Republic*, 13 Apr. 1987, 27–31.

Weigand, Gabriele. Preface to *Henri Lefebvre et la pensée du possible: Théorie des moments et construction de la personne*, by Rémi Hess, v–xvii. Paris: Economica/Anthropos, 2009.

West-Pavlov, Russell. *Spaces of Fiction / Fictions of Space: Postcolonial Place and Literary DeiXis.* Basingstoke, UK: Palgrave Macmillan, 2010.

Westphal, Bertrand. *Geocriticism: Real and Fictional Spaces.* Translated by Robert T. Tally Jr. New York: Palgrave Macmillan, 2011.

Williams, Eric. *Capitalism and Slavery.* Chapel Hill: University of North Carolina Press, 1994.

———. "The Cockpit of Europe." In *From Columbus to Castro: The History of the Caribbean*, 69–94. New York: Vintage, 1984.

Wilson, Lucy. "Age and Ageism in Paule Marshall's *Praisesong for the Widow* and Beryl Gilroy's *Frangipani House*." *Journal of Caribbean Studies* 7, nos. 2–3 (1989): 189–99.

Winks, Christopher. *Symbolic Cities in Caribbean Literature.* New York: Palgrave Macmillan, 2009.

Woolf, Virginia. *A Room of One's Own.* San Diego, CA: Harcourt, 1989.

Zobel, Joseph. *Black Shack Alley.* 1950. Translated by Keith Q. Warner. Washington, DC: Three Continents Press, 1980.

———. *La Rue Cases-Nègres.* Paris: Présence Africaine, 1974.

Index

Recent Books in the New World Studies Series

Nick Nesbitt, *Universal Emancipation: The Haitian Revolution and the Radical Enlightenment*

Doris L. Garraway, editor, *Tree of Liberty: Cultural Legacies of the Haitian Revolution in the Atlantic World*

Dawn Fulton, *Signs of Dissent: Maryse Condé and Postcolonial Criticism*

Michael G. Malouf, *Transatlantic Solidarities: Irish Nationalism and Caribbean Poetics*

Maria Cristina Fumagalli, *Caribbean Perspectives on Modernity: Returning the Gaze*

Vivian Nun Halloran, *Exhibiting Slavery: The Caribbean Postmodern Novel as Museum*

Paul B. Miller, *Elusive Origins: The Enlightenment in the Modern Caribbean Historical Imagination*

Eduardo González, *Cuba and the Fall: Christian Text and Queer Narrative in the Fiction of José Lezama Lima and Reinaldo Arenas*

Jeff Karem, *The Purloined Islands: Caribbean-U.S. Crosscurrents in Literature and Culture, 1880–1959*

Faith Smith, editor, *Sex and the Citizen: Interrogating the Caribbean*

Mark D. Anderson, *Disaster Writing: The Cultural Politics of Catastrophe in Latin America*

Raphael Dalleo, *Caribbean Literature and the Public Sphere: From the Plantation to the Postcolonial*

Maite Conde, *Consuming Visions: Cinema, Writing, and Modernity in Rio de Janeiro*

Monika Kaup, *Neobaroque in the Americas: Alternative Modernities in Literature, Visual Art, and Film*

Marisel C. Moreno, *Family Matters: Puerto Rican Women Authors on the Island and the Mainland*

Supriya M. Nair, *Pathologies of Paradise: Caribbean Detours*

Colleen C. O'Brien, *Race, Romance, and Rebellion: Literatures of the Americas in the Nineteenth Century*

Kelly Baker Josephs, *Disturbers of the Peace: Representations of Madness in Anglophone Caribbean Literature*

Christina Kullberg, *The Poetics of Ethnography in Martinican Narratives: Exploring the Self and the Environment*

Maria Cristina Fumagalli, Bénédicte Ledent, and Roberto del Valle Alcalá, editors, *The Cross-Dressed Caribbean: Writing, Politics, Sexualities*

Philip Kaisary, *The Haitian Revolution in the Literary Imagination: Radical Horizons, Conservative Constraints*

Jason Frydman, *Sounding the Break: African American and Caribbean Routes of World Literature*

Stanka Radović, *Locating the Destitute: Space and Identity in Caribbean Fiction*